READING AGAINST DEMOCRACY

The Broken Promises of Reading Instruction

Patrick Shannon

HEINEMANN
Portsmouth, NH

Heinemann
A division of Reed Elsevier Inc.
361 Hanover Street
Portsmouth, NH 03801–3912
www.heinemann.com

Offices and agents throughout the world

A previous edition of this book entitled *Broken Promises* by Patrick Shannon was published by Bergin & Garvey, an imprint of the Greenwood Publishing Group, in 1988.

Library of Congress Cataloging-in-Publication Data
Shannon, Patrick, 1951–
   Reading against democracy : the broken promises of reading instruction / Patrick Shannon.
     p. cm.
   Includes bibliographical references and index.
   ISBN-13: 978-0-325-00976-6
   ISBN-10: 0-325-00976-7
   1. Reading—United States—History. 2. Literacy programs—United States—History.
I. Shannon, Patrick, 1951– Broken promises. II. Title.

   LB1573.S4665 2007
   428.407'1073—dc22   2006035477

Acquisitions editor: Lois Bridges
Editor: Maura Sullivan
Production: Patricia Adams
Typesetter: Valerie Levy / Drawing Board Studios
Cover design: Jenny Jensen Greenleaf
Manufacturing: Steve Bernier

Printed in the United States of America on acid-free paper
11 10 09 08 07 VP 1 2 3 4 5

To Kathleen Shannon

Contents

Introduction

Why write a new version of *Broken Promises*? Consider the following events, which occurred since that book was published in 1989:

- Reid Lyon, director of research on learning and behavior at the National Institute of Child Health and Human Development (NICHD), told educators at a conference that he'd "like to blow up colleges of education."[1]
- President George W. Bush proposed the Reading First Initiative, which promises more federal funding to school districts that are willing to reorganize their reading programs according to federal guidelines.
- Susan Newman, while serving as the assistant secretary of education, stated, "I want to change the face of reading instruction across the United States, from an art to a science. . . . I suggest they [school districts] purchase a core reading program."[2]
- The California Department of Education made whole language its official curriculum, and then later, it outlawed whole language instruction in elementary school classrooms.
- Four educational publishers gained control of 85 percent of the elementary school reading instruction market through mergers and takeovers of nine other publishing firms.
- McGraw-Hill Educational Publishing, Voyager Expanded Learning, and other companies with direct ties to President Bush are directing school districts' efforts to compete for additional federal funding through the Reading First Initiative.
- On the stipulation that every teacher would use the materials according to the system's directions, Hewlett Packard heir David Packard Jr. donated money in order to enable the Santa Barbara school district to buy the complete Open Court core reading system.
- Accelerated Reader, New Standards, and other corporations have turned more and more aspects of the art of reading instruction into commodities that they can sell to school districts.

- The International Reading Association and the National Council of Teachers of English accepted a federal government contract to produce national standards for English language arts.
- The National Reading Panel established the official definition of reading instruction, limiting it to only those activities that experimental studies have proven to raise students' scores on standardized reading tests.
- The Coalition for Evidence-Based Policy recommended that the federal government fund only reading research that employs large-scale randomized control trials (methods used in pharmaceutical research for Federal Drug Administration approval).
- Officials in the Bush administration selected seventy psychologists, special educators, teacher educators, businessmen, and literacy advocates to judge the eligibility of school districts' proposals to be included in Reading First Initiative funding. Not one teacher was included among these experts.
- A 2006 report from the office of the Inspector General calls into question the credibility of the Reading First Initiative because of systematic bias and conflict of interest.

Taken separately, any of these events would not necessarily disturb the regular routines among teachers and students during reading instruction. If the Reading First Initiative were not supported by business and reading experts, or federal officials and educational publishers ignored reading research and reading researchers, then teachers could plan reading programs based on students' and communities' needs. With business, reading experts, and the state working separately, the public would deem most teachers to be successful and would consider most students able to read sufficiently well to graduate from high school and enter the workforce.

Yet as these twelve events suggest, the efforts and interests of business, government, and science in reading education overlap in both simple and complex ways. Note, for example, that the president's Reading First Initiative compels school districts to compete against one another for needed funds, and that businesses and reading experts have recognized this new market, selling new products, services, and expertise to districts seeking an advantage over their competitors (that is, other school districts). Educational businesses publish the core reading programs that former assistant secretary Newman recommends for all schools seeking federal funds. Reading experts decide which commercially based programs have enough scientific evidence to warrant funding. Although reading experts invent the science of reading instruction and they help businesses to translate it into core programs that the government recommends (and will fund), they cannot invent any type of science they desire. The government requires that the science of reading instruction be made of reliable and replicable experiments that establish causal links between specific instructional acts and designated learning outcomes—evidence-based acts that will raise test scores and can be duplicated economically in classrooms around the country. Rather than the art of reading instruction (which I assume to include the history, traditions, culture, politics, and ethics of teaching reading), business, government, and reading experts seek the one best system to be employed in every classroom in the country.

We're told that the global economy demands that schools redesign their reading programs according to scientific evidence. We're warned that if schools allow reading instruction to remain an art, then too many American children will fail to acquire the high levels of technical skills necessary to compete in the world of work. While this would certainly be a personal tragedy, we are reminded that it would eventually cause irreparable harm to the United States economy because businesses would not be able to hire skilled workers in order to compete successfully in international markets. Reading reform, then, is considered a national priority, not simply a local concern or a personal matter. In order to ensure that America reads and no child will be left behind, the federal government has passed legislation and adopted policies over the last decade to hold teachers and students accountable for students' progress in meeting high academic standards according to fixed schedules for their development. The early interest in national standards was followed quickly by a scheme for testing each student annually. Federal funding induces schools to comply with the current one "best" system. Ultimately, the federal government promises citizens that uniform implementation of scientific core reading programs will prepare all young Americans to obtain the high-skill, high-wage jobs that are waiting for them in the global economy. Everybody wins, they tell us.

This new promise, however, distorts the original promises made to American students and the public since the inception of schooling in America. For example, in the Massachusetts Bay Colony in the 1640s, reading instruction promised to lead Americans who read the Bible to salvation of their souls and away from that old deluder Satan. During the last half of the eighteenth century, Benjamin Franklin proposed public libraries to free American minds from religious tyranny, and Thomas Jefferson promised that reading would keep Americans free from political and economic tyranny as well. Horace Mann, in the 1840s, declared that reading education would bring personal and social order. "A republic form of government, without literacy in the people, must be on a vast scale, what a mad-house, without a superintendent, would be on a small one."[3] Learning to read at school, then, promised to make the public both strong and wise—strong enough to defend itself against moral, political, and economic temptations likely to lead it astray and wise enough so that all members could participate in the governance of their own lives individually and collectively. The new promise, however, directs our attention exclusively to the economic possibilities and consequences of reading, hiding the other aspects of the original promises from our vision of reading education and removing them from further discussions. In this way, the new promise limits our relationships to text (and therefore each other), reducing them to the accumulation of skills in order to raise our human capital, later to be sold to others in employment.

Promises Made, Promises Broken

Right from the beginning, however, the promises of reading instruction have been problematic for women, minorities, and the poor living in America, who for one reason or another were excluded from formal instruction. Until the turn of the twentieth century, reading among these groups was thought to be a threat to the social, economic, and political status quo. Since industrialization, however, it is the lack of reading abilities among these groups that is considered threatening. The promises of reading instruction are still often broken for these marginalized groups, despite laws requiring compulsory school attendance. Minorities and the poor continue to lag well behind white middle- and upper-class students in reading achievement. Although women seem to fare somewhat better overall on tests, they find themselves behind in the scientific and technical literacies required to gain power in the world of work. Moreover, their demonstrations of general reading skills on tests have earned them neither equal wages in the American economy nor equal representation in the government beyond local levels.

Promises have also been made and broken to those who teach reading. In order to be effective, teachers must demonstrate the possibilities of reading, inviting all who study with them to join their literate acts. Reading instruction —their work—is supposed to make a difference in the lives of their students, enabling them to gather and evaluate information necessary for them to live fulfilled lives (however defined) and empowering them to have greater control over their lives. Implicit in this work is the promise made to teachers that they should enjoy these same benefits of reading during their teaching. Yet the tighter controls on reading education in order to ensure student learning have narrowed the promise of teaching reading as they have narrowed the promise of reading for students, and as I will argue in this book, these tighter controls have also restricted the range of relationships among teachers, students, parents, and administrators. Over time, the simple control of administrators has been augmented with both more direct and more invasive bureaucratic controls of mandatory time of instruction, directed standards for each grade level, yearly testing, and the technical controls of commercially prepared, scripted lessons in core reading programs. Consequently, elementary teachers' engagements in reading instruction actually reduce the possibilities of their intellectual and social development and freedom.

Twenty years ago, I began the first edition of *Broken Promises* with the charge that the original promises of reading instruction had been broken for most Americans. Few students learned to read texts critically at school in order to understand the word and the world in ways that allow them to see through the mysteries, ambiguities, and complexities of modern living in order to make sense of their lives, to understand the connections among their lives and those of others, and to act on that new knowledge to construct a better, more just democracy. Because business, reading experts, and the state continue to mediate the human interactions of reading and teaching in school classrooms, the original promises are still broken, and now they are twisted so that we cannot see that those promises are even valuable. Think about faith-based initiatives, the Patriot Act, and the end of welfare as we know it as they direct our reading of moral, political, and economic America. Although process writing and whole language approaches brought glimmers of hope that reading education might change during the late 1980s and early 1990s, nearly all teachers and students continued to follow the directions in core reading (basal and other scripted) programs daily during times designated for reading instruction, and virtually every school district tested its students on reading abilities annually. As if these technical controls were not enough to ensure the success of the one best system, George W. Bush's administration increased its bureaucratic surveillance of teachers and students, requiring the technical control of commercially prepared core reading programs and standardized reading tests based on reading experts' scientific evidence.

Recently many educational writers have criticized this increased regulation of teachers' and students' lives during reading instruction in elementary schools. Some contrast the best efforts of teachers from the 1980s and 1990s against the current enthusiasm for compelling teachers to follow scripts that others have prepared for reading instruction in order to boost students' scores on standardized tests. The titles of their books—*Literacy at the Crossroads, Testing Is Not Teaching, In Defense of Good Teaching*—indicate how Regie Routman, Donald Graves, and Kenneth Goodman have addressed current legislation and policy. Although they refer to the macro-level politics of reading education, they focus primarily on the art of teaching reading and provide ideas for teachers to negotiate on the micro-level politics of schooling. In other writings, Goodman distinguished his critique from these others by describing the limited scope of the federal government's definition of reading and reading research. Other critics—Stephen Krashen, Jeff McQuillan, Elaine Garan, and James Cunningham—question both the research and the interpretation of that research, which federal officials and the reading experts have selected to constitute the science of reading instruction. This second group of critics implies, and sometimes states explicitly, that factors other than science drive federal decisions on these matters because the flawed designs, unique subjects, and unclear results do not fit well with the policy recommendations that the research is supposed to justify. A third group of critics names political ideology as the driving force behind current policies and legislation for the No Child Left Behind initiative. In *Big Brother and the National Reading Curriculum,* for example, Richard Allington writes, "[federal and state] mandates aren't really about improved curriculum materials as much as they are about asserting external authority and ideological control over the educational process."[4] In *Reading the Naked Truth,* Gerry Coles doubts George W. Bush's compassionate conservatism, which underlies his reading initiative, because his administration has actually injured the social and economic status of poor children in America while requiring them to meet the same academic standards as all other students.

Each of these critiques is useful in naming some of the politics that teachers and students face when negotiating current policies on reading education in their classrooms. Most defend teachers as artists and assume students capable of learning much more than they are offered at school. They raise questions about increased surveillance of classroom practices, and they encourage teachers, students, and parents to become political about reading instruction in order to make changes in schools. However, there are also limits to their critiques as well. Most write as if the new promises and policies of reading education were invented within the last decade during Bill Clinton's and George W. Bush's presidencies. Although they decry unprecedented federal government intrusions into school practices, the tyranny of bad science in classrooms, and the boldness of textbook publishers and other educational corporations when supplying commodities to these new markets, they argue as if the federal government has not been directly involved in reading education for fifty years, reading experts have not encouraged science to replace art in classrooms for the better part of a century, and educational businesses just became interested in profits. Although the individuals involved currently in government, science, and business may act meaner, more aggressively, and more clumsily than their predecessors, their actions are not new or all that different from the practices of government, reading experts, and business before them. The same market ideology that led to the rise of reading experts, changed reading textbooks into core reading programs, and invited the federal government to intervene in local schooling during the middle of the last century drives the new promises, policies, and practices of reading education in this one.

Although these critics name many of the problems facing teachers and students today, they do not explain why market ideology pervades reading education, dominating current thinking about schooling, reading, and our lives. Moreover, they do not consider how the loose coupling among business, science, and the state has outmaneuvered all challenges in order to maintain its influence on the day-to-day practices in elementary classrooms for many decades. Because these critics neglect this ideology, they cannot explain why and how most teachers and students learn to accept and even perpetuate the new promises, policies, and practices in reading education. Without careful analysis of market ideology and its impact on the macro and micro levels of reading education, the critics cannot recommend effective means for becoming political around these problems.

A New Argument

This revision and extension of *Broken Promises* is intended to address these absences in the critiques of current reading policy and recommended practices. The book is intended for teachers, would-be teachers, and friends of teachers who are currently experiencing increasing pressures to conform to a lifeless system that treats reading, teachers, and students as factors for manipulation in the official calculus of reading education, designed to fit the needs of a global economy, but not the needs of a democratic public. I start from a different set of assumptions than either advocates of the new promise or their critics. I do not assume that science holds the answers to social questions. Neither good nor bad science provides laws for social action that are universal in time or space. As critics have demonstrated, the science of reading instruction is a site of struggle in which science becomes a tool of politicians and not a determiner of generalizable truth. The critics are correct that the definitions, policies, and rules of acceptable behavior are negotiated among participants rather than discovered through science. Reading education, the science of reading instruction, and core reading programs are constructed and are socially maintained. Most critics, however, do not seem to recognize that these social negotiations are not conducted among equals because social, economic, and political circumstances have given certain groups license to assert undue influence over the outcomes. Consequently, these outcomes benefit the negotiators unequally, and the less dominant groups become dependent on the dominant group's definitions. Because these present conditions are rooted in the social relations of the past, they often seem opaque and immutable to present-day negotiators, and the inequality of participation and benefit appears benign, appropriate, and just the way it is.

But as the twelve events listed at the opening of this introduction suggest, and as seems to be becoming clearer each day in schools across America, the new promises, policies, and practices of reading instruction are not benign, appropriate, or necessary. This new book illuminates the past and current relations that created and maintained the inequalities in the continuednegotiations of possible meanings of reading education; it documents the consequences of past and current negotiations and programs; and it identifies contradictions between the consequent social structures from past negotiations and the individual and social needs of a democratic public. These contradictions are opportunities to work for more just social relations in and out of reading education. To make sense of the present, to envision a different future, and to take more strategic action, we must understand the past and how the market ideology of capitalism became the most dynamic force in reading education. I begin, accordingly, with three chapters that review the original promises of reading education and their imperfect pursuit, from the inception of formal reading programs in America through the intrusion of the industrial ideology and promises of the early and middle twentieth century to the recognition during the 1980s that a market ideology would be employed. Chapter 4 presents the opposition to the industrial rationale for reading education from the turn of the nineteenth century until the 1990s, when it appeared for a moment that a learner-centered reading education was possible, perhaps likely. Chapters 5, 6, and 7 describe the dynamic influences of the state, business, and reading science upon reading education during the last two decades, including the new promises, policies, and practices of Educate America and No Child Left Behind, focused exclusively on reading as human capital. Chapters 8 and 9 detail the consequences of these new laws for teachers and students. Finally in Chapter 10, I describe new efforts to reinsert the promise of civic reading into American classrooms.

I started this project as a second edition of *Broken Promises*, an update of that argument. I do understand recent policy and laws as extensions of past efforts to rationalize reading instruction to make its outcomes predictable. Across the last century, the economic rationale for reading instruction trumped the civic rationale. The market ideology and its new promise—that reading education will make all students capable of fulfilling the high-skill, high-wage jobs waiting for them in the global economy—distort the balance between the economic and civic rationales to such a point that the civic rationale has all but disappeared. Students are to learn to read in order to perform in the economy, and not to understand themselves, others, and ways texts work for and against them in a democracy. In effect, under the market ideology and its laws concerning reading education, we are teaching and students are reading against democracy. When I came to that realization, I recognized that this new text was not a revision, but a rewriting of the original. And I thought that a new title was appropriate—*Reading Against Democracy: The Broken Promises of Reading Instruction*.

Although the current situation in reading education seems bleak in the United States, if you examine it closely, you'll see it is far from hopeless. If students, teachers, researchers, and parents become aware of the reasons for the present conditions and work together strategically, then they can develop reading programs that keep the original promises of democratic life.

Chapter One

Reading Instruction Before the Turn of the Twentieth Century

Type the words *Dick and Jane* into any search engine on the Internet, and you will receive pages of addresses for websites devoted to the characters from the *New Basic Readers* published by Scott Foresman between 1930 and 1965. Tagnwag Books sells vintage editions of the original primers and provides free shipping on orders over $125. Fridgedoor.com offers magnets with scenes from the primers. If you scroll down the addresses, you'll find sites marketing full-size replicas of Dick and Jane's furniture, Dick and Jane T-shirts, and Dick and Jane dolls. Not all the sites are vendors, however. Some consider the *New Basic Readers* more seriously. For example, *Growing Up with Dick and Jane* presents a sentimental cultural treatment of the series' story lines, suggesting that the books taught schoolchildren about the American dream before, during, and after World War II. In *Reading Dick and Jane with Me*, Clarissa Sligh studies race, gender, and sexuality by writing poems using the limited vocabulary of the early Dick and Jane books over collages made from her photographs. In these ways, Dick and Jane are still alive and well in the hearts and minds of many Americans because they represent a past that many choose to remember.

What makes these sites so effective is the immediate familiarity of the names Dick and Jane to millions of Americans who followed their lives while learning to read at school. At one point, the *New Basic Readers* were used in 85 percent of elementary school classrooms across the country. If you close your eyes, perhaps you can see the faded watercolor pictures with short cryptic sentences like "Run, Dick, run" printed below them. You might also remember the classroom routines of your reading instruction: sitting around a table with book in hand, reading aloud in turn to your teacher, listening to the teacher talk about the shapes and sounds of words, returning to your desk to complete seatwork, and receiving a star at the top of a perfect assignment. Although the materials and routines have changed a bit over the years since Dick and Jane populated elementary school classrooms, one thing has not changed since the birth of Dick and Jane—most reading lessons consist of teachers and students following reading programs that are prepared commercially. Perhaps it seems that American reading instruction has always taken this form.

One way to gain some perspective on current reading instruction is to look at the past to see what factors contributed to the development of current structures and relations and to determine why those factors proved to be persuasive. Looking back enables us to identify points at which decisions were made that defined our current practices and to consider when possibilities for different structures and relations were either dismissed or neglected. This is not an easy task because most analyses of reading instruction before the turn of the twentieth century are limited to studies of materials, expert opinion, or educational policy.[1] Better evidence would be found in firsthand accounts of classroom practice from teachers' journals, students' diaries, or itinerant observers' reports. Although I risk misrepresenting the actual activities of reading instruction, I rely solely on descriptions of materials and policy for the colonial period of American schooling.

The Colonial Period

Many among the first immigrants to what would become the United States were intent on building the kingdom of Zion in which the word of God would provide the rule of law as a defense against Satan and other temptations of the spirit. In order to accomplish this goal, leaders sought ideological unity through a common understanding of the principles of faith among all believers. Those principles were to be found in the Bible, and the ability to read became a civic as well as spiritual duty of all who inhabited the New World. As Cotton Mather explained in *Cares About the Nurseries*, "We have in our hands the holy Scriptures which are a storehouse of saving truths and contain all that must be known by all that would be saved." All colonists were expected to "be wise unto salvation" in all endeavors of their lives.[2]

During the earliest colonial days, reading education was a family matter in which children learned to sign their name and to repeat Bible catechisms. However, responsibility for literacy was considered a community matter among American colonialists; "it being viewed . . . as the most important bulwark after religion in their incessant struggle against the satanic barbarism of the wilderness."[3] Independent schools appeared as early as 1635 in Virginia and Massachusetts and 1642 in Connecticut, although literacy rates among colonists remained relatively low in comparison with those of England. In 1642, the Massachusetts legislature passed a law requiring towns to make certain that all "youth under family Government be taught to read perfectly the English tongue, have knowledge in capital laws, and be taught some orthodox catechisms, and that they be brought up to some honest employment, profitable to themselves and to the Commonwealth."[4] Families who failed to teach their children to read were subject to punishment. By 1647, the Massachusetts colony enacted a second bill for the establishment of formal schools for larger communities.

> It being one chief project of that old deluder, Satan, to keep men from the knowledge of the Scriptures, as in former times by keeping them in an unknown tongue. . . . It is therefore ordered that every township in this jurisdiction, after the Lord hath increased them to fifty households shall forthwith appoint one within their town to teach all such children as shall resort to him to write and read, whose wages shall be paid either by the parents or masters of such children, or by the inhabitants in general.[5]

Most New England and Mid-Atlantic colonies followed with similar laws within the next fifty years, although some southern colonies waited one hundred years before establishing publicly funded schools.[6] These petty schools, as they were called, were expected to render children literate in English, taking two or three years to complete the task. Affluent graduates of petty schools attended grammar schools, which, according to the Massachusetts Old Deluder, Satan Act, were available in towns of one hundred households. Those unable to attend grammar schools entered the workforce and learned limited practices of reading commensurate with their employment. Grammar schools prepared students in classical languages, mathematics, and history in order to enable the brightest and most well-to-do to attend college. To be sure, school laws were unevenly enforced and many towns and many citizens within towns failed to comply.[7] Teachers for petty and grammar schools came from a wide variety of backgrounds, ranging from literate mothers who taught in their kitchens to college-educated scholars who were waiting for a ministry posting. Regardless of the location, the size, or the teacher in the school, the purpose of education, the materials, and the instructional methods were directed toward salvation.

As explicitly stated in the Old Deluder, Satan Act of 1647, petty schools were designed to enable individuals to fulfill their Protestant responsibilities to know the word of God and to learn proper religious behavior. In a sense, schooling was a device for promoting uniformity of thought and character based on the popular ideology of that time. This intent came through most noticeably in the rhetoric of community leaders and in the materials used in these schools. Until the middle of the eighteenth century, instructional materials for reading came in three forms. Students' first instructional texts were hornbooks, small paddles made of wood with a thin layer of cow horn stretched across to protect the writing—the alphabet, a syllabary, and the Lord's Prayer. After students mastered the content of the hornbook and were able to recite it upon demand, teachers used either a psalter or the Bible, depending on the availability of materials and the abilities of the students. A psalter was a book of spelling lessons that progressed from syllables to words to sentences.

By the beginning of the eighteenth century, the *New England Primer* replaced the hornbook and the psalter in most colonies.[8] The Primer began with Bible passages to be memorized aurally in order to convey to students the ideological intent for learning to read. The alphabet followed with the same religious tone—"A In Adam's fall, We sinned all." The contents of the Primer give some insight into the expected relationship between teachers and students during reading lessons. Students were asked to memorize the following verse in the first few pages:

> I will fear God, and honour the KING.
> I will honour my Father & Mother.
> I will obey my Superiors.
> I will Submit to my Elders.

As best can be determined, appropriate application of Bible verses to everyday life was the ultimate goal of reading instruction for most students during the seventeenth century. Teaching methods at that time followed basically two forms. Students listened to a teacher's rendition of the lesson and then were expected to engage in independent practice, leading to mastery. After a time, each student went before the teacher to recite the lesson she had learned. A second method employed choral learning, in which a teacher or older student led others in joint drills of lesson content. In either method, lessons continued until each pupil could read the contents of the primer perfectly. For more than one hundred years, the *New England Primer* was the schoolbook of America, and it was a remarkably successful enterprise, selling more than three million copies in its first 150 years of printing.

With rapid population growth, westward migration, urbanization, and ethnic and religious diversity during the eighteenth century, the power of religious leaders began to wane. In the Massachusetts colony, colonial leaders used secular ideologies to set the criteria for more and more of its structures. For example, before 1691, religious affiliation determined community status and suffrage rights. After that date, property ownership gave one the right to vote, suggesting that wealth was deemed a more important marker of community status than membership in any particular church. Changes in the social structures led to challenges to the religious tones and purposes of the petty schools, the pious content of the primers, and the solely classical content of the grammar schools. In 1749 Benjamin Franklin proposed a different kind of early education, one that would include a useful curriculum for average citizens based on republican texts. Franklin encouraged teachers to use *Cato's Letters*, which argued that freedom of thought and speech was essential for economic and social development. Cato (and Franklin) argued that this freedom was incompatible with schools dominated by religion.[9] In order to ensure that such reading was possible apart from schools, Franklin established the first subscription library in the United States.

> These libraries have improved the general conversation of the Americans, made the common tradesman and farmers as intelligent as most gentlemen from other countries, and perhaps have contributed in some degree to the stand so generally made throughout the colonies in defense of their privileges.[10]

With John Newbery's *A Little Pretty Pocketbook* in 1744, the publishing of children's books began in earnest, and some of these books were published for the first time in America during the War of Independence. Their contents reflect a general change in the child-rearing philosophies of the times from instilling a fear of God in each child to developing a positive moral character and entrepreneurial spirit among children. There is little evidence that children's books were used widely during reading lessons, but the instructional materials of the period show a similar change in tone. For example, Noah Webster's *Blue-Backed Speller*, first published in 1793, included lessons that were patriotic and morally didactic, and the 1800 edition of the *New England Primer* began not with a reminder of Adam's and our sins but with "A was an angler who fished with a hook." The general purpose for education was also modified, as suggested in Thomas Jefferson's words: "If a nation expects to be ignorant and free, in a state of civilization, it expects what never was and will never be." Jefferson proposed universal schooling for white males in reading, arithmetic, and history "at common expense to all" as the primary protection against tyranny.[11]

These events and actions are examples of the ideological changes in society, in schools, and in school materials with regard to adult expectations of youth. The young were not expected to create and maintain of the kingdom of Zion. Their primary virtues were no longer piety and the observance of the statutes of the *Covenent*. Their identities were no longer solely in service of salvation. During the seventeenth century, American youth were expected to learn to be useful to their country, to know things for their utility, to act with modesty and civility, to be dutiful to society's needs, and to serve people, not God. Their schooling, schoolbooks, and reading instruction reflected these new expectations.

Reading Instruction in the Nineteenth Century

In "Governing the Young: Teachers' Behaviors in American Primary Schools, 1820–1880, A Documentary History," Barbara Finkelstein surveys nearly one thousand diaries, journals, and reports from that period in order to develop descriptions of the daily practices in classrooms.[12] She devotes nearly one-seventh of her discussion exclusively to reading instruction, arguing that it is the only thread that connects all types and levels of schools. At times, her summaries dispute previous histories of reading instruction for this period. For example, the journals relate that instructional methods and early editions of textbooks lingered late into the nineteenth century, contradicting educational historians' claim that new methods and texts supplanted the old on a regular basis.

According to teachers and students, teachers emphasized word identification over meaning and required oral reading rather than discussion during most classes. Textbooks continued to direct reading instruction. In some rural schools where texts were scarce, children brought books from home, which teachers taught them to read individually. This required teachers to make individual assignments, hear individual recitations, and render individual appraisals. Most teachers of the time, however, whether rural or urban, created classes among their students so that the same lessons could be taught to several students simultaneously. Standardization of textbooks made teachers' practice of grouping easier. Clara Barton's journal describes how the text content set both the curriculum and the organization of the classrooms:

> The majestic schoolmaster seated himself, and taking a primer, called the class of little ones to him. He pointed the letters to each. I named them all, and was asked to spell some little words, "dog" . . . whereupon I hesitatingly informed him that I did not spell "there." "Where do you spell?" I spell in "artichoke," that being the leading word in the three-syllable column in my speller. He . . . conformed to my suggestion, and I was put in to the "artichoke" class to bear my part for the winter.[13]

Finkelstein concludes that "the descriptive literature suggests that most teachers of reading confined their activities to those of the overseer and drill-master,"[14] who carved assignments from the pages of primers. Motivation for both reading and writing lessons was seen as a disciplinary rather than an instructional matter. "Throughout the period under discussion, we find that teachers more or less consciously devised a variety of rewards and punishments which reflected the belief that the route to literacy was neither interesting nor stimulating."[15] Overseers left learning almost entirely to students, limiting the master's role to defining assignments and later listening to recitation.

> The class, composed of eight or ten scholars, takes its place on the floor, each one toeing the mark. The master commands "attention" and "obedience," the boys bow their heads and the girls curtsey. . . . One end is called the head, the other the foot, of the class. . . . The teacher opens the book, which is of course Webster's *Elementary*, and turning to the lessons, pronounces the words, beginning at the head. If a scholar misspells a word it is given to the next one.[16]

Drillmasters organized exercises—choral readings, spelling bees, and contests—that would help students memorize information without the teacher becoming overly involved in either illustration or explanation.

> The teacher had a queer contrivance nailed to a post set up in the middle of the room. It was known as a "spelling board." When he pulled the string to which the board was fastened, the school could spell out words in moderate tones. . . . If he proceeded to pull the board uptight everybody "spelled to themselves." When he gave the cord a pull until down dropped the plank and the hubbub began. Everything went with a roar. Just as loud as you pleased, you could spell anything. People along the road were happy to know the children were getting their lessons.[17]

During the first half of the nineteenth century, overseers and drillmasters used the spelling method to teach reading—students learned the names of letters (lowercase, capital, and italic), spelled and pronounced lists of two- and three-letter nonsense syllables, and then spelled and pronounced lists of words of various lengths before they began to read sentences orally. Often the journey from letters to sentences was long and hard. For example, in Webster's *American Spelling Book*, the most popular spelling method textbook of this time, students were not asked to read sentences until they could successfully render the first one hundred pages of the book on demand. Regardless of teachers' pedagogical choices, their goal remained the same. "Teachers proceeded as though learning had occurred when their students could imitate the skills or reproduce the knowledge contained in each of the assignments."[18]

By the 1860s, most urban teachers had shifted the emphasis of their reading instruction from the letter and spelling to the syllable and pronunciation, although many rural teachers continued with the spelling method for several decades—even into the twentieth century. By far the most successful textbook promoting the phonics method was William Holmes McGuffey's *Eclectic First Reader for Young Children*. McGuffey's approach and sequence proved to be satisfactory for both overseers and drillmasters. More than 120 million copies of the reader were purchased between 1836 and 1920. McGuffey removed spelling as a prerequisite to reading and used it as a means to aid and assess students' mastery of the recognition of words. In the phonics method, teachers directed students' attention first to the alphabet, then to the pronunciation guide for words, and finally to simple sentences and stories. To help teachers concerned with the lack of correspondence between symbols and sounds in English spellings, a reader was published with a modified alphabet (Leigh's *McGuffey's New England Primer and Pronouncing Orthography, 1868*). McGuffey offered the following advice to teachers:

> To the teacher: This is simply a reprint, in pronouncing type, of the one hitherto in use. It may be used with any method of teaching. Even the pupil taught to spell by letter will be guided by it to the right pronunciation of every word.
>
> But it is better to spell by sounds—to pronounce the word so slowly as to stop an instant after each sound.
>
> To teach the sounds and the signs used to denote them, exercises like the following may be printed on the blackboard for dictation to the class and recitation in concert. First pronounce the syllables in order, *m e* me, *m a* ma, then spell by sounds *m e* me, *m a* may.[19]

Just as the content of the *New England Primer* and Webster's spelling books represented the dominant ideologies of their times, McGuffey's readers presented the continued ideology of nationalism in times of increased immigration and the emerging social philosophy of business and industry. Beyond the primer and spelling book, the readers offered five volumes of progressively more sophisticated readings, including essays on nature and history, descriptions of manufacturing, and stories concerning appropriate deportment. These texts suggested that women should be tidy, appreciative of learning, and submissive and that men should be industrious, thrifty, and charitable. Moreover, these stories attempted to foster a respect for private property, a religious rationale for the contemporary class structure, and a distrust of Jacksonian democracy.[20]

McGuffey understood his role in the shaping of the American mind, extolling the social importance of both clergy and teacher. Yet in the fourth reader, he published, "much as I respect the clergy, I believe that they must yield in importance to the office of the teacher . . . the office of the teacher is the noblest on earth."[21] At their core, the readers taught Christian virtues with a

Calvinist twist. Their texts reiterated that those who worked hard would make something of themselves because industry and a government supportive of industry and business would ensure their opportunities.

> Little child, now learn of me.
> Let thy youth and seed-time be. And,
> When wintry age shall come, richly
> Bear thy harvest home.[22]

According to Finkelstein's interpretation of the firsthand accounts that she gathered, teachers' "tendency to rely almost completely on the texts meant that students, as they learned to read, write, cipher, and draw maps, imbibed the moral maxims, the political pieties, and the economic and social preachments of the writers whose books the students were commonly asked to memorize."[23]

Despite Horace Mann's advocacy in the 1840s and 1850s, the word method made little headway as a teaching method until the late 1860s and the 1870s. Finkelstein argues that the method failed to attract teachers' enthusiasm because it required them to become "interpreters of culture" rather than overseers or drillmasters. That is, the word method in its pure form eliminated the alphabet, syllabary, and spelling exercises from reading textbooks, beginning instead with familiar words complete with discussions concerning their meaning. Perhaps the earliest large-scale attempt to implement the word method was Edward Austin Sheldon's "objective system" for primary education, which became the mainstay of the Oswego Movement from the 1860s until the mid-1880s.

During an inspection of Toronto schools, Sheldon, then superintendent of schools in Oswego, New York, discovered the English Home and Colonial Institution's methods and materials, which were oriented "not to communicate knowledge but . . . to lead the children to take an interest in all objects that surround them; to cultivate attention, the power of accurate observation, and correct expression."[24] From his experiences in Toronto and his subsequent examination of the three hundred dollars' worth of English Home and Colonial Institution materials (objects, pictures, and teacher's manuals) he purchased, Sheldon rewrote the Oswego course of study to include the following statement on reading instruction:

> The children first begin by reading words, without spelling, as printed on the board by the teacher. At first, they only learn the names of animals, or objects, or actions perfectly familiar to them, and as far as possible, these objects or pictures of them, should be presented to the children and made subjects of familiar conversation that they may become interested in them before the words are put upon the board.[25]

Acceptance of the word method, then, required teachers to redefine their goals of education from the reproduction of the facts within textbooks to the examination of objects within their daily experience, and then to the interpretation of textbook facts in light of their observations. And according to Finkelstein's journals, most teachers seemed unwilling or unable to redefine their goals.

> The evidence suggests that whether [teachers] taught in urban or rural schools in the North, South, East, or West, whether they instructed students according to the literal, syllabic, or word system, they typically defined reading as reading aloud—an activity which required the teacher to do little more than assign selections to be read, and if he chose, to correct the pronunciation of his students.[26]

In 1861, Sheldon established the Oswego State Normal and Training School to train teachers to provide instruction in all subjects using the objective system. The school became immediately popular, with hundreds of teachers enrolling over the next twenty-five years and graduates finding employment in most states of the union and several foreign countries. Although the objective system created much enthusiasm within the educational community, the system was not without its contradictions and its critics. Reading instruction was at the center of many of these controversies. While the word method was the official position of the methods and materials advocated at Oswego State Normal, the sample lessons developed by Oswego teachers to direct reading instruction at the school and for sale to others dealt primarily with the phonics method. "A few simple words were permitted to be learned as words, but in the main, the reading proceeded from the use of letters and phonetic combinations of letters."[27] According to the critics of the system, teachers followed these sample lessons to the letter.[28] Thus, two forms of reading instruction coexisted within the objective system of the Oswego Movement—a word method of vocabulary study conducted during science and social studies lessons and a formal phonics program during separate reading lessons. By 1872, the Oswego schools began to withdraw some support for the objective system, and by 1900 the system was virtually indistinguishable from the lessons of overseers and drillmasters.

In fact, most teachers who used the word method textbooks combined that method with a phonics approach—pronouncing the word, requiring students to repeat it in unison, breaking it immediately into its phonic elements, blending those sounds to the original pronunciation, and finally discussing its meaning. In this combined method, definition rather than discussion was the main treatment of meaning. In this way, the word method was rendered acceptable to overseers and drillmasters. Curriculum historian Larry Cuban suggests that the co-optation of the Oswego object method and the word approach demonstrated the conservative nature of the schooling, the power of classroom routines, and the lack of teacher training concerning proposed innovations.[29] When left to their own devices, teachers often assimilated new ideas, methods, and materials into their existing teaching habits. Consequently, teachers retained the notion that the purpose of learning to read was to bring ideological unity among a disparate group in order that individuals would fit productively into the status quo of their communities. In effect, the task of teaching others to read had a civilizing function, which required neither consent nor interest among a teacher's charges. The goal was to transfer the right thoughts into the heads of the young. Textbooks provided the vehicle and the map to reach this goal, and teachers were merely the drivers.

The Beginnings of the New Education

Lest this account of nineteenth-century reading instruction seem overly pessimistic, it is important to remember that there were some "interpreters of culture," to use Finkelstein's phrase. These were teachers who sought to extend children's understanding of their world beyond the memorization of textbook information. In fact, because of increased immigration and a greater exchange of ideas between educators in the United States and in Europe, the number of interpreters of culture increased slowly during the latter half of the century but never approached 10 percent of the teaching population.[30] These teachers sought to integrate children's interests, needs, and inclinations with their curricula, making reading and writing natural consequences of children's study of their physical and social environments. Their assumptions about people and learning distinguished their work from that of their peers.

Most rejected the doctrine of child depravity, which supplied the rationale for authoritarian didactic teaching and moral training of colonial, eighteenth- and nineteenth-century schooling. Borrowing from Rousseau, these interpreters of culture sought to turn the ideology of control on its head. Interpreters of culture believed that the individual was born innocent, inquisitive, and able, and that social impositions of cultural and moral traditions pulled the youngster away from goodness. Rather than organize their instruction in order to constrain children's temptations and urges, thereby overcoming original sin, these teachers sought classrooms and schools organized to foster and develop children's natural goodness. Toward that end, they devised curricula based on the truths children brought with them to school as well as the ones they might discover while there. In this way, the process of a child's discovery became just as important as the content of the discovery. As Finkelstein notes, few teachers or students described their educational experiences using these words.

Perhaps the most coordinated effort to build a school system around these assumptions at the time was the Quincy School District, under the direction of Colonel Francis Parker. After studying the educational philosophy of Comenius, Pestalozzi, Froebel, and Herbart while in Europe, Parker was given full responsibility to examine and improve the seven schools of Quincy, Massachussetts. In his initial report to the Quincy Board of Education in 1875, Parker commented that he was appalled that children came to school after five years of successful development in "nature's great methods, object training and play," only to find imagination, curiosity, and love for mental and physical activity destroyed "by dull, wearisome hours of listless activity upon hard benches."[31] Parker began immediately to reorganize the primary grades into a "pleasant, cheerful home," providing demonstration lessons for Quincy teachers, insisting that teachers study themselves as they worked, and rewriting Quincy's course of study.

For reading, Parker proposed the word method because he believed that students should learn to read as they learned to talk, by discussing topics of interest in a supportive atmosphere. His new course of study required that the language arts be integrated with other subjects. Drills on the rules of grammar were replaced by opportunities for students to write sentences, draft letters, and compose short texts concerning the day's events. Spelling would be developed through these writing exercises, with an emphasis on students learning to spell the words in their own vocabularies. Speaking would be taught by having children share their day's work. Listening would be cultivated through short presentations on the objects and topics students found most interesting.

Charles Adams, president of the Quincy School Board, remarked that "in all, children were being taught to read, write, spell, and think all at the same time without really taking notice."[32] The rules of grammar and phonic analysis were to be considered formally later in the curriculum, after students had literacy well in hand and they were intellectually able to embark on the detailed study of the English language. All students were to be allowed to progress through this curriculum at their own pace rather than according to their age, and slower students were expected to receive more of the teacher's attention than the students who caught on quickly.

Observers of Quincy teachers, and there were many, reported that Parker's course of study was indeed implemented in classrooms. The most detailed account of the Quincy system in practice is *The Quincy Method Illustrated*, by Lelia Patridge.[33] Patridge, a former teacher and "teacher of teachers," spent much of 1880 and 1881 observing classroom instruction and recording actual lessons in the Quincy schools. Her first observation was that there was no Quincy system, wherein teachers were expected to follow one text or set of plans. Rather, she observed what she called "a unity of principle" among the teachers, without the uniformity in classroom practice noticeable in most schools. For example, in the lowest primary class, Patridge observed a lesson centered on Jumbo, P. T. Barnum's circus elephant, which had passed through Quincy by train the previous day.

> The lesson began with a listless group of students and a teacher's remark, "This is what I'm thinking about," as she drew a clumsy figure of an elephant wearing a blanket inscribed with JUMBO. When finished, the teacher asked "What is it?" and with that she had the attention of all her students. They replied, "Jumbo!" "Yes, that's its name, but what is it?" "An elephant," came the reply. "Tell me something about him?" To which the students responded with a long list of sentences which the teacher wrote on the blackboard to provide the text for reading and context for further discussion.[34]

In another classroom of more advanced children, Patridge found students "talking with the pencil,"[35] a practice in which the students discussed a picture, "first with their tongues and afterwards with their pencils." The classroom teacher explained that talking with the pencils did not immediately follow the conversation about the picture because then students memorized their sentences and copied them in their essays. Memorization limited the benefits of the exercise in composition and reduced the number of different texts for other students to read later. In all, Patridge describes scores of these lessons, each holding to Parker's principles.

To be sure, not all visitors to the Quincy schools were as impressed with the Quincy system as Patridge. Parker met almost immediate opposition from parents and even some of the school board members who had hired him. As early as the second year of his tenure, the town council entertained a resolution to dismiss Parker as school superintendent. Most of his critics questioned whether or not it was prudent or even possible to ask students to think, read, and figure without first memorizing the traditional skills to do these tasks. When Quincy students did poorly on their traditional year-end examinations, critics wondered aloud about the cost of Parker's expansion of the curriculum to include practical topics such as sewing and gardening, when so few students seemed to know or value academic information. At times even Charles Adams and Parker showed concern about their school reform project. Adams was shocked that at one school only one in six students could read a common book at sight and Parker referred to the primary program as "fairly a success" and the grammar school changes as "by no means a failure."[36] Adams explained, however.

> I doubt if one in ten scholars knew what a noun, a pronoun or an adjective was or could have parsed a sentence or explained the difference

between its subject and its predicate. They could however put their ideas into sentences on paper with correctness and facility, and though they could not define what they were they showed that they could use nouns, pronouns and adjectives in writing as well as they could in speech. Out of five hundred grammar school children taken indiscriminately from all the schools, no less than four hundred showed results which were either excellent or satisfactory.[37]

After failing to secure a raise or an appointment to the board of directors of the prestigious Adams Academy, Parker resigned from Quincy in 1880 and within three years became the director of the Cook County Normal School in Chicago.

The Public School System of the United States in 1892

One way to determine the immediate impact of Parker's influence on reading instruction is to look closely at Joseph Mayer Rice's survey of elementary schools in thirty-six cities conducted in 1892 as a prelude to a series of articles published in *Forum Magazine*.[38] Rice, a New York City pediatrician, had spent two years studying the "science of education" at universities in Jena and Leipzig, and he had published several short critiques of American instruction in small weekly journals. These articles brought Rice to the attention of *Forum Magazine*'s editor, who offered to sponsor Rice's firsthand appraisal of schooling from St. Paul to Washington, D.C., and from St. Louis to Boston. During his survey, Rice placed "no reliance whatsoever on reports published by school officials"[39]; rather, he visited several classrooms in each city and interviewed more than 1,200 teachers. He returned in June of 1892 with notebooks crowded with observations, statistics, and illustrations detailing his tour. His nine articles quadrupled *Forum*'s circulation.[40]

In the best muckraking tradition, Rice reported that reading instruction in nearly 90 percent of the schools in these cities was outdated, mechanical, and totally ineffective. "I found the results in reading and writing language almost universally poor in schools where reading matter, at least during the first two years, consisted of nothing but empty words, silly sentences, and baby-trash, and where the time spent writing was devoted to copying such words and sentences from the blackboard or reading book."[41] Even Quincy schools did not escape Rice's criticism because they abandoned Parker's ideas of unified curriculum. In all, Rice divided the schools into three categories based on their integration of literacy instruction into other subject areas and whether or not students' interests were taken into consideration during classroom instruction.

Rice labeled the least effective reading instruction "mechanical," driven by textbooks, uninformed teachers, and the ideology of control. He offered many examples of poor practice to ensure that readers would be able to examine local instruction. He included the following observations from Baltimore, with an overseeing teacher attempting the word method, and from Chicago, where a drillmaster attempted phonics instruction.

> The reading was fully as mechanical as the arithmetic. It amounted simply to calling off words. Not only was there no expression, but there was not even an inflection, or a pause at a comma or a period. Nor did the teacher ever correct mispronounced words, or make any attempt to teach the pupils how to read. Before the children began to read the designated lesson, there was a ludicrously mechanical introduction, including the calling off of the words placed at the top of the page, then: "Page 56, Lesson XVIII, the Dog and the Rat. Dog, Rat, Catch, Room, Run, Smell, Wag, Jump." And then came the story.[42]

> After entering the room containing the youngest pupils, the principal said to the teacher, "Begin with the mouth movements and go right straight through. . . ." About fifty pupils now begin in concert to give utterance to the sounds of a, e, and oo, varying their order, thus: a, e, oo; a, e, oo; e, a, oo, etc. . . . When some time had been spent in thus manoeuvering the jaw, the teacher remarked, "Your tongues are not loose." Fifty pupils now put out their tongues and wagged them in all directions. The principal complimented the children on their wagging.[43]

Rice characterized the second group of schools as programs in transition, wherein children's interests were considered in some, but not all classes, and the supervisors were attempting to elicit change. However, the language arts curriculum was still separated into isolated subjects of reading, penmanship, and grammar. In most schools in this second group, Rice attributed lack of progress toward unification of curricula to political interference, to poor execution of reasonably progressive plans, or to both, as in these examples from Rice's description of Philadelphia schools:

> The public schools of Philadelphia offer a striking example of the difficulties involved in advancing schools, when those in authority use their offices for selfish motives, whether political or other, instead of for the purpose of furthering the welfare of the children entrusted to their care.[44]

> The influence exerted upon the schools by the new course of study, together with the attempt on the part of the superintendent and his

assistants to break up the mechanical work without materially increasing the professional strength of the teachers, has been a most peculiar one ... so that we find the instruction at the end of ten years of supervision neither mechanical nor scientific. What we do find, however, in very many instances, is the weakest teaching conceivable.[45]

Rice drew roughly the same picture of reading instruction in 1892 as had the one thousand teacher and student reports that Finkelstein used in her study of schooling from the 1820s to the 1880s. Although Finkelstein blamed teachers for the poor state of reading instruction, Rice distributed blame among (1) unconcerned parents who did not acquaint themselves with the principles of scientific education or the practices of schooling, (2) meddling politicians who appointed cronies as superintendents and teachers and tampered with school budgets, (3) uninformed and overworked supervisors and superintendents who could not possibly overcome the problems of schooling, and (4) poorly educated teachers who were not well versed in either content or pedagogical knowledge. While Rice cajoled parents to take an active part in their children's education, he offered three "laws" that must be obeyed if schools were to improve.

> The school system must be absolutely divorced from politics in every sense of the word, the supervisors of the schools must be properly directed and thorough ... the principle aim of which is to increase the professional strength of the teachers, and the teachers must constantly endeavor to grow both in professional and in general intellectual strength.[46]

In contrast to these mechanical schools and isolated literacy instruction, Rice described the schools in four cities as "scientific" and "progressive" in their approach to reading in particular and education in general. Teachers in these schools attempted to implement principles of Rousseau, Pestalozzi, Froebel, and Herbart in their primary programs and were often quite successful in reorganizing their grammar school curricula to approximate unification of subjects. Rice argued that in these schools "it is no longer the textbook or the arbitrary will of the superintendent but the laws of psychology, that now became the ruling spirit of the school."[47] Concerning reading instruction, Rice reported that

> in schools conducted upon the principles of unification language is regarded simply as a means of expression and not a thing apart from ideas. Instruction in almost every branch now partakes of the nature of a language lesson. The child being led to learn the various phases of language in large part incidentally while acquiring and expressing

ideas. . . . And, strange as it may seem, it is nevertheless true that the results in reading and expression of ideas in writing are, at least in primary grades, by far the best in those schools where language in all its phases is taught incidentally.[48]

Rice based his conclusions on personal testing of students' sight reading; the results demonstrated that students read more fluently and with expression when taught through the unification method.[49] For writing assessment, Rice collected first drafts of compositions from each child in the schools in "several cities" and compared the seven or eight thousand examples he received. He found the compositions from the unification schools so superior to the others that he devoted the final seventy pages of his subsequent book to present several examples.

According to educational historian Lawrence Cremin, Rice's descriptions and conclusions were generally accepted as fact because he combined the moral indignation against partisan politics, the public's fascination with science and technology, and optimism about the future.[50] Despite educators' protests to the contrary, many citizens became concerned about schools after reading Rice's report that public schools were unprepared and unable to help Americans adapt to the changes caused by rapid industrialization, urbanization, and immigration. Although there was a growing public consensus that schools needed to change, there was little consensus about the direction that change should take. Businessmen sought vocational education and financial efficiency, settlement and social workers recommended instruction in hygiene and child care, and patriots of every stripe demanded a curriculum based on American values. For the local superintendents of schools, whose jobs depended on public support, the problem of change was one of degree. Should schools be completely overhauled, abandoning the traditional emphasis on teachers and textbooks in order to adopt an emphasis on children's needs and unified curriculum, or should the traditional emphases be technically fine-tuned?

Chapter Two

Early Attempts to Reform Reading Instruction

In order to understand why the technical fine-tuning of traditional reading instruction ultimately won out over the unified curriculum of the New Education, it is necessary to digress for a brief consideration of the spirit of the times in which this recognized crisis in school literacy took place. One hundred years after the U.S. Declaration of Independence, some limitations of the Founding Fathers' assumptions were becoming apparent. The economy was depressed for many, while fortunes were amassed by a very few; the government was scandal ridden; the southern half of the nation was under federal military occupation; the army was at war with the country's natives in the West; many newly emancipated slaves were still disenfranchised, illiterate, and unemployed, and the Declaration of Rights for Women demanded justice and equality for all citizens. Over the next fifty years, twenty million immigrants would be added to the country's population of fifty million. This increasingly variegated population with respect to race, religion, language, and culture challenged the American Anglo national identity. There was also a shift in population from farm to city (from 30 percent in 1890 to more than 50 percent in 1920). Americans were facing new and different challenges than the Founding Fathers had anticipated. Steam (later electricity and oil) and reason were the progressive tools Americans would use to face and overcome these challenges in order to enjoy moral and social improvements in the human condition.

Business

At the time, the power of business and industry seemed capable of producing a secular kingdom of Zion in which everyone might find material happiness on earth.[1] Civil War profits from government contracts enabled young (draft-dodging) entrepreneurs from the Northeast to push the American economic base from shipping and real estate to railroads, iron, coal, and oil. During the early 1870s, America's net worth passed that of England, and in the 1880s, manufacturing passed agriculture as the leading contributor to the country's economic growth. The Vanderbilts, the Rockefellers, the Morgans, Andrew Carnegie, and the like, who had accumulated fortunes through smart business practices and government largess, became the recognized gods of this kingdom.[2] And rule the kingdom they did by securing loyalty from local, state, and national politicians. Before the Seventeenth Amendment to the U.S. Constitution in 1913 provided for the popular election of senators, political pundits made reference to Standard Oil senators, sugar trust senators, iron and steel senators, and railroad senators, who were known more for their business affiliations than for their state.[3]

The tensions between rural and urban communities, citizens and immigrants, and management and labor provide a context for muckrakers', populists', and socialists' concerns about the negative consequences of extraordinary industrial and population growth during the last quarter of the nineteenth century and the first decade of the twentieth. Despite the Meat Inspection Act; the Hepburn Act to regulate the railroads; a Pure Food and Drug Act; the Mann-Elkins Act, which put telephone and telegraph companies under the Interstate Commerce Commission; the formation of the Trade Commission to regulate monopolies; the formation of the Federal Reserve to regulate interest rates and banking; the Sixteenth Amendment, allowing graduated income tax; the Seventeenth Amendment; a variety of state laws regulating wages and work hours; and safety inspection of factories and workers' compensation, Rockefeller's fortune reached one billion dollars, Carnegie's remained at half that amount, and scores of others rose to one hundred million by the turn of the century. Farmers' and industrial workers' incomes, however, fluctuated with the economic booms and busts of American capitalism. To provide some perspective on income, the ratio of the richest individual to median family income increased from 210,000 to 1 in 1875 to 800,000 to 1 in 1912 (the ratio currently hovers at 1,416,000 to 1).[4] Whether you agree with Arthur Schlesinger that these acts were a triumph of liberalism or with Gabriel Kolko that this era was the beginning of political capitalism, you can see that business and economics were at the center of public life.[5]

With this newly accumulated wealth came social and political power, displacing the local patricians whose power had been based upon inherited wealth and lineage. Like the commodities that they marketed, the new captains of industry moved on a national arena of prestige. The backlash of local civic and economic leaders can be seen in contemporary essays and novels, in which the captains were portrayed as uneducated, rootless, and corrupt, and in the newly formed patriotic societies, whose membership criteria included descent and length of family residence in the area.[6] Many of the newly wealthy hired publicists to ensure that their public relations would remain positive and their influence would grow and continue. Often, their lives were represented as living characters from Horatio Alger Jr. novels. Some began to use their wealth to improve society according to their designs. Andrew Carnegie began to redistribute his wealth in 1902, with just this in mind.

> This, then, is held to be the duty of the man of wealth: . . . to consider all surplus revenues which come to him simply as trust funds . . . for his poorer brethren, bringing to their service his superior wisdom, experience, and ability to administer, doing for them better than they would or could do for themselves.[7]

Americans had been prepared to admire these philanthropic values through the content of their school textbooks used during their reading lessons, particularly by McGuffey's readers.

> I would build a great many pretty cottages for people to live in, and every cottage should have a garden and a field, in order that the people might have vegetables, and might keep a cow, a pig, and some chickens. They should not pay me much rent. I would give clothes to the boys and girls who had not money to buy clothes with, and they should all learn to read and write and be very good.
>
> I have been told, and I have read, that it is God who makes some poor, and others rich; that the rich have many troubles which we know nothing of, and that the poor, if they are but good, may be very happy, indeed. I think that when I am good, nobody can be happier than I am.[8]

These philanthropic gifts were not limited to financial donations. The new captains of industry offered their advice on political matters and projected the principles that drove their business success as the means to address other social concerns. The first principle was a rebellion against traditional industrial practices, substituting managerial systems for "rule of thumb" methods, which resulted in confusion and waste. The second was to rely on experts—professionals—who advocated rigorous formal systems based on calculation and reason in the pursuit of profits from production. The gaze of these experts did not stop at the factory gates. They sought to direct the public's attention to how the principles of business could be applied to social institutions and private life. Schools did not escape this public scrutiny, which came in a standard form—unfavorable comparison between schools and business using economy and efficiency as the criteria, followed by suggestions that schools be more businesslike in their organization and instructional methods.[9] The introduction to William C. Bagley's popular textbook *Classroom Management* gives some indication of how quickly educators adopted the language and practices of business: "Primarily [classroom management] is a problem of economy; it seeks to determine in what manner the working unit of the school plant may be made to return the largest dividend upon the material investment of time, energy, and money."[10] As a consequence of these comparisons, superintendents, supervisors, and educational leaders began to identify themselves as businessmen rather than scholars.

Reason

The appeal to reason was simply a continuation of the American test of the practical validity of assumptions of the Enlightenment upon which the country was based. Primary among these assumptions was a fundamental faith in reason to decipher the mysteries of the physical and social worlds in order to enhance the human power, as Benjamin Franklin explained, "over matter, and multiply the conveniences or pleasures of life."[11] Before the War of Independence, Franklin developed a plan for scientific cooperation among the colonies that would lead to the invention of labor and timesaving devices, improvement of health care, and eventually alignment of the social order with newly discovered laws of nature. Identification of the natural laws would demonstrate the limits of traditional cultural and religious explanations of the world and its workings. By assuming that men (and the assumption was limited to white men of means) could act for and by themselves without the need of clergy or king, followers of the Enlightenment became "the architects of their fortune." Science, then, was conceived as the organized and systematic use of reason to secure individual and collective freedom from the problems and limits of the past.

At the end of the nineteenth century, scientists sought to codify proceedures by which scientific laws could be discovered. In *The Grammar of Science*, Karl Pearson wrote, "the scientific method consists in the careful often laborious classification of facts, the comparison of their relationships and sequences, and finally in the discovery by aid of the disciplined imagination of a brief statement or formula, which in a few words resumes a wide range of facts. Such a formula is called a scientific law."[12] The business of science was to maximize the discovery of facts from which scientific laws would eventually emerge, minimizing the risk of false theories because of the impartial nature of the scientist. Psychologist E. L. Thorndike's description of the scientists echoes Carnegie's assessment of the intellectual and moral character of the wealthy.

The judgments of science are distinguished from other judgments by being more impartial, more objective, more precise, and more subject to verification by any competent observer and being made by those who by their nature and training should be better judges. Science knows or should know no favorites and cares for nothing in its conclusions but the truth.[13]

Thorndike believed that science could supply an objective tool in order to shape human beings and ultimately a better, true social order. That order would be based on a meritocracy, which Thorndike sought to establish scientifically through testing and experimentation. A product of his time, Thorndike's test confirmed scientifically that white men of means were intellectually superior to women, people of color, and the poor. Because they were more intelligent, he reasoned that they were more fit to rule.

But, in the long run, it has paid the masses to be ruled by intelligence. Furthermore, the natural processes which give power to men of ability to gain it and keep it are not, in their results, unmoral. Such men are, by and large, of superior intelligence, and consequently of somewhat superior justice and good will. They act, in the long run, not against the interests of the world, but for it. What is true in science and government seems to hold good in general for manufacturing, trade, art, law, education, and religion. It seems entirely safe to predict that the world will get better treatment by trusting its fortunes to its 95 or 99 percentile intelligences than it would get by itself. The argument for democracy is not that it gives power to all men without distinction, but that it gives greater freedom for ability and character to attain power.[14]

The search for a science of individual differences and appropriate pedagogy led to the emergence of the new academic discipline of psychology and a new category of expert on knowing, learning, and teaching—the psychologist. Although a social form of Darwinism directed early efforts to study the development of the mind, American educational psychologists concentrated on the accurate measurement of human behavior, following the general creed of the scientific method. This practice of science required educational experts to develop mathematical scales in order to measure accurately the change in social and mental activity directly attributable to experimental treatments. During the first two decades of the twentieth century, educational science was considered "one long orgy of tabulation."[15]

Through experiments with animals, Thorndike theorized that mind and body were connected through a reflex arc. Learning could be explained, therefore, by the connections of a specific external stimulus to specific behaviors, which were to be stamped into an animal's neural system through direct intervention and continuous rewarding of the animal for its performance. Thorndike's experiments simultaneously rejected religious explanations of human nature through original sin and the new educational explanation of children's natural state of grace. He replaced those theories with the notion that personality, will, and inclination, whether good or bad, were learned, not predisposed phenomena and their composition depended on how an animal's environment shaped its actions. Thorndike challenged the contemporary views of teaching as a battle against evil within children (the traditional approach) or as an impediment to children's natural development (the New Education).

From the results of his experiments and the work of other psychologists, Thorndike fashioned laws of learning by which he described how knowledge was composed of stimulus-and-response connections and how teachers could best manage their students' learning environment in order to evoke the desired changes:

> From associationist psychology, Thorndike adapted the notion that learning was ordered and that efficient learning followed one best sequence (later to be called the law of readiness).

> From John Watson's writings, he accepted the idea that practice strengthened the connection between a stimulus and a response and led to habit formation (the law of exercise).

> From his own experiments, he concluded that rewards influenced the stimulus-and-response connection—positive rewards increased the frequency and the strength of the response and negative rewards decreased the frequency (the law of effect).

> In collaboration, Thorndike developed the idea that instruction and curriculum had specific rather than general effects on students' knowledge, thus challenging the notion that certain subjects and activities, such as Latin or Greek and grammar lessons, generally facilitated intellectual development. He argued generally for the effectiveness of specific instruction toward desired goals and suggested that learning could be tested only in situations similar to the ways in which the connections were formed (law of identical elements).[16]

Like many other psychologists, Thorndike interpreted the social role of psychology as helping individuals know the possibilities and limits of the social system in which they found themselves and to make the most of it. "We ought, to change what is to what ought to be, as far as we can."[17] This interventionist spirit accounts for some of the vast influence Thorndike and his associates exercised over American schools. At least as important, however, is the fact that psychologists' empirical findings were essentially what business-minded Americans wanted to hear. Certainly, their experimental correlations between wealth, morality, intelligence, and social power upset no one in the upper end of the American power structure.

Scientific Management

More than any other invention of the progressive era, Frederick Winslow Taylor's scientific management captured the spirit of the times.[18] This system of factory management rejected traditional commonsense explanations, embraced professional expertise, employed the experimental method, and applied associationist principles of learning theory in order to maximize the productivity of each worker. Toward that end, Taylor sought to establish rules and procedures for each job, which would supplant personal judgment and rule of thumb in the daily practices of both workers and managers. The new rules and procedures would be discovered through scientific investigation of the required tasks to be completed with particular attention paid to ways in which technology and standardization could increase both efficiency and quality of the work. Those investigations were to follow a typical pattern:

1. Divide the work of a man performing any job into simple elementary movements.
2. Pick out all useless movements and discard them.
3. Study, one after another, just how each of several skilled workmen makes each elementary movement and, with the aid of a stopwatch, select the quickest and best method.
4. Describe, record, and index each elementary movement with its proper time, so that it can be quickly found.
5. Study and record the percentage that must be added to the actual working time of a good workman to cover unavoidable delays, interruptions, and minor accidents.
6. Study and record the percentage that must be added to cover the newness for a good workman to a job, the first few times he does it.
7. Study and record the percentage of time that must be allowed for rest and the intervals at which the rest must be taken in order to offset physical fatigue.[19]

Once the one best method of work was discovered from observing, disassembling, measuring, and then reassembling workers' actions, the elemental tasks were distributed among workers in order to optimize the efficiency of production. The rules and procedures for each task were encoded on instruction cards to ensure that workers would employ the scientifically developed method without deviation. In many ways, the instruction cards lay at the heart of scientific management. Sometimes the cards were just memos to remind the workers of the new rules and procedures. More often, they were pages of instructions permanently mounted near machines to enable workers to follow the steps precisely without relying on their memories or their judgments. The instruction cards severed the connection between planning and performance at work. Some level of management would assume the responsibility for planning each job in the factory because managers were more able to discern rules and procedures scientifically, and workers would perform those plans without the burden of emotional attachment or specialized thought. To mediate between these two levels of employees, series of foremen were employed to ensure worker compliance and quality control of product. In the most elaborate forms of scientific management, foremen were appointed for each step of the one best method of production, instruction cards were written for their jobs as well, and no one was necessarily knowledgeable about the entire production process.

After a U.S. congressional hearing on a proposed railroad rate hike in which Louis Brandeis used Taylor as an expert witness to explain that the railroads did not require a hike because they had not employed the best managerial practices, scientific management became widely known and popular among more than factory owners. Taylor claimed during the hearings that he sought a complete mental revolution in the United States in which citizens would employ similar scientific and management principles to accomplish broader social goals. Stores, offices, governmental agencies, and even household tasks fell under scientific scrutiny of efficiency experts, with the expectation that all parts of life could be run more smoothly, more modestly, and with greater productivity. Taylor's intentions for scientific management were by no means modest, as his remarks before a House of Representatives subcommittee suggest:

> Scientific management would bring about the substitution of peace for war; the substitution of hearty brotherly cooperation for contentions and strife; of both pulling hard in the same direction instead of pulling apart; of replacing suspicious watchfulness with mutual confidence; of becoming friends instead of enemies.[20]

Within this general milieu of business, science, and psychology, the New Education did not stand a popular chance. Its philosophy and radical changes seemed inefficient, sentimental, and overly optimistic concerning both human nature and learning. (See Chapter 4 for a history of New Education's challenges to the industrial ideology as the rationality for schooling and reading instruction.) Indeed, Francis Parker, whom Rice had celebrated at the end of his articles in 1893 as leading the ideal school, was forced to resign from Cook County Normal School in 1899. Amid rising public criticism of his pedagogical principles, he spent the last few years before his death in 1902 working in a private school connected with the University of Chicago. According to historian Lawrence Cremin, even America's most famous progressive educator, John Dewey, was concerned about the lack of rigor in many schools subscribing to the New Education at the turn of the century.[21] Dewey questioned whether or not teachers from these New Education schools had a deep enough understanding of the character of the graduate they wished to educate or sophisticated enough understandings of the academic disciplines involved in students' activities to truly recognize the teachable moments in children's development and experience.[22] Dewey called for more deliberate forms of teacher education in order to prepare a new generation of teachers who would be able to deliver the promise of the New Education. By 1910, however, scientific management was front-page news; in 1911, the National Society for the Study of Education's Department of Superintendents appointed the Committee on the Economy of Time in Education; and in 1914, Joseph Mayer Rice published his second book, *The Scientific Management in Education.*

The Early Science of Reading Instruction

The Committee on the Economy of Time in Education was charged with broad responsibilities to render schools more productive and able to address the rapidly changing needs of society. They were to use science to eliminate nonessentials from the elementary school curriculum, to set minimum standards for each school subject, and to improve teaching methods toward those standards. Among the committee members were Frank Spaulding, then superintendent of Minneapolis schools, who boasted that he "landed the job by cleverly convincing the school board that he was an efficient, business-like, cost conscious administrator,"[23] and J. F. Bobbitt, an assistant professor of educational administration at the University of Chicago and author of "The Elimination of Waste in Education." The committee transformed Taylor's system into a three-step procedure in order to design curriculum and instruction scientifically:

> First, analyze the learning environment during instruction to identify the best instructional methods.
>
> Second, measure the effects of various methods with specifically designed tests.
>
> Third, adopt the methods that yield the highest results.

These were precisely the steps that the committee used, substituting test scores for timed efficiency, in conducting their studies of elementary schools. They published their reports in four yearbooks for the National Society for the Study of Education (NSSE) between 1915 and 1919. The authors of the reports became more prescriptive in tone across these years.

The first committee yearbook begins with the results of a questionnaire study of fifty school districts, and it includes four essays specifically addressing reading instruction.[24] According to the survey, reading instruction was offered in all fifty districts sampled to represent elementary school programs in the Northeast, Midwest, Northwest, West, and Mid-Atlantic states. This reading instruction constituted on average 26.3 percent of the time allotted for instruction (from a high of 30.6 percent in first grade to a low of 9.6 percent in eighth grade). Language, spelling, and penmanship (composition was not considered a subject on the questionnaire) were treated as separate lessons, and if combined, all language arts activities occupied an average of 53.4 percent of the school day. The questionnaire results identified a hierarchy of importance for researchers, planners, and teachers. Those subjects that occupied the greatest amount of time during the day were the ones that could most benefit from a scientific approach.

The four essays in the first committee report addressed vocabulary, reading rate, formal testing, and literary content of available textbooks. Each essay offered recommendations for the improvement of the efficiency of instruction. For example, the vocabulary study suggested the recurrence of words in stories as the criteria to determine which words deserved more attention. The researcher cautioned teachers to attend to the potency of words because "it is a greater error for a pupil to miss the word 'man,' which has a recurrent value of 633, than it is to miss the word 'cap,' which has a recurrent value of only 104." The second essay offered similar scientific encouragement in an attempt to establish average reading rates for each grade level. Although there was a great range of reading rates at any grade level, a constant rate was found for any large group at a given grade. "The great range of individual variation is a sign of inefficient teaching . . . it is the duty of elementary school to see that each individual attains this optimum degree of skill. Otherwise he does not know how to read." The third and fourth essays were surveys of the materials available to help teachers make better judgments about their reading instruction. William S. Gray presented the formal tests of reading ability that were currently on the market and described the benefits and limitations of their use. James Fleming Hosic studied the literature texts available for elementary school classrooms. They advised teachers to read the scholarly journals in their field if they hoped to stay informed concerning effective means of providing reading instruction.

In 1917, the second committee report divided language arts into reading, literature, handwriting, spelling, and grammar (again composition was not considered a subject). Different authors packed each essay with charts, graphs, and tables attesting to the scientific validity of its conclusions.[25] For example, W. S. Gray described the importance and economy of silent reading, the most appropriate periods of schooling in which to provide silent reading instruction, and the methods to improve students' silent reading. Relying completely on experimental data, Gray argued that silent reading was more practical, more efficient, and more effective than the regular regime of oral reading in elementary classrooms. To determine the optimal times for silent reading instruction, Gray reported the results from the first iteration of his Standardized Oral Reading Paragraphs and Silent Reading Tests. He concluded that there should be a gradual transition from the legitimate use of oral reading in primary grades to silent reading during the third grade. Moreover, Gray maintained that intermediate and high school years should be devoted exclusively to silent reading.

In the final portion of his essay, Gray suggested necessary modifications for reading textbooks if the new scientific emphasis on silent reading was to be profitable. "Most of the reading texts in current use have been organized for purposes of oral-reading instruction." In order to improve them, educational publishers were to reduce the difficulty of the vocabulary in order to diminish the chance that students would stumble over words and lengthen the stories in order to provide extended practice to help students increase their reading rate. Additionally, Gray cautioned teachers to prepare students for silent reading, and he presented brief suggestions for instruction. He told them to emphasize speed and purpose before giving assignments and to prepare teacher-directed assessment in order to determine whether or not students comprehended the important information from passages after reading them.

The literature essay included in this second Committee report listed the library books and reading textbooks recommended for each grade level in the reading courses of study from fifty cities across the United States. Including only titles mentioned more than five times, 817 library books and 95 different reading textbooks were listed by grade level in what appears to be an inverse relationship. First-grade recommendations included the most textbooks (38) and fewest library books (8), and this ratio switched across the grades toward eighth. Library titles began to outnumber textbooks at fourth grade. The authors cautioned "while this tabulation of books cannot be considered an absolute standard of practice for all schools, it is sufficiently extensive to represent the prevailing practices with a fair degree of approximation."

The third committee report contained only a six-page essay on reading, discussing the recurrence of words in second-grade reading textbooks.[26] The study found great variability among vocabularies included in these readers. Teachers were warned that some textbooks might be incompatible with others because their vocabularies overlapped so little that students who were trained in one reader would not be able to read the other text independently. Accordingly, teachers would find it more efficient to use only one set of textbooks for at least the primary-grade years. Perhaps the most startling finding was the fact that more than 50 percent of the words in any textbook appeared less than three times, "thus failing to develop drill on these words."

H. B. Wilson, chairman of the Committee on the Economy of Time in Education, stated succinctly the purpose of the fourth report: "Its effort throughout has been to put its recommendations in simple, direct language, that its report may constitute a handbook and guide for the use of teachers and supervisors who are interested in planning classroom procedures with due regard for both economy and efficiency in teaching and learning."[27] In fact, each of the six essays in the report was to serve as a "clearinghouse for [published and unpublished] experimental data" on one elementary school subject. After four years of study, the committee was finally ready to publish the rules and procedures for the scientific management of elementary schools. According to Lawrence Cremin, this fourth report, with its emphasis on instruction, was by far the most widely circulated and implemented of the committee's reports.[28]

Three essays were directed toward improving literacy instruction. "Principles of Method in Teaching Writing as Derived from Scientific Investigation" presented twenty-eight rules for penmanship concerning posture, stroke, development, and materials as well as tips on testing and record keeping. These rules were gleaned from twenty-two experimental studies on legible script. "Principles of Method in Teaching Spelling as Derived from Scientific Investigation" identified forty principles from 133 studies, which Professor Earnest Horn reduced to five rules: "pretest all words to be taught, teach only those words that students spell incorrectly, provide rigorous review, show students progress continuously, and keep up the interest."[29]

From thirty-five experiments, William S. Gray deduced forty-eight principles for reading instruction, covering norms for student progress across grade levels, suggestions for oral and silent reading instruction, and even specifications for the printing of books to maximize the economy of reading. Gray emphasized that experiments demonstrated that no single textbook method of teaching reading was necessarily superior to all others regardless of circumstances. Rather, he argued that instructional effectiveness varied according to how teachers used the materials, the backgrounds of the students, and the amount of materials available for instruction. Similar to what Frederick Taylor had found in the steel mills, Gray found that there were master teachers of reading working in classrooms beside teachers who had little idea of how to teach reading. As in the second report, Gray stressed the relative efficiency, utility, and overall superiority of silent reading in developing students' reading rate and comprehension, as measured by standardized tests. Although Gray acknowledged that science confirmed the importance of oral reading in primary grades, he adopted a moral tone concerning how it ought to be used: "Oral reading exercises should emphasize the content of what is read"; "Two different types of oral reading exercises should be provided for second and third grades" ; and "The oral reading which is required in the fourth, fifth, and sixth grades should be conducted under the stimulus of real motive."[30] However, Gray returned to a voice of scientific authority when he later addressed rate and comprehension: "Much reading of simple interesting materials is effective in increasing rate of reading," and "knowledge, while reading, that the material is to be reproduced improves the quality of the reading."[31]

Clearly, Gray's essay demonstrated the committee's intent to improve the typical patterns of instruction in public schools through the application of scientific findings. However, a close analysis of Gray's words suggests that these changes were not to be all that radical. To be sure, influences of the New Education were present in Gray's rhetoric—"emphasize the content of what is read," "a real motive," and so on. However, there was no mention of the student-initiated project method (very popular at this time), learning to read incidentally while pursuing an interest (Dewey's suggestion), or Parker's notion of unified curriculum. Gray directed teachers toward formal lessons according to the principles induced from the experiments on reading. Moreover, the goal of Gray's reading instruction was not to be the evaluation or use of information. Rather, the goal was to develop students' abilities to retell or to answer questions about the content of a passage. As Gray put it, reading was to learn that "the material is to be reproduced." While Gray recommended rules and procedures for the routine of reading instruction that rejected the traditions and rules of thumb for teaching reading, his scientific conclusions confirmed both the basic structure of traditional reading instruction—lessons, drill, textbooks, and testing—and the separation of the planning from the doing in reading instruction: Gray's forty-eight principles were to serve as the scientific management instruction card for the teaching of reading in elementary schools.

A Technology for Scientific Reading Instruction

If scientific reading instruction were to improve classroom practice, then it had to penetrate the classroom door in order to alter the day-to-day interactions between teachers and students. Since at the time many elementary school teachers were poorly educated, knowledgeable superintendents and supervisors were in short supply, and teachers already relied heavily on textbooks, the National Society for the Study of Education sought to identify and develop educational materials that would move teachers toward scientifically based instruction with a minimum of expense.[32] In 1918, NSSE formed the Committee on Materials in Education, combining the Committee on the Measurement of Educational Products and the Committee on Economy of Time in Education. "At this point, the Society assigned to the present Committee the task of embodying, in concrete materials to be used in classrooms, the principles arrived at by the earlier committees."[33] To be certain, the new materials for reading instruction altered the content of the textbooks, emphasizing silent reading, reducing the multisyllabic words in early readers, and increasing the repetition of vocabulary words across lessons. However, the most significant change to reading materials was the development of teachers' guidebooks designed to direct teachers' and students' actions during reading instruction. The most significant change to reading instruction was the use of a single textbook series across elementary school grades.

Prior to the 1920s, most reading textbook series printed only brief directions for teachers within the students' books.[34] Authors of the series assumed that classroom teachers were able to interpret and present the lessons according to their experience and judgment. For example, D. C. Heath Publishers included a simple three-page introduction to explain why it combined the sentence, word, and phonics methods in its new primer. Butler and Company's second reader offered a one-page introduction titled "Suggestions for Teachers," which told teachers to read the lessons for their students the day before in order that "they will be ready to receive the printed words the next day." The single-page "Words to Teachers" in the Rand McNally *Lights to Literature* related, "The teacher is expected to introduce and supplement each new lesson by appropriate blackboard exercises, talks, drawings, and readings; and when possible, to use songs adapted to the central thought of the lesson." Rand McNally expected teachers to prepare these supplements on their own. Book Four in Ginn and Company's *Cyr Readers* had a one-page preface for teachers and six pages of advertisements for the company's textbooks in other subjects. The American Book Company's *Reading with Expression* presented a one-page note to teachers, which suggested that "the pupils should be encouraged to seek for and point out the particular passages in each selection which are distinguished for their beauty, their truth, or their peculiar adaptability to the purpose in view." The publisher and author did not mark the spots of beauty or truth because they were certain that teachers could identify these qualities without aid. From first books to last, all publishers supplied only the contents of lessons and expected teachers to deliver the lessons as they saw fit.

After 1920, however, the number and the specificity of the new scientific maxims about teaching reading could no longer be accommodated in this manner. Textbook historian Nila Banton Smith concluded, "every author of new reading textbooks furnished generous instructions for the use of his materials. Furthermore, authors of texts which had appeared during the preceding period without detailed instructions now came forth with manuals . . . to furnish rather definitely prescribed instructions."[35] These guidebooks usually were bound separately for grade levels and provided specific information on appropriate instruction for each lesson, questions to test students' comprehension of each story, and brief explanations of the science of reading instruction. In her survey of the teachers' guidebooks from ten textbook series published at this time, Smith found that the length of the first-grade guidebooks ranged from 219 pages to 434 pages. Marjorie Hardy, teacher at the Elementary School at the University of Chicago and the author of the first-grade manual for the Child's Own Way series, began her manual with a statement about the unsatisfactory situation in elementary schools.

> While the light of scientific research has cleared up several questions in regard to the pedagogy of many elementary school subjects, there have been but few, if any conclusive studies offered for guidance in the beginning stages of reading. The result is a multiplicity of methods that is even more startling than most persons realize. A recent investigation shows that twenty-one widely used reading methods offer the following variations:
> In the method of approach,
>
>> 2 systems start with individual letters
>>
>> 9 systems start with individual words
>>
>> 2 systems start with individual phrases
>>
>> 3 systems start with individual sentences
>>
>> 5 systems start with paragraph or story units

> Also, the extent of the pre-primer work varies from no work whatsoever to twelve weeks of work. The same wide variance holds for content, vocabulary, supplementary devices, etc. Where procedures are so varied, it is inconceivable that all can be of the highest value. This fact is a challenge to the inquiring mind. There must be some fundamental method which is best, and the wonder is that it has not been worked out and universally adopted years ago.[36]

In the general introduction of the *Teachers' Manual for the Newson Readers Playtime Primer*, Yale University professor Catherine Bryce and the assistant superintendent of schools in Washington, D.C., Rose Hardy, provided an outline for lesson plans in order to direct teachers toward more scientific and standard instruction.[37] They listed authorized alternatives for each part of prescribed lessons—vocabulary, procedures (approach, development, silent reading, and oral reading), and related activities. In order to conduct these lessons, teachers needed an assortment of materials: the teachers' manual, the pupils' text, charts for each alternative, flash cards for vocabulary, supplemental readers, journals, storyboards, and tests—all of which could be purchased from Newson and Company. The authors directed teachers through each page of the manual, and the register and tone of their statements changed as they moved into directions for lessons. In the general introduction, the authors quoted NSSE yearbooks and employed an invitational voice. "Playtime introduces children to the reading process by means of material of immediate interest to every child, namely, birthdays and toys." Their voice turned imperative, however, once the lessons began. Their directions included scripting for teachers to ensure the precision of lesson delivery.

> Approach through the following game.
> Teacher: I know a new game.
> It is a guessing game.
> Would you like to play it?
> This is the way to play it.
> Guess what day this is. . . .

Birth of the Basal

The production of the teachers' guidebook was the beginning of basal reading materials as known today—teachers' manual, textbook, supplementary materials, and tests. Authors sought to embed the scientific knowledge of the time into the form and content of the materials in order to improve the quality of instruction and learning in every classroom throughout the school and district and across the country. Publishers recognized that the expanded directions and the need for specific supplemental materials would increase their profits. The logic of a teachers' guidebook made perfect sense given the context of the time. First and foremost, the guidebook was an expression of educators' and the public's deep faith in the power of science to explain the mysteries of life and to solve the practical problems that they faced. The guidebooks were marketed as the embodiment of that science. Not only were the guidebooks' originating maxims the results of scientific investigations, but their entire rationale was founded on the idea that theory should direct practice. That is, the science of the manuals would standardize the idiosyncratic behaviors of particular teachers and students.

The directions to teachers, then, were offered as scientific facts to be followed regardless of the social context of the instruction or the abilities and attitudes of students or teachers. It was assumed that if all teachers would use the textbooks and supplementary materials according to the directions in the guidebooks, then all students would learn to read efficiently and effectively. This general tone of scientific authority was important because the directions in the manuals required teachers to modify their previous instructional practice from overseer and drillmaster. Moreover, the aura of science used the language of change in tradition from the New Education. Although, as Cuban explained, few teachers were eager to alter procedures that seemed successful previously, the new teacher manual directions seemed compatible with traditional teachers' control and absolved them of decision-making responsibility.

Although the directions in the guidebooks were not as restrictive as those of the instructional cards of scientific management in factories, the teachers' guidebook enabled a scientific management of reading instruction. To begin, the preparation of the guidebooks separated the planning of instruction from the practice of instruction. Although removed from and unfamiliar with individual classrooms, guidebook authors would plan both the content and the process of instruction for teachers across the country through publishers' national marketing schemes for their reading series products. Decisions on what to include in the guidebooks would be made according to science, with the use of standardized tests to determine student progress. Together the guidebook and the tests provided school districts with an objective measure of the effectiveness of each teacher because teachers' performance could be judged against guidebook prescriptions. As with scientific management in other fields, a distinction had to be made between the roles of teachers and those of administrators. While teachers remained the ones who worked directly with children, someone at a higher level of authority had to select the instructional goals and plans in order to ensure uniformity of that work. The guidebooks, then, provided the rules and procedures for both the administrators and the teachers, reducing the relative authority of both in order to deliver effective and efficient reading instruction to all students.

If the wide variation among methods was considered a primary cause of the poor reading performance, then the teachers' guidebook could also be understood as a direct application of Thorndike's connectionism. The proper stimulus, the guidebooks, would elicit the proper response: standardized, efficient instruction. The guidebooks employed some of Thorndike's laws of learning in order to teach teachers how to use scientifically based methods. The general introductions and lesson overviews ensured that the teachers were prepared to learn to teach each lesson. This was a simple application of the laws of learning. Because the guidebooks provided daily lesson plans for instruction and those lessons were always parallel in form, they afforded teachers sufficient opportunity to practice scientific instruction (law of exercise). The satisfaction of providing scientifically sound instruction would affirm teachers' new instructional behaviors (law of effect). Administrators could use the lessons plans and scripts during observations in order to determine if teachers had learned to use the materials appropriately. Accordingly, the guidebooks were a sufficient environment to ensure that teachers learned to teach reading scientifically.[38]

Thorndike's laws of learning were also incorporated in the new components of basal materials. For example, the law of readiness was demonstrated in the more refined and detailed sequencing of skills that students were expected to master. The supplemental materials were a direct attempt to standardize practices across classrooms in order to increase the impact on student learning (law of exercise). The new guidebooks provided directions to teachers on how to use the supplemental materials in order to enhance students' attitudes toward reading (law of effect). Finally, publishers supplied new tests to sample students' developing abilities to read silently and to answer questions (law of identical elements). By following the prescribed lessons across their elementary school experience, students would develop the simple and complex connections necessary to read in a sophisticated manner.

In summary, the new materials—basal reading series—met the expectations of a public and educational community enthralled with business, science, and psychology. This new technology promised to address the crisis in reading instruction by preparing students for the demands of the rapid changes of an industrialized America. Without the expense of reeducating teachers or the development of new schools, the application of basal materials would do for schools what scientific management had accomplished for industry. Promoted as the embodiment of scientific study, basal materials promised increased productivity and efficiency in teachers' instruction and in students' learning. Although the contents of basals would change modestly during the next eighty years, the rationale for and the format of basal reading materials were set by the spirit of the first two decades of the twentieth century.

Chapter Three

A Real Rationalization of Reading Instruction

During the late 1970s and 1980s, I conducted a series of studies to examine the empirical reasons for the triumph of Huey's "real rationalization of the process of inducing the child with the practice of reading."[1] I considered objective factors in which power and authority beyond teachers' control promoted, cajoled, and required a scientific management of reading instruction. Using observation, questionnaires, interviews, and school district documents, I explored basal-directed instruction, mastery learning, test score quotas, teacher effectiveness systems, and class size adjustments in rural, suburban, and urban schools in open and closed textbook markets, and I found that the objective factors of rationalization had become subjective beliefs for many school personnel. Many teachers and school administrators in these districts justified their reading programs primarily by invoking the metaphors of the marketplace and the conclusions of reading experts without significant references to the human interactions of reading, learning, and teaching. At the same time, many of these teachers described their anxiety over the mechanical nature of their work and the poor fit between rationalized reading programs and individual student needs. My efforts to explain these results led me to sociological theories on the concept of ideology and the processes of rationalization in western society.

Ideologies are systems of thought, belief, and action by which groups explain to themselves how the world works and what principles it exemplifies.[2] Accordingly, ideologies are considered truths in both the material and the moral sense because they influence individual group members' actions and thoughts daily, and they define the parameters of behavior and thoughts to be considered normal. The ideologies of more powerful social groups exert direct influence over the thoughts, beliefs, and actions of less powerful groups. The principles of business and science used to rationalize reading instruction over the period from the mid-1920s to the mid-1980s could be considered an expression of a powerful ideology because they explained how the structures of reading education should work and they defined the normal dispositions of all participants. Of course, this ideology operated on a much larger scale as well, defining proper organization, beliefs, and behaviors for industry, government, and most other public and private institutions. Collectively, the consequent structures of these institutions defined individuals' lives at work and at home, which in turn reinforced and modified ideological principles directing the institutions, making the ideology to appear both universal and necessary.

According to sociologist Max Weber, the spread of capitalist ideology—the real rationalization of public and private life—has been a continuous process for two hundred years.[3] Through rationalization, business attempts to make human behavior more predictable (in work, in social relationships, and in consumption) in order to bring progress, peace, and prosperity through a decrease in the risks to capital investment and an increase to the chances and amounts of profit. Think about Frederick Taylor's ambitions for the social consequences of his principles of scientific management. Beginning with economic activity, then, rationalization spread to law, medicine, science, and even popular culture.[4] In order for rationalization to be successful, people must learn to disenchant the nature of their spiritual life, to define people as individuals without relationships except for market exchange, and to value accumulation as the definition of the good life. Only under these ideological conditions does the capitalist organization of society make sense, in which nature and human welfare become subordinate to, even dependent on, the calculus of maximum production. Consider, for example, the working conditions of miners or the natural consequence of mining during the early and middle parts of the twentieth century. If progress, production, and profits were not favored over human and natural welfare, then women, children, and men would not have been sent into unsafe tunnels hundreds of feet below the earth's surface to follow their instruction cards while they worked, and the environment would not have been left poisoned and scarred.[5]

Following the general media and religious trends of the times, these values were encoded in the McGuffey and other reading textbooks in the 1900s with the intention that they would become the driving principles of modern America. After the turn of the nineteenth century, the scientific management of instructional procedures complemented the craftsman-entrepreneurial content of reading education in order to train students' and teachers' bodies as well as minds. This combination of text and procedure occupied teachers' and students' thoughts and behaviors accordingly, at once encouraging and extending the industrial phase of capitalist ideology. Business, experts, and the state attested to the truth of these values and this course of educational action, establishing economic, scientific, and governmental structures that made the scientific management of reading instruction seem natural and normal. As Herbert Marcuse explained:

> The private and public bureaucracy thus emerges on an apparently objective and impersonal ground, provided by the rational specialization of function. . . . For, the more the individual functions are divided, fixated, and synchronized according to objective and impersonal pattern, the less reasonable it is for the individual to withdraw and withstand. The material fate of the masses becomes increasingly dependent upon the continuous and correct functioning of the increasingly bureaucratic order of private capitalist organizations. The objective and impersonal character of rationalization bestows upon the bureaucratic groups the universal dignity of reason. The rationality embodied in the giant enterprises makes it appear as if men, in obeying them, obey the dictum of an objective rationality. The private bureaucracy fosters a delusive harmony between the special and the common interests. Private power relationships appear not only as relationships between objective things but also as the rule of rationality.[6]

During the early 1980s, the private and public bureaucracies about which Marcuse wrote directed reading instruction in more than 90 percent of the classrooms in America. The multiple iterations of the scientific management of reading programs compelled teachers' and students' dependence on the continuous involvement of business, reading experts' science, and the state in daily classroom practices. The real rationalization of reading instruction was made possible by the scientific disenchantment of reading and teaching, in which reading became nothing more than the complex association of discrete skills and teaching was understood as the optimal transmission of these skills from text to student. At its core, that transmission was considered an exchange relationship in which students put forth proper effort, for which they were paid in skill knowledge. The teacher was successful when the student had accumulated sufficient skills to score highly on tests, enabling the student to secure first academic success and then economic prosperity after graduation. This rationalization of reading instruction was summarized succinctly in the National Academy of Education's federally funded, state-of-the-art report on reading education in 1985: "America will become a nation of readers when verified practices of the best teachers in the best schools can be introduced throughout the country."[7] This statement implies that more rationalization of reading instruction would be necessary because too many Americans could not be considered readers.

To explain why most teachers (90 percent) would accept rationalization that reduced reading to skills, denied the human qualities of teaching and learning, and demonstrated a lack of promised success for many students, I employed Georg Lukacs' theory of reification.[8] Writing at the time when Frederick Taylor was traveling the world to introduce scientific management to business and other social institutions, Lukacs argued that rationalization was always accompanied by two psychological and social forces—reification and alienation. *Reification* is a philosophical term for the treatment of an abstraction as a concrete object or an immutable procedure. In my studies, I found that many teachers and administrators reduced all the possible ways of teaching reading (the abstraction) to the directions within the scientifically managed reading programs. By following the directions and using the commercial materials, they were teaching reading because the directions, scripts, and procedures embodied the science of reading instruction and they led to students scoring highly on standardized reading tests. If it were not true that the directions and materials taught students to read, they argued, then the state would not compel students and teachers to use rationalized systems or standardized tests, business would not claim scientific authority for the materials, and reading experts would not endorse them directly or indirectly through professional organizations or teacher education programs.

Teachers' and administrators' reification of reading and instruction as rationalized, scientifically managed reading programs had three consequences.

> First, when they reified reading instruction, teachers and administrators lost sight of the fact that reading and instruction are human processes.

> Second, their reification of the scientific study of the reading process and instruction meant that their knowledge of reading and instruction was frozen in a single technological form.

> Third, school personnel's reification of science required that they define their work in terms of efficiency of delivery and students' gains on standardized reading tests.

Alienation is the process of separation between people and some quality assumed to be related to them in natural circumstances. This process can be consciously recognized (subjective alienation) or beyond the control of the individual (objective alienation). The historical processes of the rationalization of reading instruction employing various iterations of scientific management over the course of the twentieth century meant that both forms of alienation were in play in 90 percent of the classrooms in the United States. Outside of schools, the teaching of reading is naturally related to the teacher, who must plan the content and process of teaching, picking the materials, the goals, the pace, and the means of assessment. As Marcuse alluded, the rationalization of reading instruction divided the teaching function into parts, fixated them, and synchronized them according to apparently impersonal and objective patterns of business and science. State, district, or school directives to employ rationalized reading instruction in classrooms, therefore, objectively alienated teachers from the teaching of reading. In a similar way, students were objectively alienated from their reading—its plan, goal, process, pace, and outcome. Moreover, the process of rationalization set structures in place that made it seem natural and necessary that teachers and students accepted and participated in such programs for both personal and national reasons. Accepting and participating in this system without continuous anxiety and objection—seeking more rationalization through expanded commercial programs—meant that teachers acknowledged their separation from their teaching of reading.

How Did This Happen?

The victory of scientific management within reading instruction during the twentieth century required the active participation of reading experts, business, and the state. Each contributed in its own way to the transformation of the nineteenth century overseers and drillmasters into modern teachers, prepared to follow the dictates of science in their classrooms. The experts supplied scientific authority through experimentation, control of educational publications, and commitment to professionalism. Business produced and aggressively marketed the tools to translate that science into classroom practices—basal readers, standardized tests, and other management schemes. State and federal laws and policies ensured that those tools were available to all students and teachers, supplied research funds to further science and its translation, and then monitored teachers' and students' use of the tools. All were driven by the same faith in rationality that had directed social, political, and economic thought in America since its inception. During this century, however, this belief was guided by a new science, a more powerful corporate presence, and a progressively more interventionist state.

Narrowing of Expertise

In 1908, psychologist Edmund Burke Huey captured the research and political agenda for a century of educational science in one brief statement. "After all we have thus far been content with trial and error, too often allowing publishers to be our jury, and a real rationalization of the process of inducing the child with the practice of reading has not been made".[9] By ridiculing trial-and-error methods and deference to textbooks in the classroom, Huey sought to reduce the role of teachers and publishers in future discussions of reading instruction. He completed his proposed hierarchy of authority by chastising psychologists (the implied "we" in his statement) for acceding power to publishers. Finally, he identified psychologists as the only group capable of performing a real rationalization of reading and instruction and, therefore, the primary group to assume authority over scientifically managed reading instruction. Psychologists would develop true understandings of reading and the teaching of reading by subjecting both to scientific scrutiny. Huey's tone implied that it was psychologists' duty, their moral obligation, to address these in order to set reading instruction right. Through their basic and applied research, psychologists would formulate the guiding principles for both curriculum and instruction. Publishers would use those guidelines to prepare instructional materials, and then teachers would follow these guiding principles using the scientific materials in classrooms across the country. Huey presented separate roles for each contributor to the scientific management of reading instruction.

In *An Elusive Science: The Troubling History of Educational Research*, Ellen Condliffe Lagemann contends that this process of separation and specialization was also apparent among psychologists as they began to focus on reading and instruction.[10] Before the 1880s, education and reading were two of many concerns of philosophy. Plato, Aristotle, St. Augustine, Locke, and Rousseau wrote treatises on both subjects. At the turn of the nineteenth century, however, philosophers attempting to employ new scientific methods to the study of learning, thought, and memory established specialized professional organizations and journals under the label of psychology (the study of the mind). By the 1920s, psychologists interested in the process of reading called themselves cognitive psychologists and studied perception, eye movements, and memory. Those interested in investigations of the teaching of reading were called educational psychologists. Across the century, new specializations emerged—psychometrics and neuropsychology—and accordingly the list of reading experts with the recognized authority to address the topics of reading and instruction grew narrower and narrower still.

With the invention of the basal reading programs, most reading experts (educational psychologists and teacher educators) were certain that they had an answer to Huey's challenge. Educational publishers would hire reading experts to write the guiding principles for the teachers' manuals and to oversee the design of daily lessons within the textbooks. Publishers would substitute the new basals for the old textbooks. And then teachers would follow the experts' directions in order to teach children to read in their classrooms. In this way, the new teachers' manuals could substitute the objectivity of science for the teachers' subjectivity. In the beginning, this plan did not work smoothly. For example, in 1928, educational psychologist Harold Donovan explained:

> One of the most potent factors in spreading the results of research is through a well-prepared set of readers and their manuals; yet we find teachers still instructing children as they themselves were taught, absolutely ignorant and oblivious that science had discovered for us truths and that little children are entitled to the benefits of these discoveries.[11]

The new challenge facing reading experts, then, was how to entice teachers to follow the teachers' manuals in the new basal programs. Although drillmasters and overseers relied on textbooks during their instruction, they had devised their own unique patterns of use of these materials, including goal setting, instructional decisions, and the pace of their teaching, according to their knowledge of reading and instruction and their experience as students and teachers. Those unique patterns were now considered to be the primary barriers to effective reading instruction. Donovan provided two clues on how teachers' subjectivity might be overcome. First, the basals, and particularly the manuals, would be associated with research, science, and truth, making them the legitimate tools of scientifically managed instruction. Second, teachers' work in teaching reading would be redefined as guiding children through the basal materials according to the directions in the manuals. Just as Huey had made rationalization of reading instruction the moral duty for psychologists, Donovan implied that modern teachers owed it to their students to follow the teachers' manuals. Many reading experts joined Donovan enthusiastically in the promotion of basals and the definition of teaching, using all the tools at their disposal—research reports, methods textbooks, and academic and professional organizations. As a result, wherever school administrators and teachers sought guidance about reading instruction, they found reading experts advocating scientific reading instruction through the use of basal reading materials and other forms of rationalization. By the 1960s, national surveys demonstrated that nearly all teachers were using basals according to the teachers' manuals on a daily basis. In fact, basal control of reading instruction became so complete that some experts began to remark that the materials were using the teachers rather than the teachers using the materials.[12]

NSSE Yearbooks

The National Society for the Study of Education's Committee on Reading published a volume devoted exclusively to reading instruction, materials, and research in 1925 and continued to report at twelve-year intervals until 1961.[13] In its first report, the committee was careful not to recommend one set of books over another because it lacked sufficient scientific data to substantiate any such claim. However, the committee gave its explicit endorsement of any basal that included interesting stories and a balance between instruction on decoding and comprehension skills, and stated, "there should be a brief, simple, efficient manual." The committee's second report in 1937 was more emphatic in its endorsement of the use of basal materials over the teacher-directed instruction of the New Education or the traditional use of supplemental readers based on teachers' judgment.[14] For instance, University of Chicago professor William S. Gray compared "experience-based" instruction with "commercially prepared materials" and concluded, "prepared materials are, as a rule, more skillfully organized and are technically superior to those developed daily in classrooms. Because they follow a sequential plan, the chance for so called 'gaps' in learning is greatly reduced." Gray advocated that teachers should not deviate from the arrangement of lessons in the guidebook. "[The stories] may be read in the order in which they appear in the book. This is not only a safe procedure, but also one that reduces the possibilities of unexpected handicaps in progress."

A second essay in the thirty-sixth NSSE yearbook dealt with teachers' use of basal materials, and it is perhaps most remarkable because it was prepared by a subcommittee with representation from the three leading educational publishers of that time—Ginn, Scott Foresman, and Macmillan.[15] Although previous NSSE yearbooks considered instructional materials, this was the first time that publishers were formally represented on an NSSE committee. To begin its report, the subcommittee presented its interpretation of an informal survey of elementary schools in which it estimated that 90 to 95 percent of all teachers used basal readers during their reading instruction. Accordingly, the subcommittee directed its comments to the appropriate use of the materials during reading instruction. Among its suggestions, it warned teachers to avoid using different sets of basal readers, library books, or supplemental materials within and across grades because the vocabularies did not match sufficiently well to allow beginning readers to practice their reading independently. Rather, school administrators should adopt a single published program for all levels of instruction. Finally, the subcommittee warned that "individual and local groups of teachers are increasingly unlikely to improve upon the product of professional textbook-makers." Using phrases like "perfected to such a degree," "can be used effectively," and "systematic" to describe basal readers and "seldom justified," "scattered," and "aimless" to characterize teachers' independent instruction, the committee left little doubt about experts' position on basal use and scientific reading instruction.

By comparison, the subsequent NSSE yearbooks were tame in their promotion of basal use in classrooms. Yet each report was firm in its support. For example, in the forty-eighth NSSE yearbook, contributors suggested that "improvements in the construction and use of basal reading materials have contributed appreciatively to the improvement of primary grade reading instruction"; "the teacher is referred to the manuals accompanying whatever readers are to be used. . . . it should be remembered that as a rule, pupils gain most from the use of a reader when the selections contained in that book are taught as the authors of the reader intend them to be taught"; and "the teacher who attempts to prepare substitutes for basic readers ought to make the substitutes better than the readers available."[16] *Development in and Through Reading,* the sixtieth NSSE yearbook, began to report some controversy over basal publishers' claims that their wares provided a complete instructional program to meet all students' needs. In its conclusion, the Committee on Reading stated, however, "The content, structure and format of present reading materials can be improved; this review indicates, however, even greater need exists to improve teaching methods and over-all instructional planning for reading development." Yet, in the sixty-seventh NSSE yearbook, the committee acknowledged that the only thing that wouldn't change in reading instruction in the 1970s and 1980s was that "basal readers will continue to be used." Finally, in the eighty-third yearbook, Harvard University professor Jeanne Chall commented on the research base for basal readers, noting "some critics of basal reading series have failed to consider the many changes during the past decade."[17]

Textbooks

Professional books on reading and methods textbooks for training teachers also carried the message that scientific reading instruction depended on teachers' systematic use of basal reading materials according to the directions in the teachers' manuals. In the 1927 edition of *Supervision and Teaching of Reading,* Harris, Donovan, and Alexander promoted basal use because "the authors of the newer readers have grouped the materials for instructional purposes."[18] The authors listed fifty-two different sets of basals that met their criteria for classroom use. Similar to the NSSE yearbooks' enthusiastic authors during the 1930s and 1940s, textbook authors became more emphatic in their endorsements of basal use and clearer about which part of the basal was most important for teachers. Reading experts Donald Durrell and E. W. Dolch explained:

> The advantage of orderly procedures in reading instruction is such that few, if any, teachers can serve all pupils well by incidental or improvised reading methods. . . . The well planned basal-reading systems presented by experienced textbook publishers have many advantages. . . . A detailed study of the manuals of basal-reading systems is the first step to learning how to teach reading.

A basic reader is really one part of a "system for teaching reading." This system includes the basic books themselves, the workbooks that go with them, and the teacher's manual, which tells what to do with the textbooks, what to do with the workbooks, and also tells all the other activities a teacher should go through in order to do a complete job teaching reading.[19]

Throughout the 1960s and 1970s, reading methods textbooks offered three reasons for their relatively unqualified support of basal materials: the reading selections were considered to be high quality, the teachers' guidebooks offered suggestions for comprehensive and systematic instruction, and the materials were based on scientific investigations of the reading process.[20] In reading methods textbooks from the 1980s, authors demonstrated their commitment to basals by their allotment of page space and the language they used during their descriptions of the materials. For example, these textbooks included between eleven and thirty-six pages of explanation with between six and nineteen reproductions directly from basal materials to illustrate points, but they allotted only between zero and one and a half pages to discussions of comprehending the main idea while reading. Textbook authors' choice of phrases such as "best routines," "developed by teams of reading experts," and "objective, tightly structured and logically ordered" conveyed their support of the use of basals in teaching reading. Perhaps the most extreme example of a methods textbook's endorsement of basal readers and their use was Robert Aukerman's *The Basal Reader Approach to Reading*, in which he described the fifteen leading sets of basal reading materials for 333 pages.[21]

Journals

The articles published in professional journals between the 1920s and the 1980s suggest more complexity in reading experts' support for basal readers than do the NSSE yearbooks or methods textbooks. During the late 1920s, through the 1930s, and into the 1940s, with few exceptions, journal articles provided unquestioned advocacy of basal use over other methods. By the late 1950s and the early 1960s, however, it became apparent to some reading experts that the balanced relationship between experts and basal publishers had tipped in favor of the publishers and that profits rather than science directed the contents of basal series in their increasingly more frequent revisions. Yet within the logic of the decades-old real rationalization of reading instruction, these critics lacked alternatives except to beat basal publishers at their own game. Rather than advocate that teachers inform themselves about the processes of reading and instruction in order to abandon increasingly unscientific teachers' manuals, critics and advocates of basals called for "more scientific" methods, which would produce greater gains in test scores to be included in the manuals. In the 1950s and 1960s, this call meant to increase the direct phonics instruction in early grades. During the late 1970s and early 1980s, critics suggested more emphasis on comprehension in all grades.

Consider the articles that appeared in *Language Arts*, the National Council of Teachers of English's elementary school journal, which has published continuously since 1924, making it an ideal candidate for this illustration, and the oldest American journal devoted exclusively to literacy instruction.[22] Until 1984, *Language Arts* published three types of articles concerning basal readers: analyses of the content of the anthologies and other basal components, descriptions of teachers' use of these materials, and arguments concerning appropriate methodology. Although these themes are represented in most volumes of the journal, the analyses-of-content articles were most prominent during the first two decades of publishing, when reading experts were eager to explain the contents of basals to teachers and other school personnel and to prepare teachers for changes to come in the materials.[23] For example, William S. Gray commented on the possibility of "blocs, strikes, and even religious and racial persecution" without proper attention to the selection of readings in basal anthologies, and Emmett Betts, E. L. Dolch, and Arthur Gates discussed the appropriate vocabulary for basal readers. By the thirtieth-anniversary issue of *Language Arts*, the use of basal readers had become so commonplace that Gerald Yoakam challenged reading experts to find the most effective balance "between basal, curricular, recretory, and corrective reading" (430) in order to prepare students for the future.

Between the 1950s and the 1980s, contributors to *Language Arts* described and argued about teachers' uses of basals in elementary classrooms. In 1958, Ralph Staiger, then director of the International Reading Association, presented the results of his survey of 474 school districts from forty-eight states and Hawaii, which suggested that 99 percent of the school districts responded that teachers' guidebooks directed reading instruction in elementary classrooms. By 1972, A. Byron Calloway, then director of the University of Georgia reading clinic, rejected all nonbasal forms of teaching reading because Georgia teachers would simply not use them. In a similar way, most descriptions of teachers' practice suggested that reading experts and publishers had convinced most teachers to follow the teachers' guidebooks. In other articles, the growing ambivalence of some experts is apparent. Some contributors compared test scores for students experiencing nonbasal instruction with those of students receiving basal-directed instruction, and on every occasion the results provided unintended support for teachers' continued use of basals because the studies found no statistically significant differences between the alternate and the basal method. Although the contributors suggest that this was good news and that teachers now had little to lose in trying a new method, within the scientific logic on which their studies were based, the opposite was also true. Teachers could and did infer from these reports that they had little to gain from such a switch.[24]

The largest investigation comparing methods for teaching reading is the U. S. Office of Education's Cooperative Research Program in First-Grade Reading Instruction, which included twenty-seven separate studies conducted in various regions of the United States and which was discussed in several *Language Arts* articles.[25] Initiated by Boston University professor Donald Durrell, this project sought to determine once and for all which method was superior to all others in terms of raising students' scores on several standardized tests of letter and word recognition, oral reading, and sentence comprehension. Of the twenty-seven studies, twenty-one explicitly compared nonbasal approaches—initially teaching the alphabet, phonics, language experience, and so forth—to "the basal reader method" during an entire year of instruction (1964–65). Summarizing the results, project coordinators Guy Bond and Robert Dykstra concluded that only by adding additional formal phonics instruction to basal-led instruction could a teacher surpass the typical results from following a basal teachers' manual.[26] All other methods of instruction were described as "not of much practical significance in terms of actual reading achievement." In short, the largest research project ever conducted on reading instruction unintentionally confirmed what reading experts had claimed unconditionally for nearly forty years—basal reading instruction in which teachers followed the guidebook was as good or better than any other form of instruction. This conclusion has been used for decades to exclude alternatives to basal methods from schools.[27]

If these articles in *Language Arts* are typical of other journals' treatment of basal materials and their use, then despite the occasional critical essay, reading experts promoted teachers' use of basal readers through their professional writing. Even when they expressed criticism, they confirmed the primacy of teachers' manuals. Consider three articles in James Hoffman and Nancy Roser's 1987 special issue of the *Elementary School Journal* as an indication of this ambivalent support.[28] Jeanne Chall set the tone by redirecting growing criticism of basal materials to teachers' inappropriate use of the materials because "we know that basal readers are perhaps the most effective way to improve students' reading achievement." Gerry Duffy, Laura Roehler, and Joyce Putnam explained the shortcomings of teachers' manuals for making rational instruction decisions but then concluded, "the solution does not lie with abandoning basal textbooks because all teachers appreciate the guide." Finally, Roger Farr, Mike Tulley, and Deborah Powell exposed the extravagant claims and lavish gifts that representatives of basal publishers made, but then assured all that "by and large, however, American educators are fortunate to have available such a large quantity of high quality textbooks and other materials to support reading curricula."

Professional Organizations

The National Council of Teachers of English (NCTE) was organized in 1911, largely to protect high school teachers from efforts to align their English curricula according to college requirements.[29] By 1929, some members formed an elementary section of the organization and adopted *Elementary English* (now *Language Arts*) as its voice to articulate language arts curricula and instruction for young children. Four years later, Harry Greene and Emmett Betts founded the National Conference for Research in English in order to elevate the importance of science within the organization. Each of these moves further reduced the number of groups and individuals who could speak with authority about reading and reading instruction within the organization. Professional teachers joined the organization. Those interested in reading and teaching children to read became members of the elementary section to distinguish their work and authority from secondary school teachers. Researchers protested the emphasis on classroom practices by developing a parallel organization for themselves.

Apparently these roles were not specialized enough, because in 1947 Professor Betts participated in the founding of the International Council for the Improvement of Reading Instruction (later the International Reading Association, or IRA).[30] The organization's purpose was stated in its constitution—to stimulate and encourage research on all types of reading, diagnosis of reading disabilities, readability, and "the improvement of textbook construction and publication from the point of view of the reading problems therein and of their effects on reading instruction." This final purpose was complicated by the association's dependence on publishers for early (and continued) financial support. Nancy Larrick, a children's magazine editor for Random House, elicited donations and advertisements for the association's early publications. D. C. Heath and Ginn and Company were the first to advertise in the association's journal, *The Reading Teacher*, as soon as it graduated from mimeograph copies to printed issues in 1953. In *Reading Reflections: A History of the International Reading Association*, past president and historian of the organization Bob Jerrolds was direct about the relationship:

> From its founding, the organization had welcomed those who produced materials for reading instruction. Those who started the organization were well aware of the profound influence the publishers had on the children and young people for whom they wrote. They were also aware of the influence of sales persons on teachers and administrators. The founders wanted to make sure these people were included in the organization with the full benefits and responsibility

of membership. Publishers and their sales persons have amply rewarded the ICIRI and the IRA for that welcome with their support, financial and otherwise.

The publishers' influence on the IRA has come in three forms. First, many of the organization's presidents and members of the board of directors have also served as basal authors. Second, basal publishers often covered the expenses of their authors and consultants to speak at local, state, regional, national, and world IRA conferences. Frequently local, state, and regional conferences must rely on publishers' generosity in order to secure speakers because the groups cannot afford speakers' fees by themselves. Third, the publishers are always well represented at these conferences by sales personnel who emphasize the connection between the scientific rhetoric of the speaker and his association with their basal materials, even if the speaker does not mention this connection.

The presence of sales personnel with their basal wares also supplies much-needed capital for conferences and the IRA organization in general. According to Kenneth Goodman, a former president of the IRA, this third type of publisher influence was responsible in one year for a $300,000 surplus of receipts over expenses after an annual conference.[31] In return for this capital, publishers are granted their own display room and set times in the conference proceedings when only the materials rooms are open to the conference participants. Most recently, this financial connection between the publishers and the IRA became even more direct as the IRA board sought and received sustaining contributions from publishers of as much as $5,000 a year. In return for their "donation," publishing companies received special membership status in the IRA.

Thus, wherever teachers and other school personnel turned in search of information on elementary school reading instruction since the late 1920s— whether they consulted research yearbooks, read methods textbooks, perused journals or professional books, or attended conferences—they found reading experts advocating the use of basals according to the directions in teachers' guidebooks in order to render reading instruction more systematic and scientific. Even when they witnessed infrequent complaints about the contents of the basals, teachers were told and continue to be told that only minor technical modifications are needed to renew basal readers' service as the science of reading instruction. Huey's remarks on the real rationalization of reading and instruction from 1908 still rang true in proceedings from a 1984 conference held by the National Center for the Study of Reading.[32] Cognitive psychologist Richard Anderson, then a consultant for a basal publisher, remarked, "currently there would appear to be a lag as long as 15–20 years in getting research findings into practice. It stands to reason therefore that researchers who wish to have scholarship influence practice ought to give high priority to interacting with publishers."

Other Types of Scientific Management

Anderson's statement echoed the sentiment of the Committee on the Economy of Time in Education from the earlier part of the century, when reading experts were importing the principles of scientific management into reading programs. In the beginning, the basal seemed to be the catalyst to scientific reading instruction; however, after cornering the market in the 1960s, basal publishers slowed the rate of innovation while reducing the shelf life of each edition. By the 1980s, some psychologists and reading professors thought basals were insufficient to render the desired results for all students enrolling in American elementary schools. While some experts replaced basal systems with systematic alternatives, others sought greater control of teachers' use of basals.[33] Consider three examples: mastery learning, merit pay for test scores, and teacher and school effectiveness programs.

During the 1970s and 1980s, advocates of mastery learning argued that universal literacy was possible if reading instruction were reorganized according to three assumptions: (1) reading is segmented into separate skills, which are arranged in a curriculum according to tested sequence; (2) teachers engage in a teach, test, reteach, retest instructional cycle; and (3) students are given unlimited time to learn one skill before progressing to the next skill in the sequence. "Provided that mastery learning is placed productively within its larger instructional setting, and provided that serious attention is paid to predictable problems in implementation, mastery learning will result in impressive improvements in the quality of reported success."[34] In the late 1970s, the Chicago Public School District decided to reorganize its reading program according to the principles of mastery learning.[35] It hired experts, wrote its own basal and teachers' manual because commercially available basals were considered too loosely organized, and developed tests and retests for each of the several hundred skills that it defined as essential. To monitor student progress, district administrators set minimum skill levels within and across grades. Those students who did not reach the thresholds were retained in grade.

Chicago school administrators sought the one best method of scientifically managed reading instruction by exerting greater and more focused control of the daily classroom activities. However, from the onset, the Chicago Mastery Learning Reading Program experienced predictable problems. Teachers challenged the design of the materials as inappropriate for some students and too detailed in their articulation of separate skills. (The district used the complaint during contract negotiations, trading a reduction in essential skills for a lower-percent pay raise for teachers.) Teachers complained that they were slavishly tied to the test-retest format, leaving them little time to teach and students little time to read books. Moreover, success within the CMLR system did not translate into success on standardized norm-referenced reading tests. In the end, the tightly closed system of the Chicago Mastery Learning Reading Program did not achieve its desired results and was abandoned by the district in 1986.[36]

A second attempt to improve teachers' use of basals employed the business principle of merit pay. Teachers who performed reading instruction successfully would receive a bonus for their efforts; teachers who were considered unsuccessful would receive help in order to improve their performance, but not a bonus. All such systems focused on student outcomes in order to define success. During the early 1980s, the Houston School District adopted a merit pay model in order to improve the reading achievement test scores across the district.[37] District administrators replaced a school-based decision model with a centralized five-step plan for the use of a single basal program; they established target goals for each school to reach in order to qualify; and they offered a significant financial incentive (5 percent of salary) for compliance. Unique to the Houston system was the school as the unit of analysis. Other merit pay programs centered on individuals; however, the Houston program required that the school average for student test scores had to reach the target for any teacher, administrator, or other school staff to receive a merit award. This encouraged the school personnel to work together toward improved test scores. Schools were ranked according to increase in average test scores, and teachers and administrators of the top ten schools received an additional 3 percent of their salaries.

The centralized planning, five-step instructional card, and financial incentives were direct copies of the original plans for the scientific management of business. The coordination within schools maps the role of foremen in those plans. The Houston plan also brought much of the labor strife of the original as well. Although all faculty and administrators acknowledged the rise in students' test scores, many teachers complained about the regimentation and the pressure to manufacture test scores on demand. Teachers reported that test scores were posted on classroom doors, training was required for teachers who were "behind" in their basals, and administrators engaged in surprise observations. During interviews, one teacher explained:

> We have to show all five steps on our lesson plans and the principal checks these every week. I'm pushed harder to get my kids through (the basal). I have to be at a certain point in (the basal) by the end of the year. Otherwise I'm in trouble. I have to make my lessons quicker, I'm pushed so I push, and we do get there whether we're ready or not. . . . That sounds terrible I know . . . but what else can I do?

After initial success, the student scores began to regress back toward the historical mean for the district. Although no doubt some students profited from focused, scientifically managed instruction, teachers reported that success on reading achievement scores did not necessarily translate into success in other subjects. The Houston merit pay program ended when the superintendent accepted employment with the basal publisher of the text used in the program.

A third approach to a real rationalization of reading instruction developed from a series of federally funded studies in the 1970s.[38] Loosely coupled under the label of school and teacher effectiveness research, these studies attempted to identify the primary factors that led to student success on achievement tests. As a result, the best practices would be encouraged and unproductive aspects would be eliminated from programs. Stanford University professor Larry Cuban articulated the effectiveness formula: top officials demonstrated leadership by clearly specifying goals tied to student achievement, a centralized decision was made concerning the curriculum and instructional materials to reach those goals, individual schools aligned themselves with these goals through curricular and procedural review, evaluation of school administrators and teachers was linked to the curricular objectives by the tests that accompanied the instructional materials, and staff development programs were developed to help all participants adjust to the new system.[39] In turn, teachers were to use direct, explicit instruction concerning each point in the curriculum, to provide meaningful activities that highlighted the important cues to be learned, to ensure that students devoted their attention to the task at hand, and to promote persistence in learning.

School and teacher effectiveness models proved popular with school administrators because they used current research to legitimize the practiced principles of scientific management. The principles of each were quickly translated into district plans for curriculum because educational experts designed instructional rubrics to direct teachers' attention and practice toward the expected student outcomes. For example, Madeleine Hunter marketed her version of these century-old principles as a staff development program complete with lesson formats that established a correct way of thinking about teaching and learning as well as correct procedures for both. In 1984, *Becoming a Nation of Readers*, the state-of-the-art report on reading education in America from the National Academy of Science, recommended teacher and school effectiveness principles as the driving forces for improving reading instruction across the country.

Over the course of sixty years, from the 1920s to the 1980s, both of Edmund Burke Huey's challenges were addressed. First, the authority to speak about reading education was limited to those who could engage in scientific investigation of reading and instruction. According to Anthony Barton and

David Wilder in a national survey of teachers and principals during the 1960s, less than ten university professors were listed as authorities concerning the teaching of reading at all levels of schooling.[40] Second, many attempts had been made at a real rationalization of reading instruction. During this time, most reading experts engaged in the project to legitimize scientific management as the core value of an effective reading program. Whether conducting research, writing for teachers, or working for professional organizations, they encouraged teachers to trust and follow the equivalent of Frederick Taylor's instructional cards for workers in his plants. Substituting test scores for the speed and quality of worker output, reading experts defined the real rationalization of the process of inducing a child with the practice of reading as the directions in basal teachers' manuals or the hyperrationalized schemes to more closely control teachers' and students' lives during reading instruction.

Standardized Reading Tests

Any real rationalization of reading instruction was not possible without a measure of instructional effectiveness. Frederick Taylor's scientific management measured workers' productivity by two criteria—the speed and the accuracy with which they worked. These two factors became the defining features of workers' effectiveness and they were translated as the criteria used in the psychological mapping of mental processes. In the *Handbook of Reading Research*, Peter Johnston located the origins of this translation in Wilhelm Wundt's psychological laboratory in Germany before the turn of the nineteenth century.[41] The mapping of the mental processes crossed the Atlantic Ocean with James McKeen Cattell's interest in word and letter perception as good indicators of mental activity and Joseph Meyer Rice's survey of American classrooms and subsequent articles in the 1890s. Their translations differed, with Cattell focusing on the psychological mapping project and Rice measuring reading and writing as educational achievements. Rice's early study of spelling as a measure of the effectiveness of teachers' instruction evoked disdain among educators in the 1890s but later became the blueprint for the scientific management of schooling. For example, E. L. Thorndike turned his attention toward the measurement of reading in 1914.

> It is obvious that educational science and educational practice alike need more objective, more accurate, and more convenient measures of (1) a pupil's ability to pronounce words and sentences seen; (2) a pupil's ability to understand the meaning of words and sentences seen; (3) a pupil's ability to appreciate and enjoy what we roughly call "good literature"; and (4) a pupil's ability to read orally, clearly, and efficiently. . . . Any progress toward measuring how well a child can

read with something of the objectivity, precision, comeasurability, and convenience which characterize our measurements of how tall he is, how much he can lift with his back, squeeze with his hand or how accurate his vision, would be a great help in grading, promoting, and testing the value of methods of teaching.[42]

E. L. Thorndike's adaptation of Rice's approach for testing literacy began with his 1909 scale for measuring handwriting. Other tests followed soon after: Hilligas' composition scale, Buckingham's spelling examination, and finally, William S. Gray's Standardized Oral Reading Paragraphs were published in 1915. Gray's test—with periodic adjustment—was still in print in the 1980s. Between those decades, Guy Buswell, W. F. Dearborn, Charles Judd, E. L. Thorndike, Arthur Gates, Emmett Betts, Donald Durrell, George Spache, and Roger Farr published some type of standardized reading test. While each tested the capabilities of individual students, it also enabled evaluation of teachers' instruction in decoding and comprehension. As instructional emphasis shifted from students' oral to silent reading during the 1920s, reading tests came to consist of the silent reading of a passage, followed by the solving of brief, generally text-related problems, typically questions.[43] These tests allowed groups of students to be assessed simultaneously and set the goals for efficient reading instruction in both classrooms and remedial programs. As Columbia professor Arthur Gates explained in 1937, standardized reading tests directed the scientific management of reading instruction.

> Within recent years various types of organization of materials similar to published standardized tests have appeared. . . . The better types represent an effort to develop a comprehensive series of exercises that include in well printed and illustrated forms the best informal devices and tests that the teacher would otherwise have to prepare herself. They are organized systematically to provide learning of the basal words, word recognition, comprehension, appreciation, and study techniques and simultaneously to test and diagnose ability and difficulty. Their purpose is to provide the nearest possible approach to the policy of daily diagnosis with the least expenditure of time of pupils and teachers.[44]

The connection between teaching and standardized reading tests became law during the Johnson administration's War on Poverty through Title I of the Elementary and Secondary Education Act. Senator Robert Kennedy was concerned that school administrators would divert the federal funding for Title I reading programs away from the intended poor unless there was an objective reporting system by which parents could monitor their children's progress.[45] The federal Planning, Programming, and Budgeting Systems Office translated

Kennedy's concern into a requirement that all Title I programs would use standardized reading tests to admit students to the program and to measure their periodic progress. Those scores would be made public. Echoing the remarks of early advocates of scientific management and presaging current opinion, Education Commissioner Frances Keppell argued in 1964 that public reporting would provide performance comparisons among schools, districts, and even states, and would thus stimulate competition. In this way, reading test scores based on speed and accuracy became the government's official measure of teaching effectiveness and efficiency.

Business

In 1991, the second *Handbook of Reading Research* included a chapter on the publishing industry and textbooks written by Harvard University professor Jeanne Chall and James Squires. Just the presence of the chapter denoted the importance of business in the teaching of reading in America.[46] The handbook editors' choice of Squires as an author of that chapter demonstrated the intimate connection between researchers, publishers, and professional organizations. At that time, Squires had served as a professor at the University of California at Berkeley in the 1950s, executive secretary of the National Council of Teachers of English during the 1960s, and senior vice president, publisher, and editor-in-chief at Ginn and Company during the 1970s and 1980s. In the chapter, Squires made it clear that educational publishing was a business—a $1.6-billion-a-year business. Capturing educational publishing in the 1980s, he wrote:

> The total investment by a publisher to bring a complete basal program to the market has been estimated to range from $15 million to $35 million, including editorial and authorship costs, permission fees, research and field testing, printing and distribution costs, promotion and sales training, and warehousing. Since the first dollar in sales is seldom returned until a year after publication, and six years must pass after publication until every school has had an opportunity to purchase, the high risk/low return involved in educational publishing becomes manifest. . . . Average school publishers achieve less than 9 percent profits, and smaller publishers report less that 4 percent. At a time when the federal government guarantees a return of 6 percent to 8 percent on non-risk savings accounts, profits not in excess of 10 percent are not designed to stimulate widespread investment. . . . Given the high total investment in basal reading programs, one can understand why reading publishing is dominated by a relatively limited number of large companies, and why the industry is basically conservative.

Right from the start in the 1920s, publishers recognized that they needed reading experts in order to legitimize their products in the redefined reading education market. To that point, several educational publishers had been successful in selling their products based on their approximation of the moralist format of McGuffey's Readers. The early NSSE surveys of classroom practice reported that more than forty publishers supplied the basic texts for reading instruction in American schools and more than twenty different companies sold supplemental materials for instruction—word cards, charts, and the like. Most authors for these textbooks were school personnel—classroom teachers or school administrators—some of whom had recently accepted employment at teachers' colleges. According to Nila Banton Smith, before scientific management, publishers marketed these series based on their practicality and tradition.[47] During the 1920s as research on reading became more widely known and the real rationalization of reading instruction became the goal of reading experts and school officials alike, the authors of the textbooks changed, the marketing of textbooks changed, and their content was amended. The expanding and changing school market was partially responsible for these changes as experts and school officials sought a scientific management of reading instruction. Just as certainly, however, the new materials were the catalyst for changes in elementary school in order to transform drillmasters and overseers into modern teachers. By adopting the language of science and incorporating some of the findings from experimental studies of reading and instruction, the basal materials became indispensable in the classroom.

Authors

From the 1920s to the 1980s, the list of basal authors reads like a directory of reading researchers in America. During the 1920s and 1930s, Guy Buswell, William S. Gray, and Arthur Gates began their association as authors of major reading textbooks series. In the 1940s, Emmett Betts, Donald Durrell, and David Russell joined their ranks. Guy Bond, Albert Harris, and William Sheldon became authors during the 1950s. Mary Austin, Glenn McCracken, and Russell Stauffer did in the 1960s, Carl Bereiter, Roger Farr, and Kenneth Goodman did in the 1970s, and Richard Allington, Donna Alverman, P. David Pearson, and Robert Tierney did in the 1980s. All were basal authors for major educational publishers. Many of these authors remained associated with educational publishers for their entire careers. For example, William S. Gray worked with Scott Foresman from 1929 until his death in 1961. Roger Farr has enjoyed a similar arrangement with Harcourt from 1972 through the present. Others were authors for a single edition of a series, Kenneth Goodman worked with Scott Foresman only for the Reading Systems edition.

In 1977, George Graham wrote a dissertation on basal publishing after working in the publishing industry for two years.[48] His report described the role of authors and the tension between innovation to attract new customers and stability to ensure that old customers remained loyal. According to Graham, authors did not actually write much of the materials that teachers used in classrooms. Rather, when a publisher originated a new basal, authors provided a framework for lessons and a theoretical orientation to the curricular and instructional design, and then they acted as consultants for company editors and production staff (often former teachers), who wrote and assembled the series. After the materials were completed and ready for sale, authors became important in marketing the new products. In publishing houses with established textbook series, authors began as advisers to the ongoing production of new editions. Early in the twentieth century, publishers revised editions every ten or twelve years; by the 1980s, the revision cycle was half that time. In Graham's words, "series houses have often cared more about the national prominence of their authors than about their actual ability." And they changed authors regularly in order to appear to be at the forefront of innovation in reading education.

The actual writers of the materials were in-house editors who were organized into teams, which were assigned responsibility for one part of the complete program—teachers' manual, student book, workbook, supplemental materials, or tests. Working from the authors' outlines, assistant and associate editors wrote the texts for each part, including the directions for teachers on how to teach and test and for students on how to read and learn. Supervising editors in each team ensured that the work was accomplished effectively and efficiently. Executive editors coordinated the production of all parts at particular grade levels, and editors-in-chief brought the grade levels together for the complete series. According to Graham, sales personnel had oversight at all levels of production and often commented on the possible effects of innovation on sales. As basal author Richard Allington remarked, "publishers rely heavily on research to produce their curricula, but it is market research that more often carries the day—not basic research."[49]

The Market

Although reading instruction was a potentially lucrative market, production costs and profit margins made it a highly competitive and conservative one as well. Because all basals were reported to be based on the best science available, and there was only one best science, most companies produced similar products appropriate for the largest possible market. Much like the American automobile industry, basal publishers copied their industry's most successful model. For example, the success of the Dick and Jane series for the Scott Foresman Company was followed directly by Tom and Betty from Ginn and Company and Jack and Kim from the American Book Company. The similarities extended well beyond the characters in the early primers and anthologies. Each series included a teachers' manual for each level of student anthology, workbooks, practice activities, and texts as well as some supplemental materials. Each lesson in all the series followed a similar format; after the 1940s that format was called a directed reading thinking activity. This DRTA began with an introduction of a story, vocabulary development, and story reading in short sections with questions to test readers' memory for events. When the story was completed, a skill lesson was taught and students were directed to complete practice activities individually. Regardless of the stories, the scope and sequence of skills, or the stated philosophy of the authors, all basal programs followed this DRTA for more than forty years, leaving textbook sales representatives with little of substance to distinguish their wares for potential buyers.

In order to separate their basal from others on the market, publishers spent a quarter of their budgets on advertising and promotion. In a study of the textbook selection process, Roger Farr and his associates discovered that publishers' reputations were often the determining factor in state, district, and school decisions to purchase a basal series.[50] That reputation was built partially upon company history and notoriety of its authors. However, free supplemental items, free training in how to use the materials, and toll-free numbers in order to receive advice while using the materials were common practices among textbook representatives. Publishers offered dinners, wine-and-cheese receptions, or parties at professional conferences in order to influence key people before they made their decision. Some companies hosted all-expenses-paid summer institutes for key decision-makers in order to provide extended exposure to their materials. Former IRA president Kenneth Goodman reported riverboat trips up the Mississippi River, parties at the Franklin Mint, and trips to Atlantic City for gambling, all at the expense of basal publishers during the professional organization's annual convention. Calling these practices part of the tradition of basal marketing, he lamented that the intensity of the market tainted the textbook selection process and caused potential conflicts of interest at many levels.[51]

During their first sixty years, the number of publishers producing basals steadily declined. Of the forty publishers mentioned in the 1916 NSSE surveys, only eighteen remained in the 1930s, and that number was reduced to twelve in the 1950s. The reduction was caused by many factors, not the least of which was the near monopoly enjoyed by Scott Foresman's *Dick and Jane* series. With William Gray's death and the cultural changes of the 1960s, Scott Foresman lost much of its market share, and six companies shared 80 percent of the basal market. While traditional market forces and lack of profits caused some of the attrition, mergers and acquisitions reduced the number of competitors as well. For example, in 1985, Ginn and Company merged with Silver Burdett, which had already acquired Allyn and Bacon. Macmillan owned Harper and Row, Lippencott, and Laidlaw. Moreover, many of the publishing companies were purchased by corporations without previous experience in the publishing industry.[52] Within these conglomerates, profitable basals were removed from the market simply because their profit margins were too small to help the parent company attract more investment. Mergers and takeovers reduced the number of basals on the market and froze even the possibility of innovation within the industry, reinforcing the scientific management of reading instruction.

Control in Classrooms

Across the six decades between the 1920s and 1980s, educational publishers were more than willing to supply the technology and instruction cards for teachers to work scientifically. In Chapter 2, I explained how the integration of Thorndike's laws of learning and Taylor's principles of scientific management led to the development of basal materials. Once created, however, basals were the driving force behind the spread of Thorndike's laws and scientific management in classrooms across America. The directive language of the early manuals and the array of materials deemed necessary to conduct reading instruction scientifically increased with succeeding editions of the materials.

Consider the language and design of the most popular basal between 1930 and 1960. In 1951, *The New Basic Readers* (Scott Foresman) authors William Gray, A. Sterl Artley, and May Hill Arbuthnot supervised construction of the primer *The New Fun with Dick and Jane*. This teachers' manual began with a simple but separate six-page advertisement for the series, followed by a thirty-page briefing on the theoretical foundation for the series and each lesson. Professors Gray and Artley wrote short essays concerning the reading process, informal testing through observation, and promoting skills and comprehension. Professor Arbuthnot contributed essays on reading enjoyment and poetry. In a separate section, the editors listed the materials necessary to use the basal "according to its designed sequence within and among lessons." That list had grown considerably since the early editions: teachers' manuals, anthologies for each grade, think-and-do workbooks, basic reading tests when students completed reading the anthology, flash cards, pocket charts, poetry books and recordings, and filmstrips. Directions for the coordinated use of each of these materials were printed in each lesson, telling teachers when and how to use each page, card, cut, or strip. The twenty-five stories and ten poems were divided into five units, with an explicit lesson plan for each new story. Before each unit, the editors offered suggestions on how teachers might alter the organization of their classroom to accommodate the new themes and topics to be introduced. Although the introductory sections were written in inviting and collegial tones, lesson directives were written in the imperative.

> Teacher: "Today is the day for our new book. This is a long book with many good stories about some friends of ours. It tells how all the members of a family have fun together."
> HOLD A COPY OF THE PRIMER SO THAT ALL CAN SEE THE COVER AND CONTINUE.
> "What old friends are we going to meet again in our new book. Yes, Dick and Jane are here again."

In 1974, the level F teachers' manual for *The Young America Basic Reading Program* (Lyons and Carnahan) followed the same basic format as the 1951 Scott Foresman primary teachers' manuals, demonstrating that intermediate-grade teachers were offered the same explicit direction. The twenty-eight pages of introduction blended theory and advertisement. Authors Leo Fay and Paul Anderson wrote page-long essays on early adolescents, language study, critical thinking, and the like, embedding explanations of how the *Young America* basal provided the best technology for the task of developing fifth-grade students' reading abilities in each essay. In addition to the typical assortment of supplemental materials available in the 1950s, Lyons and Carnahan provided skill tests for each unit, affording much closer monitoring of student progress. Story summaries, lists of vocabulary and comprehension questions, and scripts for skill lessons were provided to reduce teachers' preparation time. Innovation within the scripts for each lesson supplied the explicit expected student responses as well as the teachers' lines.

The teachers' manual for the 1983 edition of the Houghton Mifflin Reading Series began with a thirty-six-page advertisement explaining the basic components, the scope and sequence of skills, the authors, and the program's philosophy (in one paragraph). "When it comes to offering teachers guidance, Houghton Mifflin proves that giving you more can help you work less!" More was what teachers received from the publisher. Besides the scope and sequences of skills listed in three different forms, the materials included instructional and recreational books, large flip charts listing examples for each lesson so that teachers would not need to write them on the board, two workbooks, three forms of worksheets, bonus worksheets, two forms of lesson tests, placement tests, unit tests, book tests, and year-end tests, floppy disks for scoring all the tests, record-keeping systems, monographs on theory supporting the program format, and letters and activities to send home to parents. Each component was keyed directly into each lesson, making it essential to the delivery of the program and ensuring the standardization of each part of teachers' instruction. In order to make use of the materials easier for teachers,

> regular type is used for statements and questions that you direct to students. Ellipses (. . .) following the questions and directive statements indicate that you should give students time to think and time to follow your direction before you continue. Boldface type indicates material addressed solely to you. Boldface italic type with parentheses indicates expected student responses.

Since Houghton Mifflin conducted extensive market research, published revisions every five to seven years, and was among the six top-selling basal series during the 1980s, it seems reasonable to conclude that this level of specificity was what the market demanded. Although educational publishers were quick to point out that their consumers dictated the shape, tone, and content of their products, publishing companies created their market as much as their market created them. Publishing is a business, and businesses require profits. Because their educational products were to be based on the same science, cosmetics distinguished one from another. Under such conditions, style counts for as much as substance, and style must be marketed aggressively if one competitor is to prevail over another. The pressures of profits, then, forced the proliferation of supplemental materials (series of workbooks, reproducibles, and various forms of assessment, and the trips, free materials and services, and parties to sway customers). With each new device, the necessity of the materials seemed all that more certain. With aggressive marketing, the potential conflicts of interest seemed less important. Moreover, the reading experts the publishers employed guaranteed the validity of business efforts.

The State

The United States Constitution does not mention education, thereby making it a state's responsibility under the Tenth Amendment. The federal government has, however, been interested in schooling in general and reading instruction in particular since the country's beginnings. In 1793, Thomas Jefferson expressed this interest in his call for universal public schooling: "If a nation expects to be ignorant and free in a state of civilization, it expects what never was and will never be."[53] Jefferson proposed a curriculum of reading, writing, and history for all, with free schooling after primary grades for only those with academic promise. From this rhetorical beginning, federal attempts—first to influence research and later to intervene directly in schooling—grew until they can now be portrayed as "the overriding issue in the support and control of elementary and secondary education."[54] State involvement in schooling began in earnest with the public school movement during the decades before the American Civil War. Early policies regulated the parameters of access and quality of schooling in local areas. Later issues of school funding and curricular control and accountability occupied state legislatures and departments of education.

Opportunity and control were the competing factors in governmental involvement in public schooling. As Jefferson stated, democracy is predicated on an informed population who are willing and able to reflect on the civic events of the day and make judgments about the present and the future. If ignorant, then the citizens cannot be actively involved in governing themselves. Both state and federal officials recognized that schooling in general, and reading in particular, were vital to the political and economic survival of the United States. Without an educated populace, economic prosperity was impossible. Yet state government oversight raised questions: What type of educated citizen should the government sponsor? Who should determine what is taught and how it is taught in government-sponsored schools? Who should have the opportunity to study? For how long and to what end? Who should decide and how should they decide when students are sufficiently educated? And who should decide who is qualified to teach? Governments, be they federal, state, or local, have not historically addressed these questions well for all citizens. Consider the deplorable treatment of indigenous peoples in government-sponsored schools, the exclusion and then limits set on schooling for women, and American apartheid schools until quite recently.[55]

During the first fifty years of the twentieth century, state and federal governments let local schools make most of the decisions about who would be educated and how. After World War II, centralization of the control of schools began to follow the general pattern of politics. First, independent, often rural, schools began to consolidate into larger school districts to achieve economy of scale and to increase academic quality. Second, in the wake of the Sputnik launching and attacks on progressive education, federal and state education departments increased pressure on schools to provide students with more rigorous academic curricula from kindergarten through high school. The war on poverty and desegregation of the 1960s brought new state and federal regulations to local school districts and spawned the minimum-competency movement of the 1970s. Third, ironically in the name of small government, the Reagan administration's *A Nation at Risk* report in 1983 began the movement toward a national education system in the United States.[56] At each stage, more centralization of organization and curricular control meant an increased emphasis on the scientific management of classroom reading instruction.

State Government

State governments have jurisdiction over schools, and therefore, fifty histories of the effects of state policies on reading instruction await anyone interested in discussing the power of the state in daily reading instruction. Added to this complexity of numbers is the fact that state policies are negotiated at the district level, leaving a gap between the rhetoric of state policy and classroom reality. Some of the state policy outcomes are beautifully idiosyncratic—think about the wonderful classroom libraries that emerged from the contradiction between California's reluctance to fund school libraries and its emphasis (supported by funding) on students reading more books during the 1980s and early 1990s. Other state policies limit the possibilities of teachers and students, not only in one state but in all other forty-nine. The most compelling example of this fact is state textbook adoption policies in twenty-two states across the South and West. Those closed markets, in which state officials pick the reading textbooks to be used in elementary classrooms, command the content and style of basal materials for the entire country.

Controversy over textbook adoption began before the turn of the nineteenth century when it became apparent to local school districts that the merger of small textbook publishers into a national brand, the American Book Company, meant a decrease in variety of textbook content and higher prices for districts and students' families. At that time, educators questioned the expense of textbooks, their quality, and publishers' aggressive marketing practices. States stepped into the selection process in order to compensate for ill-prepared teachers. "The poorer the teacher, the better the textbook needs to be."[57] By 1931, the NSSE yearbook took up the topic of American textbooks, suggesting that reforms were needed in order to stop corruptions including kickbacks and direct payments for selection and to ensure that local districts had the right to select the best textbooks to meet their needs.[58] In the yearbook chapters on courts and textbook selection, however, W. L. Coffey, dean of the College of Detroit, was clear about who was in charge:

> The maintenance of public schools is matter of state, rather of local concern. School districts exist because the state finds this a convenient way to carry out its educational program. It may require these districts to do any act which it might perform directly. It may place restrictions upon them as it seems essential. It has full authority, unless its constitution provides otherwise, to prescribe the subject matter that may or shall be taught in its schools.[59]

In order to increase their chances for sales and profits, publishers tailored their textbooks to meet the curricular standards from states with centralized selection procedures. By the late 1970s and early 1980s, that meant that educational officials in California, Texas, and Florida exerted considerable influence on what was taught during reading instruction in classrooms all over the country. Being selected in one or all of those states meant considerable profits for publishers because the state bought textbooks for every student in the state. In fact, these three states accounted for 40 percent of the entire market. In order to increase their chances of being selected, publishers typically included well-known educators from these states among the authors, and they modified the content to suit the tastes of the respective selection committees and interest groups. Virtually all publishers designed their reading materials to compete successfully in these markets. State officials are sensitive to public concerns about textbooks, making them susceptible to interest groups concerns. That is why there were so many stories and passages about agriculture, so many Hispanic surnames, and so little fantasy incorporated in the texts. In these states, state adoption was organized for the public to air its complaints about textbooks.

Consider textbook adoption in Texas.[60] During the 1970s and 1980s, the Texas system was organized for three levels. At the first level, a state textbook committee composed of fifteen appointed educators was charged with the review of all textbooks submitted for all subjects and all levels. This committee enlisted the help of a permanent staff of advisers in order to contend with the large number of textbook series. The committee and its staff spent each summer meeting with publishers and reviewing textbooks. Each September, formal hearings were held in the state capital, at which groups of citizens raised concerns about topics, illustrations, or approaches in textbooks and publishers defended their books. Following the hearings, the committee recommended a maximum of five books, which were forwarded to the Texas State Education Agency. Beyond this level, no new textbook brands could be considered.

At the second level of review, curriculum experts from the Texas Education Agency and the commissioner of education analyzed each of the recommended textbooks carefully, soliciting again public concerns about each remaining brand. During these reviews, publishers were asked to correct, add, or delete specific information from their books in order to keep them in contention for adoption. If changes were not made, then the agency or the commissioner could remove as many as three of the five texts from further consideration. Textbooks remaining on the list were formally presented to the Texas State Board of Education each November.

By state board members' admission, they could not review all the textbooks submitted. "And of course, really, we had so many things to do that I did not read each book. If there was an objection or a criticism of textbooks, yes.

Otherwise, no." [61] Again, public concerns were heard. Publishers were not allowed to present or respond at this level. After deliberations, board members voted whether to include each of the remaining textbook series on the official list from which school districts were allowed to pick free of charge.

In this way, the Texas market (and those of California and Florida) influenced reading instruction across the country. Because of expense, publishers produced one set of basals designed to appease the "big three." Those were the only basals available to school districts in all the other states, whether the states had a centralized adoption procedure or permitted school districts to negotiate directly with basal publishers. Regardless of other state policies for reading instruction, the centralized state textbook adoption policies in Texas, California, and Florida affected the classroom practices in all other states through their influence over basals at the time.

Federal Involvement

The federal government has used three methods in order to influence the organization and practices of schooling. First, since 1876, it has used the prestige of its authority to speak to the public about education. Consider the first commissioner of education Henry Barnard's address on "supplementary schools" for the infirmed and delinquent, Franklin Roosevelt's promotion of informal education through the Civilian Conservation Corps, the National Youth Administration, or the Works Progress Administration for the "youth problem" during the Great Depression, and William Bennett's attempts to instill a moral tone in the elementary school curriculum during the 1980s. [62] Second, before the 1980s, federal authorities sought legislation to ensure equity. And third, since the 1960s, agencies within the federal government have solicited and funded basic research on reading and applied research on reading instruction. All three methods have been effective, and often, federal authorities have combined methods for increased impact.

In the third *Handbook of Reading Research,* Anne McGill-Franzen argued that Title I and Head Start from the Elementary and Secondary School Education Act of 1965 and PL94-142 of 1976 (which entitled disabled children to free and appropriate education) had the greatest impact on reading education in American schools. [63] Title I marked the federal government's first attempt to influence local practice directly by making federal funds available for compensatory education programs in order to supplement regular reading and math instruction for poor children. Head Start programs were to prepare poor children for their public school experience. With these two forms of added attention in place, the government assumed that all students would have an equal opportunity to learn to read at school.

Even before its inception, the idea of the ESEA was at the center of the dispute between state and federal control of education.[64] In order to get the bill past southern legislators, the proponents compromised, directing funds toward the education of the poor rather than toward improvement of schooling for African Americans, as originally proposed. Title I of the original ESEA was also open to political interpretation. Senator Robert Kennedy saw this portion of the act as schools finally giving service to powerless groups in local communities who had often been ignored previously. He insisted, therefore, that the ESEA carry a reporting requirement that would make school administrators responsive to the parents of poor children in their area. The officials in the Program Evaluation Section of the Department of Health, Education, and Welfare, who were ultimately responsible for overseeing the implementation of the law, interpreted Title I as a renewed experiment in scientific management that would yield the most efficient approach to educating the poor. They ensured that the goals would be stated, measured, and evaluated in cost-benefit terms. They selected standardized reading tests as the primary measure of individual and programmatic success.

The Head Start program took a similar turn for poor preschool children. Part of the War on Poverty, Head Start was originally conceived as a summer program to prepare African American children socially, emotionally, and academically for public schooling. Early rhetoric suggested that this quick, intensive intervention would raise students' intelligence. The same Program Evaluation Section of the Department of HEW, however, conducted a multiple model experiment that would yield the one best way to organize preschool. Again a business model for evaluation was imposed, and standardized test scores quickly reduced the possible variety among programs to academic training for three- and four-year-olds. At the time, the authors of DISTAR, an exemplar program of scientific management of reading instruction, claimed its scripted lessons and behavioral management scheme to be the only model to bring real and lasting testing results.[65]

In 1976, Congress passed into law PL94-142, which entitled disabled children to a free and appropriate public education. New in-school programs were established to allow physically and mentally disabled students to attend their local schools along with their neighbors and to provide an individual curricular plan to enable each student to achieve measured progress. Moreover, the program allowed teachers to refer students to these programs who were already enrolled in public schools but were struggling academically because of an "organic" disability that impaired their abilities to learn to read. During the first ten years of the law, teachers referred a tenth of the student population to these programs, primarily because these students were not learning to read quickly enough to meet established norms. Because of the labor-intensive nature of this special education, in time, the budget for the education of these 10 percent began to rival the school expenditures for the other 90 percent. In the mid-1980s, the federal government commissioned the National Institute for Child Health and Human Developement (NICHD) to determine the cause of these reading disabilities in order to control the costs and return students to regular classroom programs. This proved to be a Trojan horse for reading programs in regular classrooms because the NICHD studies became the basis of reestablishment of the scientific management of reading instruction during the 1990s and into the twenty-first century.

The funding of research was the third method of federal influence on reading instruction in American classrooms. Following the launching of Sputnik in 1957, Congress passed the National Defense Education Act, which provided substantial funding to improve science and engineering education and acknowledged that American schooling in general needed reform, if the United States was to win the cold war. At that time, the National Conference on Research in English established a special committee on reading in order to reform reading instruction. That committee decided upon a two-pronged approach.[66] Jeanne Chall would conduct a reinterpretation of existing research on reading instruction (funded by the Carnegie Foundation), and other committee members would begin a large-scale cooperative experiment with clearly defined goals that could provide solid evidence on which method of teaching reading brought the best results (funded by the Cooperative Research Branch of the Office of Education). Of the seventy-six applications to participate in the study, twenty-seven projects were selected to compare a variety of experimental curricula against existing basal reading series. When the study ended, the coordinators of the study concluded that "reading programs are not equally effective in all situations" because a successful treatment in one setting achieved poor results in another.[67] The studies demonstrated that the results from most innovative combinations of phonics and basal methods were superior to those of the basal alone. No combination, however, was effective for all types of students. In short, these researchers concluded that there was no one best way to teach young children to read.

Before the results of the First Grade Studies were even published, President Johnson proposed Project Follow Through in order to track the progress of Head Start graduates through the early grades. Shortly after his announcement of the project in his State of the Union message in 1967, however, Johnson reduced the appropriation for this project from $120 million to $15 million, in order to apply more funding to the management of the Vietnam War. The Office of Economic Opportunity interpreted that this reduction required a comparable reduction in the scope of the project from a complete extension of Head Start with its multiple concerns for social, health, cultural, and academic development to a planned variation experiment based solely on academic achievement in which winners and losers could be identified among the competing models. Accordingly, standardized reading and math tests were used to determine which programs were worthy of continuation. The OEO interpretation was controversial at the time because it distorted the image and work of Head Start and promoted the scientific management of early reading instruction.

> It was never made clear to all concerned that these programs were planned variation experiments whose primary purpose was to try out and evaluate different approaches to early education. . . . The shift in objectives was clear enough at the policy making level (but it was not) made clear to many of the lower-level federal, state and local officials within whose ambit Follow Through was designed to operate.[68]

Confusion over the definition of success in the Project Follow Through evaluations resulted in mixed assessments of particular models that had appeared initially successful in the Head Start program, leading Alice Rivlin to title her book *Should We Give Up or Try Harder?* This lack of clear winners prompted government agencies to fund research on both the basic psychological processes of reading and the elements that made teachers or schools effective in raising students' standardized reading test scores. In 1976, the federal government attempted to combine these projects under the direction of the Center for the Study of Reading at the University of Illinois. The original charges to the center were to investigate the processes of comprehension, translate them into classroom instruction, and review the place of phonics instruction, including which commercial programs worked best. Through two five-year cycles of funding, the center set the agenda for reading researchers. In 1983, the National Institute of Education of the U.S. Department of Education established the Commission on Reading, selecting nine reading experts to develop a state-of-the-art report on reading (five psychologists, an authority on teacher and school effectiveness research, two professors, and a first-grade teacher). The president of the National Academy of Education outlined the commission's agenda "to engage in work that can secure greater reliability in instruction and render educational outcomes more predictably beneficial."[69]

Chapter Four

Challenges to the Scientific Management of Reading Instruction

Not every American accepted business principles as the measure of progress. In 1887, Edward Bellamy penned *Looking Backwards—2000 to 1887* as a critique of the social conditions of his time.[1] In the year 2000, his protagonist, Julian West, awoke from a century-long trance to find a society that had eliminated involuntary poverty, achieved social equality, and ensured plenty for all. Everyone shared responsibility and benefited equally in this new society, which cared for its citizens because they were people, not because of their station or function in society. A wealthy businessman of his time, Julian West was startled by the possibility of such a different future and spent much of the book investigating how it had come to pass. His host, Dr. Leete, reported that the changes were simply the logical outcome of the operation of human nature under rational conditions. During the twentieth century, Leete explained, people drew the logical conclusion that, if they cooperated with each other, then industrialized society could produce sufficient goods and services to benefit everyone. Such solidarity, he argued, redirected rationality from its traditional production of wealth for a few to the construction of a new world free from want.

Although not without faults, Bellamy's vision of the future made his contemporary 1890s appear greedy, wasteful, and uncaring in comparison. Captains of industry and government officials seemed corrupt and selfish— unable or unwilling to see the egalitarian possibilities of industrialization for the benefit of society. Bellamy's book promised that a better world could be made through the appropriate application of reason, hope, and solidarity. The only barriers to this new future, he maintained, were a lack of imagination, willpower, and clear thinking. To build this new world, citizens would choose to replace the hypercompetition of social Darwinism with Lester Frank Ward's notion that humans distinguished themselves from other species by their capacity to act rationally on their own behalf.[2] Ward argued that the ravages of monopolistic capitalism during the late nineteenth century were not a natural state of affairs, as business leaders pretended. Rather, they were human constructions originated and maintained by the rich for their well-being. In *Looking Backwards*, Bellamy challenged citizens to reinvent democracy in order to distribute wealth and power more equitably.

Both Bellamy and Ward believed that schooling within a democracy should distribute useful social and academic knowledge equally among all citizens, "preventing the encroachment of the ignorant upon the intelligent and of equally great value preventing the encroachment of the intelligent upon the ignorant."[3] In Bellamy's cooperative society, compulsory free public schooling began for children at age three in infant school, and it ended at twenty-one with a university diploma for each citizen. These schools were designed to allow children time to discover their own goodness and generosity, and then over time, to recognize that all others shared these traits. Instead of requiring students to specialize as they proceeded through the grades, Bellamy's schools of the future prepared all citizens to assume and rotate among all the various roles in their community. As Joseph Meyer Rice's survey of American schools in the 1890s demonstrated, however, few schools at that time were ready to act on Bellamy's plan.

> In some cities, the schools have advanced so little that they may be regarded as representing a stage of civilization before the age of steam and electricity. In these poor schools, the work is all formal, the pupils learning mechanically to read, write and cipher without acquiring any new ideas. The real causes for the existence of the mechanical schools at the present stage of civilization are no other than corruption and selfishness on the part of school officials, and unjustifiable ignorance, as well as criminal negligence, on the parts of parents."[4]

At the time that *Looking Backwards* was published, only a few educators recognized that schools were struggling to cope with rapid urbanization, industrialization, and immigration. Even among those few, there was little agreement upon the appropriate direction of school reform. As I explained in the first three chapters, most adopted the principles of business and harnessed science to translate those principles for schools. Only a small minority questioned their appeal to business practices and sought alternatives to the scientific management of schools. These educators hoped and worked for the new worlds imagined in Bellamy's novel and Ward's sociology. At times during the twentieth century, the rhetoric, if not the substance, of this small group took hold in elementary schools across America. Their efforts demonstrated

Bellamy's and Ward's point to educators that they had choices concerning the organization and practices of schooling. By tracing the theoretical and practical threads that connect the utopian dreams of this minority with our present conditions, we can develop a better understanding of the choices we have made and the ones that have been made for us, leading to the increasingly invasive roles of science, business, and the state in classroom reading instruction.

Parker and Dewey

Francis Wayland Parker and John Dewey are the most celebrated architects of the New Education who achieved schools similar to the ones Bellamy envisioned. Both rejected the old mechanical education that Rice described and believed that the future of schools depended upon teachers' intellectual development and their hope for a more egalitarian future. Parker and Dewey argued that teachers would face the challenges of redirecting students' and citizens' reason from competition to cooperation within communities all over America. In each community, teachers would face unique challenges while helping children adapt to the rapid changes of modern life. This variation required thoughtful teachers who were able to adapt curricula to their students' needs. Dewey even went so far as to lay the responsibility for a new society at the schools' doorstep. "Democracy must be born anew in each generation, and education is the midwife."[5] Parker's and Dewey's trust in teachers' intellects and values was a drastic departure from the principles of scientific management, which sought the application of technology to supplant human decisionmaking.

Parker offered four tenets of good education to change traditional schooling. First, children had the right to be themselves—to be happy in their self-initiated, spontaneous activities that made sense for their stage of development. His intentions were grand. "The end of all education should be to promote man's happiness, not only during his present transitory existence, but throughout eternity which is to follow."[6] Parker believed in the innate and inherent goodness of all children, and he rejected the argument that original sin required that children be disciplined toward good behavior through stern control. Following Rousseau's educational philosophy, Parker advocated that students be protected from competition until they were able to understand themselves and others.

Second, Parker maintained that people learned continuously without formal instruction. Instead of requiring rigid schedules and formal rules, he said, people learned effortlessly in order to make sense of and to change their environments. Accordingly, Parker suggested that schools should accommodate this natural learning, encouraging students to address the important issues in their daily lives during school hours. This curricular change would elevate students' interests to the status of serious subjects worthy of disciplined study. Parker argued that even struggling students would quickly master the elementary school curricula once they were encouraged to use its concepts to address their own questions and problems.

Third, in order to make these changes, Parker believed that teachers must experiment continuously in order to find the delicate balance among teacher intervention, student initiative, and environmental impact on students' learning. Parker recognized that instructional experimentation was necessary in order to ensure that both the "bright" and the "dull" students developed socially useful knowledge and dispositions. Instead of imposing a single technology upon both teachers and students, Parker advocated that teachers must develop their abilities to reason in action in order to find unique solutions to challenges posed by unique students in each classroom. He understood that instead of mastering a prescribed set of instructional formulas, educated teachers must rely on their informed rational powers throughout the school day. Contrary to the popular beliefs of his time, Parker thought that schooling could not be run like a factory because a good education relied too heavily on the individual interests of students and the individual talents of teachers.

Parker's fourth tenet was that teachers should acknowledge that schooling was a social force. In addition to a standing army, religion, and philanthropy as important conservative social powers, Parker argued that the mechanical schooling of his time prepared citizens to maintain the social, political, and economic status quo. In particular, he bristled at the notion that traditional schooling facilitated social mobility among classes. He did not mince his words. "The problem was how to give the people education and keep them from exercising the divine gift of choice, to make them believe that they were educated and at the same time to prevent free action of the mind. The problem was solved by quantity teaching."[7] Parker believed that schools and teachers should work for democratic social justice.

Under Parker's leadership in the Quincy schools in Massachusetts, teachers demonstrated their brand of democratic teaching based on these four tenets. Lelia Patridge captured these lessons in her book *The 'Quincy Method' Illustrated,* published in 1885. For example, Patridge recorded first-grade lessons on the dignity of work in which the teachers and students studied the Quincy stone quarries. Overlooking the owners' interests, the teacher probed the students' understanding of stonecutters' lives, using the tools of the trade as objects to name, read, spell, and understand. The lessons included discussion and examination of the stone, interviews with workers and family members about the work, wages, and mothers' contribution to family life, and drawings of the process of stone masonry. During each lesson, objects and information became sources for vocabulary and phonics lessons in order to help first graders crack the alphabetic code while they learned about the production of culture in their town.

In an intermediate-grade classroom, Patridge observed lessons that invited students to reconsider the Pilgrims' treatment of Native Americans in their area. To give some perspective of the politics of the lesson, this classroom exchange took place just after the Battle of Little Big Horn and just before the Battle of Wounded Knee.

> *When the white men landed in the Indian country, how did the Indians treat them?*
>
> "Kindly, they were good to them," is the unanimous opinion.
>
> *The children of the Pilgrims live here now, where are the children of the Indians?*
>
> "They've gone West! They've moved away," are the vigorous answers. But the omnipresent slow boy, who sometimes says the right thing at the right time, takes his turn now and remarks in the most moderate and matter of fact fashion—"Those that they did not kill, the white men drove away."
>
> "But this was a beautiful country and the white men wanted to come here to live," reasons a small sophist eagerly.
>
> *So because they did, and because they knew more, and because there were more of them, and because they had guns, it was right for them to do it?*[8]

The lesson continued with teacher and students agreeing that all students should write a paragraph explaining their understanding of the issue in preparation for further study.

The essence of Parker's approach to teaching reading is demonstrated in these two lessons. "The process of learning to read, then must consist of learning to use the written and printed work precisely as he used the spoken words through the association of words with ideas." Because literacy lessons were to be based on speaking and extensive world knowledge, reading and writing lessons were embedded in students' study of the social, physical, and natural worlds surrounding their classrooms. Through guided observation, drawing, and discussion, students developed an extensive knowledge of the world that served as the incentive for and the object of further work with written language. The association of words with ideas and the recognition that written language could serve an important function in their lives enabled students to acquire both reading and writing.[9]

When John Dewey arrived at the University of Chicago in 1896 to assume duties as head of the Department of Philosophy, Psychology, and Pedagogy, he enrolled his son at the Cook County Normal Elementary School under Francis Parker's direction. Although reported to be happy with his son's schooling there, Dewey transferred him to his own Laboratory School when it opened two years later. Dewey believed that philosophy was a social force to be tested in the real world, and his Laboratory School was his attempt to test his educational philosophy. In turn, Dewey considered schools to be the institutions through which appropriate social knowledge, memory, thought, and habit could be developed in order to reach a democratic ideal. Schools were a place to test his thoughts on democracy. Much like Bellamy and Ward, Dewey defined democracy as a way of life in which self-realization of the individual in a community involved necessarily the equal opportunity for self-realization of every other person. At its core, his conception of democracy questioned the contemporary business practices and their consequences on all social classes. "If democracy is to achieve the higher and more complete unity for every single human being, it can fill that destiny only by substituting economic democracy for the existing economic aristocracy."[10]

This ideal was not meant to be a utopian dream. Rather, Dewey intended for it to be realized through the use of human reason acting on the behalf of all citizens. According to Dewey, any ideal was always preceded by an actuality; that was, the ideal was to be fashioned out of experiences at some more basic, simplified level. Dewey's Laboratory School was designed to be that actuality for schools in general and democratic education in particular. His vision was utopian:

> It remains but to organize all the factors to appreciate them in their fullness of meaning, and to put the ideas and ideals involved into complete, uncompromising possession of our school system. To do this means to make each one of our schools an embryonic community, active with types of occupations that reflect the life of the larger society, and permeated throughout with the spirit of art, history, and science. When school introduces and trains each child of society into membership within such a little community saturating him with the spirit of service, and providing him with the instruments of effective self-direction, we shall have the deepest and best guarantee of a larger society which is worthy, lovely, and harmonious.[11]

Dewey's thoughts on the teaching of reading were complicated. Because Dewey believed mental development to be a social process embedded in the events of everyday activities, he expected a child's recognition of the functional values of reading and writing to be gradual and to precede the actual development of the habits of reading and writing. Although classroom activities always began with children's interests, the objectives of each activity were to connect those interests with matters of the world outside of home and school and to consider the principles of language, science, history, and mathematics that were embedded in the activities and their extensions. The teachers' role was to help children to develop plans of action for their projects, to oversee students' development, and to recognize signs when children were ready to take the next step intellectually and socially. These principles placed considerable demands on teachers, and they precluded any standardization of instructional practices across classrooms. Rather, Dewey's idea of schooling relied heavily upon teachers who had a clear conception of the kind of individual the school was trying to educate as well as clear understandings of learning and curriculum content. To develop their abilities to meet these demands, Laboratory School teachers met weekly (1) to discuss Dewey's, Parker's, and others' writings on education, (2) to apply those principles in analyses of daily lessons, and (3) to receive counsel from peers who were designated as experts on particular curricular topics.

For reading, Dewey worried most about teachers pushing students toward reading before they were truly interested. Teachers and even parents feared violating the time-honored road of the alphabet and asked students to draw letters and recollect words before the children understood fully literacy's role in their lives. "This is often taken by the inexperienced teacher as an indication that he has arrived at the stage of growth where the use of this tool arises out of a genuine need. An observant teacher, however, will recognize this as premature, if in other situations the child gives evidence of immaturity."[12] A mature interest was evident when students recognized reading was a means to a functional or informational end. And they were to make this recognition by participating in school activities in which teachers and older students demonstrated reading and writing at ever increasing levels of sophistication. The modeling of the function and explicit talk about forms of reading and writing within the projects at hand afforded young students the opportunity to recognize the value of learning to read and write as tools. "The desire to read for themselves was often born in children out of the idea that they might find better ways of doing and thus get more satisfactory results. With this interest as an urge, the child himself often freely set his attention to learning to read. A rational need thus became the stimulus to the gaining of skill in the use of a tool."

Dewey and Parker negotiated the traditional dualism between the student and the curriculum by recognizing that the curriculum was important to students as a tool to make sense of their lives and communities and that the students were important to the curriculum because they brought it life and gave it new meanings. Dewey's and Parker's efforts to construct a new education featured both students and curriculum together, and not either one or the other.

At first, both feared that teachers could not easily overcome the traditional focus on curriculum and would neglect the consequences of their educational practices on students' organic understanding of the utility of school knowledge. For example, they argued that teaching skills like reading and writing out of context in assembly-line fashion meant that teachers were overlooking the impact of the skills on students' habits and dispositions. Parker and Dewey worried that when teachers ignored the ways in which their classroom practices influenced students' self-esteem, initiative, and openness toward learning, they diminished students' chances at a good life. For both, the good life grew from democratic living in which the work and the benefits were shared by all equally, and schools were the best chance to help citizens develop the appropriate dispositions to engage in reflexive democracies.

Child-Centered and Community-Centered Literacies

Parker died at the turn of the century and Dewey turned away from issues of schooling after the Great War. They left a delicate balance for teachers to achieve between individual and social needs. The individual could not realize herself outside social commitments, and at the same time, society could not achieve democracy unless individuals were free to develop themselves continuously. Although contemporary individual and social needs were not then in harmony, Parker and Dewey believed that they could and should be harmonious. Teachers were expected to manage this dialectical relationship by offering children opportunities to make sense of the fragmented realities of materialistic capitalism and develop appropriate thoughts, habits, values, and behaviors to bring about a more worthy society. Even devoted followers of the New Education found this balance difficult to maintain, and most teachers tipped the scales toward the child and away from curriculum.

For example, Marietta Johnson established the Organic School in Fairhope, Alabama, in 1907, following Parker's first three tenets of New Education—self-expression, natural learning, and teacher experimentation. Young children pursued an unspecified curriculum based on physical exercise, nature study, music, handwork, field geography, storytelling, sense culture, fundamental conceptions of numbers, drama, and games. They followed their interests without assigned lessons, examination, grading, or failures. "There is no fixed curriculum, but the teachers keep a simple record of work done as a guide to the next teacher."[13] This reliance on experience was expected to develop students as critical thinkers with "the ability to wait for data, to hold the mind open and ready, to receive new facts, to delay decisions and opinions." Learning to read too early would lead children into trusting books, curtailing their powers to recognize the more convincing truths of experience. When Dewey's daughter, Evelyn, visited the Organic School in 1915, she wrote:

> The pupils are not allowed to use books until the eighth or ninth year, and by this time they have realized so keenly their need, they beg for help in learning. The long, tiresome drill necessary for six-year-old children is eliminated. Each child is anxious to read some particular book, so there is little or no need to trap his attention or to insist on endless repetition. . . . Mrs. Johnson is convinced that a child who does not learn to read and write in her school until he is ten years old, is as well read at fourteen and writes and spells as well as a child fourteen in a school where the usual curriculum is followed.[14]

Teachers who placed the child at the center of schooling developed goals and methods to help individuals overcome the stifling effects of traditional society. Consistent with the Expressionist movement in the arts and with Freud's newly popular theories of psychology, many child-centered teachers organized school environments and practices that would enable each individual to realize his uniquely creative self. To reach this goal, students had to be freed from compartmentalized curriculum, recitation, and seatwork. These teachers trusted students to pursue their interests without coersion in order to express, develop, and clarify their characters and talents. The growth of each individual was considered the best guarantee of a larger society truly devoted to human worth and excellence. According to these proponents of the New Education, answers to contemporary social problems were not to be found in immediate social action; rather, true change would come only when future generations possessed cooperative, engaged dispositions that they developed and refined while at school.

In *The Foundations of Method*, William Kilpatrick articulated the details of the project method, his approach to free teachers and students from traditional school routines.[15] In this method, students would propose, plan, execute, and judge a series of related individual and group projects of immediate interest to them in order to explore their daily lives. The project curriculum would begin during the primary grades, in which young students would develop simple investigations and receive constructive feedback concerning how to make their inquiries more sophisticated. Over the course of a school career, students would develop the necessary balance between personal interests and social needs to become productive citizens within a democracy. Kilpatrick pushed beyond a reiteration of New Education's assumption that reading and writing did not constitute an appropriate curriculum for elementary school in order to describe how teachers could develop students' dispositions toward reading and writing. By engaging students in projects in which various types of texts were necessary for their completion, teachers would instill the habits of identifying appropriate sources of information and obtaining desired information from such texts. In this way, students would learn different habits of inquiry in order to find the information required to complete their projects. For this reason, Kilpatrick advocated cross-aged classes in which older students would demonstrate appropriate uses of texts for the younger ones, providing a model and supportive feedback on the younger students' efforts. Kilpatrick was adamant that multiple sources should be used: "I should hope my boy would consult books where all this accumulated wealth could be found, but I should hope that he would search, and he would find and he would compare, and he would think why, and in the end, he would make his own decision."

At the City and Country School in New York City, Caroline Pratt afforded her students a rich variety of firsthand experiences (trips to the park, stores, harbors, etc.) and then provided them with materials (blocks, clay, paints) through which they could imaginatively portray what they had experienced when they returned to the classroom.[16] The school's curriculum was both impressionist (students were expected to interpret, not reproduce) and expressionist (they were expected to construct their interpretations in many media). Students composed the literature and art of the classroom from their "appreciation for reality," as this dictated poem by a six-year-old attests.

The Great Shovel

The great shovel takes a bit of coal and he spits it out into another boat. Then the coal wagon comes and takes his breakfast away from the boat. The great shovel takes a bite and chutes it down into the coal wagon. Then another bite and another bite until the coal wagon fills up. Then chunk a chunk chunk, away goes the bingety, bang bang truck. And then comes another truck and gets some more coal. Then when the whole boat gets empty a tugboat comes and pulls it away and it goes back to get more coal and it does that until the end of the day's over.

Margaret Naumburg tipped the scale even further toward the individual when she taught at the Children's School (later the Walden School) from 1915 through the 1930s.[17] She believed that Freud's theories warranted teachers' attention and suggested that emotions and not intellect should be the focus of schools. She criticized Dewey, Kilpatrick, and Pratt for their neglect of emotional development in their new curricula. Through her own psychoanalysis, Naumburg sought sufficient self-realization to enable her to help children free themselves from their emotional inhibitions. "For to us, all prohibitions that lead to nerve strain and repression of normal energy are contrary to the most recent findings of biology, psychology, and education. We have got to discover ways of redirecting and harnessing this vital force of childhood into constructive and creative work." The challenge for teachers was to find the activities that would enable students to identify and develop their true selves. Students' artistic and literary expressions and responses were both the means and the end of the curriculum because, as Naumburg and her allies believed, allowing individuals to act authentically was the only way to build a better society.

During the 1920s and 1930s, Hughes Mearns of the Lincoln School at Columbia University developed a poetry reading and writing program in order to help students make "outward expressions of instinctive insights that must be summoned from the vast deep of our mysterious selves."[18] Using only the students' work as examples, "all were received and made the basis of informal personal instruction" that demonstrated in a given case how the feelings of the poet did or did not become the feelings of the reader. Mearns believed that reading and writing could not be taught; rather they could be learned only through observation and imitation as students first trained their ears and eyes on the teachers' and older students' continuous uses of reading and writing. He cautioned teachers against allowing students to direct the classroom activities without guidance. "Child activity is marvelously educative, in the proper place, but it is not a substitute for teacher activity in its proper place."

Two school surveys during the 1920s and 1930s demonstrated that a significant number of teachers across the country engaged in some form of the New Education.[19] Harold Rugg and Ann Shumaker toured the East Coast and the Midwest to find what they considered a triumph of self-expression and authenticity in a society based on superficiality and commercialism. The classrooms they visited championed freedom over control, child over teacher initiative, activity, children's interests, creative expression, and personality adjustment. Contributors to the 33rd Yearbook of the National Society for the Study of Education on the Activity [Project] Movement reported from New York to Denver to Los Angeles and from Battle Creek, Michigan, to Houston, explaining local variations on the themes of self-expression, the project method, and emotional support.[20] Uniting these schools was the premise that time was teachers' ally, and not their enemy. That is, teachers could use the hours, days, and weeks of schooling to immerse students in projects that would remake their identities as problem posers and solvers, cooperative critics of their own and others' work, and engaged citizens with the ability and the right to express their interests and desires. This work would ensure that students recognized the purpose of reading and writing in their efforts to engage in their lives fully. Once students became fully aware of what literacy could do for them, their efforts to learn to read and write would be internally motivated and relatively easy.

The origins of later alternative methods of teaching reading can be found within these early iterations of the New Education. For example, Pratt's and

Mearns' working from only children's stories and narratives laid the foundation for the language experience approach. Johnson's and Naumburg's self-selection of topic and media led to individualized reading programs. Kilpatrick's efforts to disrupt the drudgery of traditional classroom routines preceded the open classrooms and free schools of the late 1960s and early 1970s. Interest in voice, choice, and self-expression provided the experiential justification for the writing process movement in the 1970s and 1980s. The re-interpretation of instructional time, cross-disciplinary inquiry, natural learning, and teacher experimentation provided glimpses of the whole language philosophy to come in the late 1980s and early 1990s. Through these connections, the definition and meaning of the New Education was negotiated and renegotiated across the twentieth century, connecting Parker and Dewey with Lucy Sprague Mitchell, Laura Zirbes, Dora V. Smith, Jennette Veatch, John Holt, Herb Kohl, Sylvia Ashton Warner, Donald Graves, Carolyn Burke, Frank Smith, and Ken and Yetta Goodman.

The early versions of the New Education also attracted criticisms that continue to the present. Some criticisms were to be expected. For example, advocates of the scientific management found the New Education at best "a legitimate supplement to a program of systematic and sequential learning," and at worst, "a waste of valuable time."[21] These authorities lamented the lack of standard objectives, instruments of measure, and controlled studies to support its value. Other criticisms might have been surprising. In 1930, Dewey published a criticism in the *New Republic* under the series title "The New Education: Ten Years After."[22] He began with the acknowledgment that the New Education was a revolt against traditionalism rather than a movement toward a set of well-defined ideals. He excused the lack of clarity of objectives and the diversity of methods as therefore understandable. However, he found disturbing the complacency among current new educators toward these matters. He argued that although education should start and end with the child, this should not mean that the child should be left without guidance to figure out the complexities of modern life. Moreover, he criticized new educators' distrust of traditional school subject matter and the fear of adult imposition, which he believed undermined their efforts to help children become able citizens. Too often, child-centered educators left students "to operate in a blind and spasmodic fashion which promotes the formation of habits of immature, under-developed, and egocentric activity." In the end, most new educators had engaged only the first three of Parker's tenets, leaving the issue of schooling as a social force entirely alone.

> Upon the whole, new education has been more successful in further-
> ing creativeness in the arts—in music, drawing, and picture making,

dramatics, and literary composition, including poetry. But it is not enough! Taken by itself, it will do something to further the private appreciation of say, the upper middle class. But it will not serve to meet even the esthetic needs and defaulting of contemporary society in its prevailing external expression. . . . That the traditional schools have almost wholly evaded consideration of the social potentialities of education is no reason why new schools should continue the evasion, even though it be sugared over with esthetic refinements. The time ought to come when no one will be judged to be an educated man or woman who does not have insight into the basic forces of industrial and urban civilization. Only schools that take the lead in bringing about this kind of education can claim to be new in any socially significant sense.

Outcomes of New Education

As frequently occurs in school reform movements, the language of new reading education changed more rapidly than the practice of reading education in schools. Moreover, small concrete changes in practice were adopted more rapidly than larger, more philosophical ones. Educational historian Larry Cuban estimates that only 10 percent of schools in America overhauled their schools according to tenets of the New Education.[23] New teaching methods crept into many teachers' repertoires. For example, many increased student participation through small-group work, project activities, and field trips, yet most reading instruction remained traditionally focused on skills as directed in teachers' guidebooks. The new methods, however, were often divorced from their originating theories, thus subverting their possibilities of reaching new educational goals. For example, projects that were initially intended to make academic subjects more understandable and relevant for students became substitutes for academic subject matter itself. Despite these limitations, advocates of the New Education competed actively with advocates of scientific management for control of school curriculum between 1910 and 1930. They captured rhetorical control of education during the late 1940s and early 1950s, until the writings of Arthur Bestor, Admiral Rickover, and Albert Lynd used the cold war to argue for tougher academic standards in schools.[24] "The schools must now concentrate on bringing the intellectual powers of each child to the highest possible level. Even the average child now needs almost as good an education as the average middle and upper class child used to get in the college preparatory schools." Rudolph Flesch directed this argument toward reading education, explaining that a lack of direct phonics instruction was why Johnny couldn't read.

Advocates of the New Education reemerged in the wake of the civil rights movement and Great Society legislation. John Holt, Nat Hentoff, and others paraphrased Dewey's arguments for the schooling of intelligent citizens.[25] Holt agreed that risk taking, scientific thinking, malleable habits, and acceptance of uncertainty were the marks of bright students, and he charged that school curriculum and practice in the 1950s and 1960s taught complacency, rule application, rote learning, and timidity among students. Contemporary schools, Holt argued, worked against democracy by being more interested in social control than in the development of active citizens. Hentoff reported that Holt's bright students attended inner-city schools but were dulled by teachers who ignored their needs, their languages, and their cultures. George Dennison called public schooling a process of subtraction in which students who were competent in their own culture learned that they were unintelligent and unworthy in mainstream culture and that learning was difficult. For these critics, the problems of public school lay in its inability to accept or to adapt to the human differences among students. Because traditional schools still sought standardization of outcome, they reinforced rather than challenged social, economic, and intellectual biases. The critics' solution was to elaborate and adapt the new education of the turn of the century in order to establish free alternative schools or to open the public school curriculum to change. You can hear Parker's and Dewey's voices in the new critics' statements.

> Open education is a way of thinking about children and learning. It is characterized by openness and trust, by spatial openness of doors and rooms; by openness of time to release and serve children, not to constrain, prescribe, and master them. The curriculum is open to significant choice by adults and children as a function of the needs and interests of each child at the moment. Open education is characterized by an openness of self. Persons are openly sensitive to and supportive of other persons—not closed off by anxiety, threat, custom, and role. Administrators are open to initiatives on the part of teachers; teachers are open to the possibilities inherent in children; children are open to the possibilities inherent in other children, in materials, and themselves. [26]

By their own admission, advocates of New Education in the 1960s and 1970s struggled with the teaching of reading. "More free schools go to pieces over the question of the teaching of hard skills—and the teaching of reading in particular—than over any other issue that I know."[27] Similar to the debate among the early advocates, free schoolers and open educators argued over whether teachers should instruct their students directly in reading and writing or whether they should wait for students to ask for help. In *The Lives of*

Children, George Dennison made the dilemma public when he published his efforts to develop a position on children learning to read. After reading Tolstoy, Rousseau, and Dewey, analyzing his students' efforts at reading and writing, and consulting with other teachers, he concluded that students learned to read and write as they learned to talk, by producing meaning and establishing themselves in the world. "The infant, in short, is not imitating, but doing. The doing is for real. It advances him in to the world. It brings its own rewards in pleasure, attention, approval, and endless practical benefits."[28] Dennison followed his conclusion with an inventory of recommendations from other free school teachers (e.g., John Holt, Orson Bean, Vera Williams, Billy Ayers): Initial Teaching Alphabet, code breaking programs (Sullivan readers, Merrill Linguistic Readers, DISTAR), Sylvia Ashton Warner's key word methods, and children's books (with warnings about their sexist and racist content). All cautioned Dennison to remember that the answers for the questions of teaching children to read and write could not be found in instructional materials or standard curricula; rather, the answer could be found only through the interaction between teachers and students.

> Many poor and minority group people are demanding better reading programs in their schools. They might be wiser to demand jobs and to get more branch libraries in their district, or better yet, neighborhood storefront libraries or traveling bookmobiles, with newspapers, periodicals, and paperbacks—the kind of reading material that we know kids like to read. What's the point of having kids learn to read, if they've learned there's no real reason to read and nothing to read.[29]

> It is from the children's writing that the teachers have been able to discover what it was that was most important for their pupils to learn at that moment in their classes. Prefabricated curriculum was irrelevant. Teachers had to look to their own knowledge of literature to present images of life which were real and coherent. They found that many of the arbitrary limits placed on children's receptivity and performance disappeared; what was supposedly appropriate at a certain grade level became a mockery of the needs of the children. New criteria and necessities became apparent. It was not grammatical structures, number of words, but human content that determined the lessons.[30]

> A deeper understanding of what is involved in reading and in learning to read is far more important for the reading teacher than any expectation of better and more efficacious instructional materials. Nevertheless, I am frequently pressed to elaborate upon what I think are the implications of psycholinguistics for reading instruction, as if

psycholinguists have a responsibility to tell teachers what to do. Many teachers have difficulty in accepting that a child might have a better implicit understanding of his intellectual needs than the producers of educational methodology or technology.[31]

Whole Language Umbrella

On a hot evening in July 1990 at the Hilton Hotel in St. Louis, Kenneth Goodman declared John Dewey to be the Honorary Past President of the Whole Language Umbrella. Although Dewey died in 1953, Goodman and the WLU sought to identify their organization's connection with the century-long struggle over the goals and means of schooling in America. For the previous fifteen years, teachers and teacher educators in attendance had engaged in projects to wrestle control of reading and writing instruction away from advocates of scientific management by recognizing the importance of social context, acknowledging the competence of the learner, and advocating an inversion of authority in the classroom. The group that met in St. Louis attempted to bring those projects together in order to explore what might evolve from a larger, more coordinated effort. They adopted the name *umbrella* to signify simultaneously the independence of the groups and the possible strength in numbers. The stances and principles of those projects and the WLU, itself, were the most dramatic and direct rejections of the scientific management of reading instruction in the twentieth century. In a special issue of the *Elementary School Journal*, P. David Pearson confided that during his twenty-five years as an educator, he had "never witnessed anything like the rapid spread of the whole language movement."[32] The challenge to tradition, however, made practice according to whole language philosophy dangerous for some.

> Whole language teaching is a grassroots movement among teachers. Deciding to take charge of your own classroom is an act of courage in an era of a shortage of jobs for teachers and a regressive back-to-basics curricular trend. It's particularly scary if you're the only teacher in your school to do so. Many teachers have formed support and study groups. They get together to cry on each other's shoulders, to engage in self-help group therapy, to share triumphs. They discuss whole language techniques, strategies, and units. They plan ways of dealing with skeptical colleagues, threatened administrators, bewildered parents. They find themselves engaged in in-service education for their colleagues, as well as themselves.[33]

Much like the advocates of the New Education in the 1920s, whole language educators sought research and practices based upon a primary unifying principle that children constructed their understandings of the world through active engagement. In order to inform their work in schools, whole language advocates found such research in a variety of academic fields beyond psychology—linguistics, psycholinguistics, sociology, anthropology, philosophy, child and curricular studies, composition, literary theory, and semiotics.[34] This research taught whole language teachers that cultural variation among students meant that no single method of teaching reading would suffice. Rather, students' understandings and attempts to practice reading would vary according to dynamic cultural identities and opportunities. Valuing this diversity within a democractic society, whole language advocates recognized that only a teacher, and not a method, would be able to create the conditions for students to engage reading and writing productively—immersing students in a literate environment, demonstrating for students how written language was used, making time for students to read and write, and responding to student approximations. This change in basic understanding of learning to read and write meant a change in metaphor for teaching them

> At my level, junior high, there seems to be two ways a reading course can go: either a skills/drills/basal textbook approach—essentially an extension of elementary programs—or a watered-down lit. crit. approach of the type found in many high school classes. Until two years ago, my approach to reading was the latter: pass out the anthologies, introduce the vocabulary, lecture about genre or theme, assign the story or parts of the story, give a quiz on comprehension and vocabulary, conduct a whole-class post mortem, and sometimes assign an essay. A little over two years ago, I began to be aware of the contradictions between my beliefs about writing and my instruction in reading. . . . The same elements that characterize writing workshop characterize my behavior as a reader. I exercise responsibility, deciding what and why—or at the very least—how I'll read. I spend regular, frequent time reading and thinking about others' writing. I confer with other readers, talking about books naturally as an extension of my life as a reader. And much of this talk takes place at the dining room table, talk about novels, poems, articles, and editorials, and general literary gossip. That dining room table is a literate environment where we analyze, criticize, interpret, compare, link books with our own knowledge and experiences, and go inside written language. I'm dwelling on my dining room table because it's become the metaphor I use whenever I think or talk about what I want my reading course to be.[35]

E. L. Thorndike and Frederick Taylor, the two main theorists in scientific management of reading instruction, were not invited to the whole language dining room table. Whole language teachers left Thorndike uninvited because they believed he misunderstood both language and learning. Rather than adopt Thorndike's understanding of language as the sum of its parts, whole language teachers equated oral, written, and sign language as linguistic systems for creating meaning through socially shared conventions. Each system included inseparable and interdependent subsystems of symbol (phonology, graphophonics, or gesture), syntax, semantics and pragmatics, which operated according to socially negotiated rules. These rules made language predictable and allowed aesthetic representations of meaning.[36] Advocates argued that learning to read written language was similar to learning to read oral language (listening and uttering). That is, people learned to read by generating and testing hypotheses about these rules and the representations of meaning afforded by a text within a particular time and place for a specific purpose. Because the author intended to mean through the composition of the text and the reader intended to construct both the meaning of reading and the text, any attempt to reduce reading to a subsystem would subvert the roles of both writing and reading and misrepresent the purposes and process of reading and writing. Neither the process nor the text was reducible to behavioral responses or elemental symbols, as Thorndike maintained. "Whole language teachers support this process by demonstrating learning through actual participation (studying a phenomenon along with a child and offering their own ideas as co-learners) and through responding analytically but respectfully to children's current hypotheses."[37]

> Jimmy and Tricia taught me that I am not a silent partner in my classroom. I guide and direct my students by what I do and what I choose to immerse them in for reading and writing. . . . I shared what I was doing as a learner and for my purposes, not intentionally modeling my learning but sharing my authentic reading and writing, trusting that they would get what they could from it.[38]

Because whole language conceptions of learning assumed variation and spontaneity among learners and teachers within particular settings, the outcomes of teaching and learning were not completely predictable. Taylor's notions of scientific management were not welcomed at the whole language dining room table. Instructional cards could not prepare teachers to initiate and respond appropriately during classroom activities.[39] Moreover, time was not the enemy of learning to read in a whole language classroom. Rather, the diversity of experience with print and types of literacy required a flexibility with time and task in classroom programs. While both teachers and students could benefit from analytical responses to their hypotheses about teaching and learning (and the world), those analyses could not be scripted. Feedback had to be tailored to the personalities and circumstances of the immediate situation and the people in it. To improve their teaching and learning, teachers and students tested hypotheses about good teaching and learning in the company of their peers and reflected upon outcomes. Risks in learning and teaching, then, were encouraged because they stretch students' and teachers' actions beyond the typical and can lead to growth. Errors were expected, and through careful analysis and feedback, errors could be the engine that drove both teaching and learning toward more sophisticated forms. In this way, learning and teaching were never completed; they were always in the making.

These first steps of whole language challenged the traditions of reading instruction in American elementary schools.[40] For example, young children's use of oral language for a variety of purposes before coming to school and their experimentation with written language eliminated the need for traditional reading readiness training. Children's experiments with written language included their hypotheses about writing as well as reading, disrupting the traditional sequence of reading instruction before writing instruction in primary grades. Experimentation with text meant trial-and-error construction of reading and writing conventions. Teachers expected mistakes from students, rather than immediate perfection, because the errors exposed partial understanding and the thought processes behind students' learning. Because students' interests in learning more about the world drove their experimentations with oral and written language, all instruction was to honor students' efforts after understanding. This meant (1) books and other authentic texts would replace basal materials in classrooms; (2) drill and practice of isolated skills instruction would give way to students' inquiries and teachers' efforts to identify students' abilities to use text well; and (3) informal assessments of students' development would supplant standardized achievement tests administered in September and May. Moreover, this meant that students and teachers were learning in each classroom. All told, whole language views of reading instruction rendered basal reading series and standardized reading tests to be of limited value to elementary school teachers.

> There are no ditto sheets or workbooks, no basal texts, no ability groups, no readiness or "letter of the week" programs in my kindergarten. My teacher's editions are *The Foundations of Literacy* (Holdaway, 1979), *The Art of Teaching Writing* (Calkins, 1986), and *Reading, Writing, and Caring* (Cochrane et al., 1984). My consumables are paper and pencils, my reading books are trade books, and my tests are the children's work over time.[41]

The absence of Thorndike's and Taylor's theories in whole language approaches had a profound impact on authority in and out of the classroom.

Whole language challenged the traditional allocation of authority to text, teacher, and expert. Because whole language advocates believed that readers interpreted all texts, they invested the interpreter, and not the text, with authority over meaning.[42] Since texts did not have fixed meanings, the abstract absolute value could not be established for any text. Rather, the reader's purpose determined the value of any text during a particular reading. Therefore, a recognized canon of literature lost its footing within the whole language classroom as an interpretive community of readers began to stand.[43] Expert opinion on literature became "just another read" that could be useful to others when engaged in conversation about texts around the dining room table. This stance on reading and text provoked an angry outcry among religious fundamentalists because it opened religious texts to secular interpretations.[44]

According to whole language theory, students were ultimately responsible for their learning.[45] Although teachers could influence that learning, they could not determine what was learned, how it was learned or why it was learned. Scripted lessons only gave the appearance of this level of control. What was learned was always more than what was taught. How it was learned included both the expected induced behavior and the hidden values of the lesson. Why it was learned was embedded in both the immediate and the past contexts of the learner and situation. Teachers might gain greater influence by establishing caring and trusting relationships as well as through setting the conditions of learning in their classrooms. They could acknowledge the importance of students' cultural knowledge and recognize that students' dialects were wrapped up in their identities. They could make accommodations within their classrooms and activities to affirm and extend what students knew and who they were. Yet they could not make a student learn or specify the parameters of that learning. Students were responsible for, and therefore had authority over, their learning.[46] That authority shifted the teacher's responsibility to observing students closely in order to support and extend students' current approximations toward more sophisticated practices. This shift reduced the authority of commercially prepared lesson plans and standardized tests. Neither provided precise guidance to serve as aids for teachers' new responsibilities.

Yet, teachers were readers and learners too in the whole language classroom. The traditional authority they lost as teacher-experts, they regained in different forms as teacher-readers and teacher-learners.[47] As such, teachers flattened the traditional hierarchies of authority in schools and the profession. Although teachers had to continue to negotiate with other teachers, administrators, public officials, and experts, they were ultimately responsible for what transpired in the classroom. Unless they agreed to comply, they could not be controlled in their teaching. Expert advice, policy, laws, and research were all texts that whole language advocates interpreted. Even when they appeared to follow the same mandate, there were always subtle and not so subtle differences among their behaviors and, certainly, among their understandings of what they were doing. And there were sometimes wide variations in student outcomes. These interpretations produced knowledge and built theories that appeared as texts for others to interpret. In this way the traditional flow of theory toward practice was redirected so that teachers' practices and reflections on their practice created new theory and modified established theories, which in turn informed and were informed by other teachers' practices and ideas. According to whole language advocates, authority should be held as close as possible to the teaching and learning.[48]

> I've been involved in whole language projects in Cambridge and New York City, but I'm more excited about the Milwaukee project. The Cambridge and NYC projects were top-down. We had to go convince teachers that whole language was a good idea and that they needed to collaborate. Here I have teachers saying, "It's bottom up. All you have to do is listen to us and support us." And we, the administration, promise to do that.[49]

In the 1990s, whole language advocates acknowledged that many media function as language.[50] That is, media use symbols in attempts to communicate and, therefore, work like language. For example, oral language uses sound; written language uses words; sign language uses gesture. Music uses notes on a scale, and photography uses light and space. Beyond the obvious, the fashion industry uses clothes, and a traffic light uses colored lights to communicate. While these symbols—sound, words, gestures, notes, light and space, clothes, colored light—are parts of our natural and artificial worlds, their importance for language is not about what they are. Rather, what is important is how speakers, writers, the deaf, musicians, photographers, clothes designers, or traffic cops use them to mean.[51] It's what they do that counts. The symbols can be used in conjunction with specific language subsystems (syntax, semantics, and pragmatics) in that medium to construct meaning. Although the symbols do not have any clear meaning in themselves, they are vehicles for meaning when they operate within socially constructed sets of rules. Whole language teachers recognized that the process of reading remains similar across all forms of language—only the codings of the interdependent subsystems change. This expanded view of languages offered students greater flexibility and power in pursuit of their interests and challenges than the traditional primacy of written language instruction in schools.

> I acquired a different sense of what was possible when learners used various sign systems to make meaning. I started to wonder how this

experience could and should change things in my classroom. I thought a lot about how I used art in relation to literature extensions. We read books together, often wrote responses, and explored new interpretations and insights through drama, drawing, collage, music, and poetry. I valued all these extension activities.[52]

These tenets of whole language galvanized the interests of teachers around the English-speaking world during the 1970s, 1980s, and early 1990s. The New Zealand national system of education was based on compatible theories of learning and language. England's national system also worked from similar principles. Teachers in Australia and Canada elaborated and refined the British system. Teachers in these countries added their own touches to the New Education of Parker's and Dewey's time, while continuing to develop whole language through their classroom practices. Kenneth Goodman remarked, however, "what has been an evolution elsewhere has been seen as a revolution here."[53] That feeling of revolution worked for and against whole language advocates.

Dewey wrote about origins and rationales for revolution shortly after his visit to the new Soviet Union in 1922. He explained that if those in control of a country would not permit needed changes, then citizens had the right to force those changes. He referred to the American and French revolutions as justifiable precedents. "The primary accusation against the revolutionary must be directed against those who have power, but refuse to use it for ameliorations. They are the ones who accumulate the wrath that sweeps away customs and institutions in an undiscriminating way."[54] Yet Dewey also criticized many revolutionaries who failed to recognize how deeply rooted citizens' prerevolutionary habits and social knowledge are or how difficult it is to modify those behaviors and ideas. Even when officials change policies and laws dramatically, he argued, the previously socially negotiated, historically situated values of citizens remain firm. Even the leaders of revolution still carry traces of prior knowledge and values long after the revolution.

Early whole language advocates heeded Dewey's words. They began in small groups of like-minded teachers who met to share stories about their questions about teaching children to read and write. These groups began in Tucson, Arizona; Columbia, Missouri; Winnipeg, Manitoba; Durham, New Hampshire; Bloomington, Indiana; Halifax, Nova Scotia; and many other towns and cities across North America. Analogous in form to the early consciousness-raising meetings in the women's movement, these teachers' groups sought to elevate members' awareness of how children learned to read and write and to help teachers change their teaching behaviors accordingly. Judith Newman described a typical sequence of these meetings.

I had been meeting regularly with several teachers. In our study sessions we discussed current theories of reading and writing and we explored classroom application of those theories. Our primary
intention was to support one another as we tried out what we hoped
were theoretically sound curricular ideas. As we explored whole language curriculum in the classroom our understanding of theory
grew. As we learned from our students we were better able to talk
about our theoretical beliefs.

Several summers ago we decided to share our ideas with other
teachers interested in knowing more about whole language theory
and curriculum. We organized a week-long workshop, using that forum to share what we were trying in our classrooms. The following
summer we repeated the workshop.[55]

The members of these small teacher study groups reformed their ideas
and habits about their work with children who were learning to read and write.
Each concentrated upon her personal understandings and practices before the
group sought to expand its focus to what other teachers might think about and
do in their classrooms. Newman implied the careful steps that were taken. Only
after several years of study did her group become confident enough to open
its collective knowledge to public view and to invite others to join it. The spread
of influence of these groups created markets for whole language ideas, attracting publishers' interests. Heinemann, Richard C. Owen, the Wright Group, and
others began publishing texts on whole language explicitly targeted at these
teachers. New authorities arose through these texts: Nancie Atwell, Lucy
Calkins, Susan Church, Kitty Copland, Carol Gillis, Richard Myers, Karen
Smith, and many others.[56] The need for children's books to drive classroom
reading instruction significantly increased the market for children's literature
across North America. Before the Internet and chain booksellers, this market
demand was met through local bookstores, which began to stock both the professional and the children's books needed to redirect traditional classroom
thoughts and habits. The bookstores provided another piece of infrastructure
to support teachers as they attempted to change their minds and behaviors.
Perhaps the most ambitious whole language projects among these groups were
the ones that sought to change the state (or provincial) requirements for reading education in all classrooms.

Alarming new research on illiteracy in America indicates that without
a profound change in direction, most American school children will
not become life-long readers—that one of four will scarcely learn to
read at all. We launched the California Reading Initiative in May 1986
in response to this frightening problem, and the equally startling

realization that 40 percent of those Americans who can read books choose not to. The goal of the Initiative is to turn this disastrous trend around by encouraging students to develop lifelong positive attitudes towards reading and stimulating educators to change and improve their reading programs.[57]

The California Reading Initiative, the state's guidelines for teaching reading, included a list of good books and a curricular framework that "set the stage for bringing this new and integrated 'whole language' approach to the classroom."[58] Coupled with the state's rejection of all existing basal reading programs because they did not meet the new state standards for authentic reading materials or meaning-based instruction, the initiative encouraged teachers to abandon the scientific management of reading instruction. Rather, the California State Department of Education advocated student choice of their reading materials from among multicultural, multilingual children's literature included in classroom libraries. The state's decision to reject the basals left California's elementary teachers with two choices in order to achieve the goals that the state superintendent for instruction set for them: they could continue with old basal readers and teachers' manuals (but without the practice workbooks and worksheets) or they could develop reading lessons on their own. In this way, the California Reading Initiative pushed all California teachers toward whole language overnight. As one superintendent explained, the initiative did not work as smoothly as planned.

> The California Reading Initiative offered an opportunity to progressive teachers. It provided research and policy to support teachers' movement beyond basals, which had previously caused teachers' dependence on lockstep methods of teaching reading. The Initiative also provided a large list of "good books" that stimulated student interest in reading. It was well written and flexible enough to allow districts to choose the timeline for implementation, and left the degree of usage to schools. It implied that the State trusted school districts to make changes, and it encouraged teachers to take risks in designing their own curriculum. However, the Initiative failed to anticipate the resistance from parents and teachers, the "retraining" required, or the problems districts would have in implementing a new program without an assessment tool that could reflect the learning and teaching that was to go on in classrooms.[59]

During the 1980s, teachers and administrators across North America attempted to rewrite state educational policies in order to find language more conducive to whole language teaching.[60] Beyond the classroom and district levels, state department officials convened teachers to redraft state guidelines for teaching reading and writing. From Texas to Minnesota and from Massachusetts to Oregon, the official language began to change in state reading and language arts documents in order to encourage or compel teachers to reconsider their understandings of the reading and teaching processes, to use students as informants to plan their reading instruction, and to offer students more control over time and choice of their reading and writing activities during classes. Although there were differences among the paths toward such change, each state used its existing structures in an attempt to implement whole language.

Consider Pennsylvania's efforts to provide space and direction for whole language teaching in classrooms across the state. Pennsylvania had a history of teacher involvement in the development of policy and an organized dissemination plan to introduce state policy to school personnel. Although there are more than five hundred school districts in Pennsylvania, they are collected into fewer than thirty intermediate units, which help districts comply with state guidelines. In 1977, the state released a new reading and language arts curriculum that advocated responding to literature, sustained silent reading, oral and written composition, and mastering language patterns as the critical experiences of good instruction. Although the curriculum was implemented unevenly across school districts, those schools that took steps to reorganize reading instruction as suggested raised students' scores on state tests.[61]

During the mid-1980s, the Pennsylvania Department of Education commissioned Susan Lytle and Morton Botel to revise the 1977 reading curriculum in light of " a considerable body of theory and research … which pointed in some significant new directions."[62] The new curriculum was to assuage teachers' concerns about fragmented curricula and address the problems created by the rising number of students being classified as at risk of failing to learn to read and write. Reviewed by a panel of national experts and fifty classroom teachers from across the state, the newly named *Pennsylvania Framework for Reading, Writing, and Talking Across the Curriculum* is one of most clearly articulated documents on whole language principles on record. For example:

> The first critical experience focuses on the development of active motivated readers who engage in reading for a variety of authentic purposes, both in and out of school. Here reading is viewed as a complex interplay of many factors, not the simple exercise of skills. By calling reading events transactions, we emphasize the organic, ongoing nature of the reading processes to which readers bring prior knowledge, experience, beliefs and attitudes. Meanings are not simply in the text to be extracted by readers. Successful encounters with texts are constructive and interpretive: readers of all ages relate new to the known, integrate and refine concepts, make (not

simply take) meaning. Children learn to read and read to learn—both at the same time. From the beginning then, reading is about making sense of the world. Creating learning environments in school in which meaningful reading transactions occur frequently, throughout the grades and across the curriculum is the focus of this critical experience.

The framework was based on four principles: learning as meaning making, language as inherently social, the interrelationship of the language processes, and learning as human activity. The four critical experiences of the 1977 curriculum were changed and extended in the 1988 framework: reading as transacting with text, writing as composing using a wide range of genres, self-awareness of strategies for reading and writing in differing situations, investigating language in use, and learning to learn. After a detailed review of these experiences, the framework offered suggestions for the complementary planning of curriculum and evaluation of students' learning. The framework took a dim view of standardized testing—"to emerge from the constraining effects of testing, we must move to a new stance: from a narrow focus on testing to a much broader focus on evaluation." The framework concluded with a diffusion plan for implementing the framework in schools across the state based on four principles.

1. The individual school and its teachers and administrators were the unit of control for implementation.

2. Because teachers were capable and ultimately responsible for what happened, they should exercise significant control of instructional decisions.

3. Individual and group teacher research should be the means to relate theory to practices and to have practice inform theory.

4. Schools should develop leadership teams to support teachers' development of the framework in their classrooms.

In order to help schools follow those principles, the state held framework seminars, encouraged staff cross-visitations among schools, developed district-wide networks, selected intermediate unit coordinators, and published a framework newsletter (with articles on classroom and school implementations) biannually.

Although the philosophy and practices advocated in the new state reading curricula challenged the orthodoxies of the scientific management of reading instruction, the scope of statewide implementation of whole language required changes in the methods of capturing the hearts and minds of teachers in the revolution in reading instruction. In the end, many whole language advocates began to rely on the power of government, science, and business to accomplish their goals. To work on a larger scale, whole language principles were translated in official doctrines that all had to apply, rather than answers to questions that individual teachers asked about their own understandings and practices. The principles, then, became abstractions to many teachers because they could not connect them to their daily practices as early whole language advocates had done a decade before. Because whole language now had to be managed within schools, across districts, and throughout the state, contemporary business practices of site-based management were to be employed among school administrators who were not necessarily cognizant of whole language or management principles. Teachers who were not already asking questions about their teaching or students' learning were seen as resistant to change and out of touch with current theory and research. Dewey's cautions to revolutionaries were gone almost completely. In this sense, whole language had become the one best system of teaching reading and writing until a point at which, as P. David Pearson explained, it "was in danger of becoming conventional wisdom."[63]

Chapter Five

One Best Method: The Role of Government

During September 1981, an insider leaked to the *New York Times* that the Reagan White House would list ketchup as a vegetable in the federal school lunch program. Budget Director David Stockman explained that the move was warranted because scientists had found that the nutrients in tomatoes were more easily digested when the tomatoes had been cooked in some way and economists had discovered a large deficit in the federal budget. This culinary substitution would reduce the federal expense incurred when meeting students' daily nutritional requirements. Initiated during the Great Society legislation of the 1960s, the federal lunch program provided free and reduced-cost lunches for twenty-six million students from less well-to-do families in ninety-four thousand schools across the country. After a barrage of negative commentary, G. William Hoagland, the federal food and nutrition director, withdrew the ketchup proposal.

> We did not withdraw the rules because they were in error. Both President Reagan and I felt they were in tune with the administration's philosophy. Unfortunately they were misunderstood and misinterpreted. The intent and thrust will not be changed when the new rules are released.[1]

President Reagan's ketchup fiasco demonstrates some ways in which politics, science, and business are brought to bear on contemporary school issues. In this example, science and economics were used to support a political ideology concerning government service to its citizens. Reagan and members of his administration believed that governments should not be responsible for the social welfare of citizens. They used science as an authority to justify the substitution and good business sense to make the substitution appear reasonable. Without stopping to think about the issue in human terms—children consuming condiments as the nutritional equivalent of vegetables—one might think the decision and its rationale were legitimate and natural. Moreover, the scientists, economists, and politicians all appeared sincere in their proposal to help children. The move seemed legitimate until someone questioned the basic assumption about the responsibilities of government and leaked the proposal to the press. Only within the light of different political ideologies on governmental responsibilities to its citizens did the substitution become outrageous and the proposal mean-spirited.

In an editorial titled "Bumble Lives," however, *New York Times* editors listed other food-related cost-saving measures proposed in the same budget: reduction of meal subsidies for orphanages, increased requirements for eligibility for food subsidies among sixty- to sixty-four-year-old citizens, and elimination of automatic cost-of-living increases for food stamp recipients.[2] None of these proposals drew the same level of response as the ketchup-as-a-vegetable ploy. Only this last element was eliminated from the administration's next proposal.

In this chapter, I describe ways in which the animating political ideologies of three presidential administrations found common ground in the rejection of American liberalism, enabling science and business to work dialectically in order to reestablish the authority of the one best method of teaching reading in American classrooms. Although they did so for differing reasons, Reagan's conservatives, Clinton's neoliberals, and George W. Bush's neoconservatives rejected large government projects as the appropriate answer to social questions. Rather, each promoted market ideologies as the solution to social problems, assuming that the unfettered pursuit of profit would lead businesses to provide efficient, effective solutions to any problem. According to this logic, business would engage in research and development to employ the latest scientific expertise, leading toward the best option to fulfill social needs. Good solutions would chase weaker solutions from the field.

Whether to conserve the past, to develop human capital, or to learn the moral principles of western civilization, each administration made reading education a priority within its efforts to reform schools. Because profitability continues to thrive on predictability, the predictable outcomes of reading programs were emphasized in each proposal. During the 1980s and early 1990s, however, whole language critics continued the century-long project of the New Education by questioning the authority of experimental science, commercially prepared curricula, and government support for teacher and school effectiveness models. Whole language critics argued that controlled experimentation distorted the reality of reading; they exposed the mismatch between students' interests and needs and the standard lessons in basal reading programs; and they charged that the state testing policies reduced reading to its lowest functional form. To overcome these problems, whole language critics proposed expanded views of science to include interpretive approaches, the use of authentic texts, and teacher-negotiated curricula. Moreover, they worked to change state policy in order to accommodate whole language principles and practices. In sum, whole language critics recommended that teachers and students—not the state, experts, or publishing companies—should be recognized as the proper authorities on what transpired during reading instruction at school.

Although Heinemann and other publishers, independent professional development companies, and teacher research groups moved quickly to fill the void of authority created by these critiques, the criticisms left educational scientists and basal publishers floundering, upset many teachers who continued to reify reading instruction as the application of commercial programs, surprised parents raised on Dick and Jane, and enraged conservative fundamentalist Christians because meaning was to be negotiated, with the reader in charge.[3] To stem this revolution over authority and the threat to the predictability of outcome, the federal government stepped in to renew the project of discovering and enforcing the one best method of teaching reading. In order to move schools toward the market and to reestablish traditional authority, the federal government needed to discredit schools with claims that America was in social and economic decline because public school teachers were not teaching students to read as well as their counterparts in other countries.[4] Although the work of government, business, and science were intertwined in the efforts to squash the New Education and whole language challenges, I separate them into three chapters in order to show how each worked to reassert authorities behind the one best system.

First Attempt to Discredit Schools

President Reagan's election in 1980 marked the culmination of two decades of work among American conservatives to redirect federal politics toward militant anti-communism, social traditionalism, and economic libertarianism. The Reagan administration set its policies based on this agenda, increasing dramatically military spending, reducing drastically spending on social programs, failing purposely to enforce social policies already in place, and cutting strategically taxes and regulations for businesses and well-to-do citizens. Schooling was central to Reagan's conservative mission because, as Russell Kirk affirmed in *The Conservative Mind*, teachers prepared citizens to understand the past, to interpret the present, and to develop the future. "Previously, even in America, the structure of society had consisted of a hierarchy of personal and local allegiances—man to master, apprentice to preceptor, householder to parish or town, constituent to representative, son to father, communicant to church. This network of personal relationships and local decencies was brushed aside by items in that catalogue of progress which school children memorize."[5]

Shaped in the 1960s by the civil rights movement, the Great Society, and opposition to the Vietnam War, that liberal "catalogue of progress" sought to provide equal opportunity for all American students to succeed within school curricula in order to be prepared for the world of work.[6] Liberal federal policies were expected to counteract existing legal and social barriers, which, liberals believed, kept the poor, minorities, and women from these equal opportunities. According to these liberals—even if state and local officials were disinclined to provide these opportunities—the federal government was responsible to all its citizens to ensure their equal access to the pursuit of happiness as well as to defend their life and liberty. Consequently, liberal educational policies followed, favoring affirmative action, multicultural curricula, separation of religion and state, and federal regulation of school services. And by sheer numbers alone, liberal programs for great equity had been successful. In 1950, only 34 percent of the American population had completed four years of high school and only 6 percent had finished four years of college. By 1985, 74 percent had four years of high school and 19 percent, four years of college. This increase in school attendance broadened the demographic makeup of schools and consequently the backgrounds of the students taking the standardized tests at school.

Reagan's six major goals for education can be read as a conservative campaign to reverse and rewrite that 1960s liberal agenda, which he believed had favored equity over excellence. Terrell Bell, Reagan's first secretary of education, described the goals:

> First the President wanted to reduce substantially federal spending for education. Second, he wanted to strengthen local and state control of education and to reduce dramatically the federal responsibility in this area. Third, the President wanted to maintain a limited federal role that would build and enhance the capacity of states to carry out their traditional responsibilities. Fourth, the President wanted to encourage the establishment of laws and rules that would offer greatly expanded parental choice and that would increase competition for students among schools in newly created public and private structures patterned after the free market system that motivates and disciplines U. S. business and industry. Fifth, President Reagan wanted to

encourage a substantial reduction in federal judicial activity in education. Finally, the President wanted to abolish the U. S. Department of Education and replace it with a newly established agency that would be less powerful and prominent in the total structure of the federal government.[7]

The Reagan White House used a two-pronged approach to reform schooling. First, Reagan charged that educational achievement had declined sharply during the 1960s and 1970s, school expenditures had tripled, and school discipline had broken down. He argued that public schools were weak in these areas because they enjoyed a protected monopoly and that private schools were strong because they competed in the marketplace. This approach worked to secure the support of conservatives and religious fundamentalists by continuously advocating what Bell called "right-wing conservative" issues: publicly funded vouchers to enable parents to choose religious schools for their children, tuition tax credits for private schools, and school prayer in public schools.

Relying on Charles Murray's statistical analysis in *Losing Ground: American Social Policy 1950–1980*, Reagan White House officials believed that liberal federal policies were inappropriate at best and harmful at worst because they had created a culture of dependency, injuring the very people that they were intended to help.[8] Moreover, Reagan and others in his administration accepted the conservative principle that social inequalities were biologically driven and fixed.[9] Liberal public schooling, then, had corrupted America's youth, leaving them undisciplined and immoral; liberal equity programs had pushed minorities and women beyond their capacities to respond, and federal sponsorship of curricular reform had undermined American values, indoctrinating children with liberal understandings of the past and present and fostering a dangerous future for both individuals and society.

Reagan's conservative remedies often originated and always found support among some philanthropic institutions (e.g., Abell Foundation, Coors Foundation, John C. Olin Foundation), think tanks (e.g., American Enterprise Institute, Heritage Foundation, Hoover Institution, Manhattan Institute), and religious pundits (e.g., Jerry Falwell, Mel and Norma Gabler, Tim LaHaye, and Pat Robertson). Such support increased the likelihood that his conservative position would be presented forcefully and positively within the popular media and fundamentalist Christian churches across the United States. Each proclaimed the importance of excellence over equity, the moral decline in America, and guilt of the federal government in the reported dismal record of public schooling. All favored the replacement of public school districts by a free market of competing private schools supported through tax credits and vouchers.

Conservative Philanthropic Organizations and Think Tanks

Beginning in the 1970s, wealthy conservatives worked to establish institutions with members who would present the case for conservative principles to the public because they believed that left-wing intellectuals controlled the media, universities, and public secondary schools. This control, they believed, blocked the public's access to conservatism. As William Simon, the Nixon-Ford administration's secretary of the treasury, who left the cabinet to become president of the John C. Olin Foundation, wrote, "Foundations imbued with the philosophy of freedom must take pains to funnel desperately needed funds to scholars, social scientists, writers, and journalists who understand the relationship between political and economic liberty.[10] The Bechtel, Pew Freedom, Adolph Coors, Lilly, and Olin foundations acted on this directive, funding the American Enterprise, Heritage, Manhattan, and Hudson institutes, which provided the intellectual justifications for a conservative agenda throughout society and in public schools in particular. According to Joel Spring, a libertarian insider for these institutes during the 1970s, the foundations and institutes used four methods to present their case to the policymaking elites and the public:

1. Creating foundations and institutes that fund research and policy statements supportive of school choice, privatization of public schools and more recently, charter schools.

2. Identifying scholars to conduct research, write policy statements, and lecture at public forums that are favorable to school choice, privatization of public schools, and charter schools.

3. Financing conferences to bring like-minded scholars together for the sharing of ideas and the creation of edited books.

4. Paying scholars to write newspaper opinion pieces that are then distributed to hundreds of newspapers across the country.[11]

The attempt to influence educational policy directly began in 1980 when the Heritage Foundation presented President Reagan's transition team with *Mandate for Change*, a thousand-page position statement on conservative government. Beyond the call to close the U.S. Department of Education, the Heritage Foundation proposed the ending of Title I programs with perhaps a stipend for poor families to seek private tutoring for their children who were struggling in learning to read and calculate. The Cato Institute proposed the same solution for Head Start.[12] Although both arguments lacked sound empirical evidence to support their positions, the institute's media connections ensured that the ideas would appear in the *New York Times*, *Washington Post*, and *Time Magazine* and on the nightly news and political talk shows. The experts who were consulted by these media were also members of these institutes or foundations.[13] During the Reagan and Bush administrations, these experts slipped in and out between the foundations, institutes, and U.S. Department of Education (e.g., William Bennett, Lynne Cheney, Dennis Doyle, Chester Finn Jr., and Diane Ravitch). This movement continued into the new millennium.

Different groups carried the conservative argument directed at the reading instruction in pubic schools. Sidney Blumenfeld, the Eagle Forum, and the Reading Reform Foundation took direct aim at the liberal tenets of whole language instruction. As early as 1982, the *Blumenfeld NewsLetter*, with a circulation of more than ten thousand, called whole language a hoax that was failing to teach children to read. Blumenfeld claimed that whole language was undermining the authority of God's word by maintaining that meaning was in the mind of the reader and not in the authority of the text.[14] *Eagle Forum Reports*, the newsletter of the Eagle Forum, explained why conservatives should teach their children to read in order to avoid the multicultural content of school textbooks and antiauthority stance of contemporary reading education.[15] Throughout the 1980s, these groups monitored local newspapers across the country, countering stories about whole language approaches with letters to the papers' editors that questioned the veracity of the reporters' and editors' judgment for allowing the stories to run. Each letter ended by advocating reading lists of traditional literature and phonics instruction.[16] By 1989, the conservative position on whole language became the official position of the Republican Senate Policy Committee.[17] The crux of these statements was captured in the Reading Reform Foundation Basic Information and Catalogue:

> When 35 percent of the population is affected by a disability, it is epidemic. When that disability is the leading cause of emotional problems in children and adolescents in North America, we are talking about a serious public health problem. Consider also that this epidemic is a major etiological factor in school-dropouts and in juvenile delinquency....
>
> We already have the vaccine to attack reading disability, but we can't get the educators to use it. Samuel Orton, Rudolf Flesch, Jeanne Chall, Patrick Groff and numerous other researchers have urged the educators to prevent this massive problem by inoculating primary students with a steady injection of synthetic, explicit phonics.[18]

The Religious Right

Christian fundamentalists' views of the world are basically Manichean. They look at the world as an arena in which absolute good battles absolute evil. As historian Richard Hofstadter wrote in *Anti-intellectualism in American Life*,

"The issues of the actual world are hence transformed into a spiritual Armageddon, an ultimate reality, in which any reference to day-by-day actualities has the character of an allegorical illustration, and not of the empirical evidence that ordinary men offer for ordinary conclusions."[19] (Recall the Old Deluder, Satan Act that brought the first governmental mandate for reading instruction in America.) Compromise is impossible for fundamentalists because to do so would be to make a deal with the devil. America has a long tradition of religious fundamentalism, predating the American War of Independence, when America as the kingdom of Zion was still a New World dream. For fundamentalists, that dream is still a possibility.

Since the U.S. Constitution was ratified without the mention of God, fundamentalists have worked to topple Thomas Jefferson's "wall of separation" between church and state. There have been notable victories: during the American Civil War, "In God We Trust" was printed on United States currency; during the cold war, "under God" was added to the Pledge of Allegiance; and during the Reagan administration, "God Bless America" ended every presidential speech. The width and height of that wall of separation have been altered over the intervening two centuries with a decidedly effective initiative to diminish the size of the wall since 1980. Although only a small minority of the U.S. population, Christian fundamentalists are well organized and wield political power far beyond their numbers. Besides the thousands of church pulpits, they own television stations, radio stations, and newspapers. Their opinions appear on mainstream news programs, editorial pages, and the floor of Congress.

Following the plans of former Nixon advisers Kevin Phillips and Pat Buchanan, the Republican Party courted southern fundamentalists and northern urban Catholics to form a new morally conservative majority with its ranks. The strategy proved effective; however, it created a split in the party between a majority of members, interested primarily in moral issues, and a minority, which focused on protecting American big business. In 1979, the Reverend Jerry Falwell, then a televangelist, seized the name Moral Majority to promote an agenda to legalize school prayer and school choice and abolish abortion. By the time Ronald Reagan was inaugurated in 1981, the Moral Majority had more than two million dues-paying members. At a meeting of the group in Dallas in 1980, candidate Ronald Reagan stated, "I know that you cannot endorse me, but I endorse you and everything you do."[20] Leaders of the Christian Coalition, formed in 1989, negotiated a compromise among Republicans in which fundamentalists would support economic issues in exchange for unanimous support of cultural and school issues. With the consensus, fundamentalists began an organized grassroots network to promote Republican issues with particular attention to school matters.[21]

Fundamentalists are convinced that liberals control the federal bureaucracy, the courts system, the media, universities, and public schools with the unexpressed goal of eliminating Christian values from American culture. As evidence for their conclusions, they point to the many secular laws, regulations, media stories, films, television programs, and school curricula that pervade public and private spaces in America. Because fundamentalists assume their values are good, any differing values of others must be evil and beneath compromise. These so-called culture wars between fundamentalists and "free-thinkers" have been active for at least 140 years in the United States.[22] Because public schools subject all Americans to evil values—scientific realism, theories of evolution, sex education, multiculturalism, values clarification, and most recently, whole language reading instruction—without sufficient counterbalance, fundamentalists seek to eliminate public schools. Their strategies are straightforward.

> I imagine every Christian would agree that we need to remove the humanism from public schools. There is only one-way to accomplish this: to abolish the public schools. We need to get the government out of the education business. According to the Bible, education is a parental responsibility. It is not the place of the government to be running a school system. . . . [We must] shut down the public school not in some revolutionary way, but step by step, school by school, district by district.[23]

Fundamentalists believe that whole language principles threaten, if not negate, the traditional Christian view of reading. For whole language advocates, meaning is not brought by the word. Rather, the reader controls the meaning of any text. Thus, the meaning of the Bible does not come directly from God because, according to whole language advocates, meaning is socially produced through readers during conversations with themselves or others. Either way, whole language opens God's word to human interpretations. And this is unacceptable to fundamentalists. "Whole language is an attack on the notion of absolute truth and literal comprehension of a written text."[24] Whole language's secular authority and multiple possibilities of meaning are incompatible with the fundamentalist teaching—"God gave every word of Scripture, not just the thoughts"[25]—and therefore, fundamentalists must reject whole language on principle.

At a more mundane level, fundamentalists object to whole language instructional strategies as well. Student choice of reading material from among the books on library shelves, reading without expectations of precision, and identification and development of personal voice through writing and responding to literature counter the authority of the word and the church. Whole language instructional practices expose children to secular concepts that question fundamentalist values, implying that children are authorities over their own development and encouraging readers to question all texts. With these principles, it is small wonder that fundamentalists resent and resist whole language teaching.

Fundamentalist strategies for opposing whole language has varied across groups and sects, but each has included daily battles between good and evil within reading instruction.[26] The Christian Coalition, Focus on Family, Citizens for Excellence in Education, and other large fundamentalist organizations have encouraged members to challenge whole language directly by filing formal complaints about the content of books, films, and textbooks that included objectionable content. They have advocated that church members run for school boards to influence school policy, promoted the discipline of direct instruction in phonics, spelling, and grammar, and encouraged parents to remove their children from public schools and enroll them in Christian schools or teach them at home. In order to incite, organize, and maintain these challenges, fundamentalist leaders have taken their arguments directly to fundamentalist churches across the country through direct visits or information kits for local pastors to preach the end of whole language. Many have formally lobbied education departments at the state and federal levels to achieve their collective agenda.

Culture Wars Directed from the White House

During his second administration, Reagan appointed William J. Bennett as the secretary of education to lead the movement of discrediting public education. Bennett's first efforts were "to get clear answers to the fundamental questions about education: what should children know? And how can they learn it?"[27] Standing in the way of clear thinking on these matters, Bennett argued, were the "infusion of diversity in schools" and a "surfeit of confusion, bureaucratic thinking, and community apathy." According to Bennett, diversity became a concern for public schooling only after minorities and women began to question the western European focus of school traditions and inequalities of academic outcomes during the 1960s. Although diversity was not an "insuperable obstacle," Bennett explained:

> Our diversity is socioeconomic. We are rich and poor and most of us are somewhere in between. Yet the persistence of socioeconomic "underclass" in America looms as one of the largest challenges to our nation in general and to our educational system in particular. Lack of money is only one aspect of the problem, and perhaps, not even the most serious. Dependency, crime, ill health, joblessness, drug addiction—these are not, of course, confined to the poor nor do most low-income individuals experience them. But when they intersect within

the burst of poverty that sociologists often refer to as the underclass, we have an authentic and sizable problem for which the term diversity is not nearly expressive enough—a challenge increasingly troubling for our elementary schools.

Bennett's solution for this problem of diversity and worse was twofold. First, schools had to clarify their curricula, and Bennett's office offered three guides: *What Works, First Lessons,* and *James Madison Elementary School.*[28] *What Works* presented a selective sample of research findings that boiled down to "[the] belief in the value of hard work, the importance of personal responsibility, and the importance of education itself contributes to greater academic success." *First Lessons* explained "although most teachers seek to reinforce good character in their students by teaching honesty, industry, loyalty, self-respect, and other virtues, their presentation of certain issues may yet be clouded by foolish 'value-free' educational theories and by their perceptions of conflict among value systems represented in their students' diverse backgrounds." *James Madison* provided explicit elementary school curricula in order to demonstrate that "there is, in fact, no broad class of American students for whom the time-tested principles of good education do not and cannot apply." According to Bennett, schools were failing because they would not civilize the diversity of the American population.

Bennett's second solution required teachers to supplement this explicit moral curriculum with "another powerful 'curriculum,' the implicit lessons they deliver concerning the development of character and morality."[29] For example, teaching phonics first would require students to learn patience and persistence and to defer the instant gratification of meaningful reading. In a speech to the Manhattan Institute, Bennett declared that the solution to the problems of diversity was moral literacy in which students would learn the common principles of western civilization through direct instruction, skill development, and memorization. The redesign of American schools would not come from federal fiat but rather "a grassroots movement for education reform that has generated a renewed commitment to excellence, character, and fundamentals."[30]

Although many took up the call for character education and its religious foundation during the 1990s (e.g., Bill Honig, William Kilpatrick, Thomas Lakona, Kevin Ryan), Bennett turned this concern into an enterprise after he left the White House. He released a series of books intended to popularize his interpretation of American social decline and the need for moral literacy. The titles convey their content: *The De-Valuing of America* (1992), *The Index of Leading Cultural Indicators* (1994/1999), *Body Count* (1996), and *The Death of Outrage* (1998).[31] The message was consistent—liberal institutions were not prepared to cope with the social problems released in the morally bankrupt 1960s and 1970s. At the same time he was making his argument for moral literacy, he published *The Book of Virtues*, an anthology of stories and essays that exemplified the morals to be universally learned. *The Book of Virtues* was on the *New York Times* best-seller list for more than a year, and spawned more than twenty sequels, a website, and a Public Broadcasting System television show by that name. After the turn of the century, Bennett augmented his educational thrust with an online school intended to supplant K–12 public school.

The President as a Christian Fundamentalist

Although Ronald Reagan was a favorite of the religious right, George W. Bush is considered its unofficial leader. In fact, when Pat Buchanan resigned as the leader of the Christian Coalition, he acknowledged that his efforts were rendered unnecessary, as the president spoke for the organization and its constituency. George W. Bush is a fundamentalist Christian. He was born again during 1985 when he decided that Jesus Christ was his personal savior. The decision changed the direction of his life—away from hedonistic pleasures and toward service to others in God's name. Shortly after his rebirth, Bush ran for governor of Texas and won. After his reelection, he attended services in Highland Park Methodist Church in Dallas. During one sermon, the preacher used Moses as his example to explain, "people are starved for leadership—starved for leaders who have ethical and moral courage." While listening, Bush thought that the sermon was directed at him. He felt a "call," a sense that God was directing him to run for president. His mother, Barbara Bush, had the same insight during the sermon and turned to say, "He was talking to you." Later, George W. Bush told Rev. James Robinson, moderator of the Christian television program *Life Today*:

> I've heard the call. I believe God wants me to run for president. I can't explain it, but I sense my country is going to need me. Something is going to happen, and at that time, my country is going to need me. I know it won't be easy on me or my family, but God wants me to do it.[32]

Upon being appointed president in 2000, Bush displayed immediately the religious convictions of his administration. On the first day, he called for a national day of prayer and cut federal spending on sex education, banning information on abortion as one of the options offered to women in federally funded health clinics around the world. Shortly after, he established a White House office of faith-based initiatives to solve social problems. Moreover, the White House website provides technical assistance to religious organizations applying for federal funding in order to launch these initiatives. Bush contends that the First Amendment to the Constitution, which he swore to uphold when inaugurated, applies only to the federal government establishing a single sect as a national religion. He argues that nothing prevents Christian morals from directing policy or state governments from relying on religious groups for information and service. All of Bush's policies on education and public schooling must be understood through the ultimate fundamentalist goal to withdraw federal and even state responsibility to educate the American populace.

The Second Attempt to Discredit Schools

The second approach to discrediting public schools casts a wider net than the nation's conservatives and cuts across three presidential administrations. Against conservative objections, the National Commission on Excellence in Education released the *Nation at Risk* report, which blamed schools for the declining fortunes of the American economy in the 1980s. In the best cold war rhetoric, the thirty-six-page report explained that "if an unfriendly foreign power had attempted to impose on America the mediocre educational performance that exists today, we might well have viewed it as an act of war."[33] Accordingly the report called for the complete reform of the school system or America would experience a significant drop in its economic position within the world economy. With this drop, Americans would experience dramatic reductions in their standards of living. The report turned liberal rhetoric on the economic importance of schooling upon itself. "If only to keep and improve on the slim competitive edge we still retain in world markets, we must dedicate ourselves to the reform of our educational system." As Terrell Bell explained, "It was because so many lacked the basic skills to be retrained. Our loss of zest and drive and spirit would not be regained until we renewed and reformed our schools."[34] President Reagan, however, released the report, apparently without having read it, as he couched the release of the report as if it endorsed his conservative agenda for schools.

> When Secretary Bell and I first discussed a plan of action to deal with the declining quality of education in America, we agreed that it was imperative to assemble a panel of America's leading educators, an assembly of such eminence that the Nation would listen to its findings. Well, today, you've issued your report. And I'm confident that America's students, parents, teachers, and government officials will join me in listening closely to your findings and recommendations.
>
> Your report emphasizes that the Federal role in education should be limited to specific areas, and any assistance should be provided

with a minimum of administrative burdens on our schools, colleges, and teachers.

Your call for an end to Federal intrusion is consistent with our task of redefining the Federal role in education. I believe that parents, not Government, have the primary responsibility for the education of their children. Parental authority is not a right conveyed by the state; rather parents delegate to their elected school board representatives and State legislators the responsibility for their children's schooling.

So, we'll continue to work in the months ahead for passage of tuition tax credits, vouchers, educational savings accounts, voluntary school prayer, and abolishing the Department of Education. Our agenda is to restore quality in education by increasing competition and by strengthening parental choice and local control. I'd like to ask all of you, as well as every citizen who considers this report's recommendations, to work together to restore excellence in America's schools.[35]

Despite Reagan's reiteration of his conservative goals at its debut, the claims of *A Nation at Risk* captured the imaginations of the media, business leaders, and neoliberal politicians and pundits. Capitalizing on the new excitement, the Reagan reelection team used the report to create further doubt about school success among citizens in order to move on its agenda.[36] Beyond enabling Reagan to steal education as an issue from the Democratic Party, *A Nation at Risk* invited businessmen and educational scientists back to the federal policy table with a mandate to overhaul American public schooling. During his campaign for reelection, Reagan referred to *A Nation at Risk* in order to paint schools as failed governmental monopolies that lacked passion for traditional American values and lowered the achievement levels of high school graduates from those of the past. Although Reagan's rhetorical strategy appealed to conservatives, it was the contents of *A Nation at Risk* that attracted the most public attention.

The crux of the report argued for public schooling to regain its capacity to develop the human capital necessary to keep the American economy preeminent. The report's authors blamed the school decline on the overemphasis on equal opportunity during the 1960s and 1970s. That attention diverted schools from concerns of academic excellence, leaving the country's workers ill-equipped to adapt to new economic demands. "The average graduate of our schools and colleges today is not as well-educated as the average graduate of 25 or 35 years ago, when a much smaller proportion of our population completed high school and college."[37] The commission recommended higher academic standards, stronger exit measures, a longer school day and year, and better-prepared teachers. With these changes, the commissioners assumed that the students' achievement would return to the high levels of the past, enabling American students and workers to once again compete with students and workers from other countries (the Pacific Rim in particular). State and school district efforts to make these reforms consumed much of the 1980s.[38]

Neoliberalism and American Schools

During the G. H. W. Bush administration, from 1988 to 1992, neoliberals, in and out of government (e.g., Harvard professor Robert Reich, Governor Bill Clinton, and Xerox CEO David Kearns) complimented the commission on naming the problem correctly, but criticized it for underestimating the enormity of the needed changes. These critics started from a different political ideological perspective on governmental responsibilities to citizens and the role of schooling than the Reagan conservatives. While neoliberals retain the core values of liberalism—liberty, justice, and equality of opportunity—they no longer accept traditional liberal solutions to social problems. That is, they do not espouse large, centralized social programs, trade unionism, or restrictions on business as the best routes to achieving their values. Since public schools are liberal solutions, neoliberals question schools' chances for success in their current forms.

Yet, neoliberals do not accept conservative solutions completely either, being unwilling to blame individuals for the problems that beset them, to back the military without reservations, or to embrace traditional social values. Neoliberals recognize that not all citizens have received an equal opportunity to develop themselves because they have not enjoyed the same access to health care, nutrition, housing, and especially education throughout their lives. According to neoliberals, this lack of access, and not the individual habits, keeps inner-city and rural citizens impoverished and blocks their opportunities to advance themselves. "Indeed, in our search for solutions that work, we have come to distrust all automatic responses, liberal and conservative."[39]

Neoliberal solutions blend the liberal concern for equal opportunity with the conservative promotion of libertarian economics in order to advance society. For neoliberals, the economic marketplace when unencumbered by greed, traditional biases, or governmental regulation will eventually raise all citizens' standard of living to bring them out of poverty, dissolving all barriers to equal opportunity, and prepare them to compete successfully throughout their lives. Schooling is understood to be an engine for securing appropriate market conditions and for preparing workers for their globalized future.

In the first part of this century, we adopted the principles of mass-producing low-quality education to create a low-skill workforce for mass production industry. Building on this principle, our education and business systems became tightly linked, developing into a single system that brilliantly capitalized on our advantages and enabled us to create the most powerful economy and the largest middle class the world has ever seen. . . . But most of the competitive advantages enjoyed at the beginning of the century had faded by mid-century, and advances in technology during and after the war slowly altered the structure of the domestic and world economy in ways that turned these principles of American business and school organization into liabilities rather than assets.[40]

According to neoliberals then, the commission performed the wrong analysis and drew the wrong conclusions in *A Nation at Risk*. In order to refocus the concerns for school reform, neoliberals corrected the commission's charge that student achievement had declined greatly, noting that test scores for minorities and girls were actually rising more rapidly than those of white boys. Moreover, the neoliberal reports conceded that high school graduates were at least as smart as their predecessors. However, they argued that old levels of achievement were no longer adequate to meet the challenges of the new world economy because international struggles for freedom and recognition of colonized countries and oppressed groups within industrialized countries created a world in which specialized markets desired products to fit specific needs. Economies based on large corporations engaging in mass production could no longer meet the challenges posed by this new world order.[41] The transition of the American economy from mass production to one that could quickly reorganize itself unsettled traditional assumptions about work, government, community, and schools. Neoliberals pointed toward rising crime rates, a shrinking middle class, and the abandonment of cities as some of the unfortunate social consequences caused by Americans' reluctance to change their assumptions and reorder their lives in order to compete and win in the global economy.

Rather than work to uphold the standards of the past, as conservatives and the commission sought, neoliberals sought new, higher world-class standards based on the assumption that future employment would require students and workers to retrain themselves continuously in order to keep themselves useful to constantly changing business and industry. Beyond traditional curriculum, neoliberals argued that high school graduates should have a high capacity for abstract thought, an ability to apply that thought to real-world problems, mastery of a sophisticated level of oral and written

English, and a talent for working easily and well with others. During the late 1980s and early 1990s, many business leaders and governors preferred this neoliberal interpretation of the need and direction of school reform to the fiery but conservative rhetoric of William Bennett, Reagan's second secretary of education.

Goals 2000, America 2000, Educate America

In order to maintain some control over school reform, President Bush summoned state governors to meet at an educational summit on the University of Virginia campus in September 1989. Although there were deep divisions between the president's staff and the governors, they managed to issue a statement of common purpose by the end of the summit and to establish a standing committee to oversee the development of goals and procedures for school reform.[42] The six initial goals were to be met by the year 2000:

1. all children will start school ready to learn;
2. graduation rates will exceed 90 percent;
3. students will demonstrate competency in challenging subject areas at 4th, 8th, and 12th grades;
4. U. S. students will score highest among nations on math and science tests;
5. every adult will be a literate and responsible citizen; and
6. every school will be free of drugs and violence.[43]

Chaired originally by Governor Bill Clinton, the Governors' Educational Task Force declared that "to achieve the new national goals, we must invent a new education system. The system must:

a. be lifelong, recognizing that lifelong learning begins at birth, not at school, and continues throughout life, and does not end at graduation;
b. focus on prevention, avoiding damage to young children and removing barriers to learning for all, rather than paying the higher price of compensating for preventable learning difficulties after they develop;
c. be performance-oriented, with an unwavering commitment to achieving results than to maintaining existing procedures, practices, or institution;
d. be flexible. Professionals should decide how best to help each individual achieve at high levels, rather than being told what to do and how to do it by distant authorities;

e. be accountable for the results they achieve. There must be real rewards for high performances and significant consequences for failure;

f. attract and retain talented professionals and ensure that they receive continued support and professional development; and

g. provide meaningful choices to students, parents, and adult learners by recognizing and accommodating their varying learning needs and styles.[44]

With his election as president in 1992, Clinton worked to realize the remaking of schools without upsetting unionized teachers, who had become the largest organized voting block for the Democratic Party. These two lists demonstrate the compromises between conservatives and neoliberals in order to gain the legislative support of both groups for school reform. Clearly, neoliberal plans dominated, particularly in the second list, but conservative issues remained. The Goals 2000 statement features conservative values: family options, supremacy in math and science (harkening back to responses to Sputnik launching during the 1950s), and school safety. However, the neoliberal language describes the means to reach those goals: lifelong learning, removing barriers, being performance oriented, having a flexible organization, retaining and attracting quality teachers.

Clinton's reauthorization of the Elementary and Secondary Education Act displayed the neoliberal values of his administration. In 1994, Clinton signaled ideological movement by changing Reagan's term for Chapter 1 back to the original Title I. Moreover, he retitled the entire law—Improving America's Schools Act. His intention was to announce his commitment to the original goals of ESEA. "The new ESEA programs focus on ensuring that all children, especially those in high poverty areas, the limited English-proficient, migrant children and others in need of extra education supports, are taught to the same content and performance standards as all other children in the state."[45] Yet Clinton's means to reach those goals were not all that liberal. They began the use of mandatory standards for all Title I students (Reagan's version of ESEA required only voluntary standards), state testing at regular intervals, and recording of demonstrated yearly progress. Noncompliance with the law meant a withdrawal of federal funding, and lack of success required an improvement plan to be completed in order to continue federal funding. To begin the process, Clinton solicited proposals for world-class academic standards from professional organizations. (Much more on this in Chapter 7.)

While traveling by train from West Virginia to Chicago to accept his party's renomination for president in 1996, Clinton and his advisers devised the America Reads Initiative. Staring at the results of the 1994 National

Assessment for Educational Progress, which demonstrated little change in achievement despite Goals 2000 initiatives, Clinton stopped at Wyandotte, Michigan, to announce:

> To meet this challenge, we need one million tutors ready and able to give children the personal attention they need to catch up and get ahead. Today I propose a national literacy campaign to help our children learn to read by the third grade—a plan that offers thirty thousand reading specialists and volunteer coordinators to communities that are willing to do their part. People who will mobilize the citizen army of volunteer tutors we need. America's reading corp. We will succeed however, if the thirty thousand are joined by legions of volunteers—seniors and teenagers, business, and civic groups, libraries and religious institutions, and above all parents.[46]

America Reads was designed to address two educational issues—reading at the elementary level and funding at the university level. Clinton sought $2.6 billion from Congress to address illiteracy. Funds for tutoring would be channeled through university- and college-monitored programs in which college students would be able to earn additional funds in exchange for their work in schools. The metaphor of a war on illiteracy proved popular with the public: colleges valued the increased funding for public service, and schools seemed to welcome the added bodies to help. Lost in enthusiasm was the implication that classroom teachers were incapable of teaching America's youth to read. Congress set a three-year limit on the program, and the results of America Reads are still debated.[47]

Democratic President, Republican Congress

Republicans were swift in their response to America Reads. Chair of the House Education and Workforce Committee Bill Goodling (R-PA) held congressional hearings in order to assess the effectiveness of volunteers in teaching reading and proposed the Reading Excellence Act on the heals of America Reads. Responding to the same NAEP test data as the Clinton administration, Goodling's act had four goals: (1) teach every child to read in his early childhood years, not later than the third grade; (2) improve the reading skills of students and the instructional practices of teachers through the use of findings from reliable, replicable research in reading, including phonics; (3) expand the number of high-quality family literacy programs; and (4) reduce the number of children who were inappropriately referred to special education because of reading difficulties (SI293, 1998). The Reading Excellence Act was the first time that the federal government defined reading and research in legislation.

The term "reading" means a complex system of deriving meaning from print that requires all of the following:

(A) the skills and knowledge to understand how phonemes, or speech sounds, are connected to print;

(B) the ability to decode unfamiliar words;

(C) the ability to read fluently;

(D) sufficient background information and vocabulary to foster reading comprehension;

(E) the development of appropriate active strategies to construct meaning from print; and

(F) the development and maintenance of a motivation to read.

Scientifically-based reading research—the term "scientifically based reading research"—

(A) means the application of rigorous, systematic, and objective procedures to obtain valid knowledge relevant to reading development, reading instruction, and reading difficulties; and

(B) shall include research that

(i) employs systematic, empirical methods that draw on observation and experiment;

(ii) involves rigorous data analyses that are adequate to test the stated hypotheses and justify the general conclusions drawn;

(iii) relies on measurement or observational methods that provide data across evaluators and observers and across multiple measurements and observations; and

(iv) has been accepted by a peer reviewed journal or approved by a panel of independent experts through a comparably rigorous, objective, and scientific review.[48]

These definitions were meant to close debates about reading and authority in reading education. Clearly, according to the Reading Excellence Act, the text brought meaning to the reader (rather than the reader constructing meaning), and the eye (rather than the mind) drove the reading process. In this definition, a reader's interpretive authority was submerged beneath the functional skills required in the excavation of textual meaning. In order to improve those skills, reading experts designed scientifically based instruction which teachers employed. With this move, the community of the expert subsumed the teachers' authority. In the first iteration of the act, Congress allotted $260 million to change reading education accordingly.

In Clinton's proposal for the 1998 ESEA reauthorization, he conceded the field to the Republicans. According to Clinton's proposal, schools would eventually be responsible for all students passing state and national tests in reading and writing during elementary, middle, and secondary levels. Until they reached that goal, schools would be required to disaggregate students' scores into demographic categories (by race, class, and English proficiency) and demonstrate adequate yearly progress in percentage of students in each group passing the tests. All schools and students would reach the goal within ten years of the reauthorization. If schools failed in any of these steps, they could retain federal funding only if they filed improvement plans to rectify the failures, offered students from failing schools the choice of attending other district schools, or, if failures continued, employed new administration, curricula, and teachers. To help states and districts make the necessary changes, the federal government would ease the restrictions on how funding could be used. In short, the federal government would force schools to reorganize in order to prepare all students to complete for jobs in the global economy. Even after these concessions to the Republican approach, Clinton's ESEA proposal met with stiff resistance from a Republican Congress, and his ESEA bill never passed.

Third Attempt to Discredit Schools

During the 2000 campaign for president, George W. Bush presented himself as a "compassionate conservative" who was responsible for the "Texas miracle" in education when he served as governor. "I call my philosophy and approach compassionate conservatism. It is compassionate to actively help our fellow citizens in need. It is conservative to insist on responsibility and results. And with this hopeful approach, we will make a real difference in people's lives."[49] Compassionate conservatives, or neoconservatives, mix conservatism and liberalism with a different twist than neoliberals. Unlike conservatives, neoconservatives acknowledge social and economic inequalities and attempt to close those gaps, but unlike liberals, they reject the structural explanation for inequalities. They are willing to fund a modest welfare state; however, they insist that the disadvantaged be taught to make the right life choices that will enable them to prosper in the future. That curriculum is drawn from the transcendental nature of European Christian values, which are considered to be the basis for both a civil society and personal well-being.

Upon being appointed president by the Supreme Court during a voting fraud investigation in Florida, Bush began the policy process that led to the reauthorization of the ESEA law under the title No Child Left Behind (NCLB). Bush invented none of the components of this law, which maps closely onto

Clinton's proposal for his second reauthorization and includes four explicit attempts to discredit practicing teachers: an external testing system, a tighter coupling of federal and local programs in reading education, a mandate for highly qualified teachers, and a national study of teacher education programs. Bush did, however, pattern the implementation of NCLB after his Texas miracle. The story of the miracle is based on Texas Department of Education data that suggested that a tightly centralized system of curricular and instructional standardization enforced by strict school, teacher, and student accountability procedures drastically lowered the school dropout rates, improved students' scores on state tests of reading and math, and narrowed the gap between poor and middle- and upper-class students and between minority and white students across Texas.[50] The system required teachers and students to follow commercial reading and math programs explicitly and to convert time devoted to science and social studies to the formal study of reading and math in the elementary grades. As president, Bush appointed Rod Paige, the former superintendent of the Houston City School District, as secretary of education to replicate the Texas system on a national scale. According to NCLB, through discipline, responsibility, and perseverance, American teachers would ensure that every child could demonstrate proficiency on all state standards for reading, writing, mathematics, and science by 2014.

> When it comes to our schools, dollars alone do not always make the difference. Funding is important, and so is reform. So we must tie funding to higher standards and accountability for results. I believe in local control of schools: we should not and we will not run our public schools from Washington, D. C. Yet when the federal government spends tax dollars, we must insist on results. Children should be tested on basic reading and math skills every year, between grades three and eight. Measuring is the only way to know whether all our children are learning—and I want to know because I refuse to leave any child behind in America. Critics of testing contend it distracts from learning. They talk about teaching to the test. But let's put that logic to the test. If you test a child on basic math and reading skills, and you're teaching to the test, then you're teaching math and reading. And that's the whole idea.[51]

Bush's statement demonstrates his neoconservative ideology. In the first sentence, he rejects the liberal position of more funding in order to provide equal opportunities for all. According to Bush and other neoconservatives, money is not the answer. However, he is not willing to accept the conservative notion that many children cannot be taught to read. Therefore, he acknowledges that money must be spent. If it must be, then students and teachers must be held accountable for their actions. With the moralizing tone at the end of his statement, Bush implies that the discipline of testing will be good for all involved. His rules for implementation continue in that vein. A problem with Bush's logic is that the Texas miracle was wildly exaggerated. Although all Texas elementary school reading programs were thoroughly rationalized according to officially approved core reading programs and testing schedules, reported improvements in students' reading test scores were not confirmed by national tests, high school dropout rates did not decline, and achievement gaps between rich and poor and black and white students did not close.[52]

NCLB – External Testing

Because schools would not be run from Washington, DC each state government was responsible to develop a plan of compliance and to submit that plan to the federal Department of Education for approval. If a state failed to submit a plan, to gain approval, and to implement it accordingly, then the federal government would withhold ESEA funding. Some federal officials and education pundits interpreted the lack of national standardization as a sign of weakness within the federal position.[53] Most, however, recognized that the threat of financial loss and the strictures of NCLB would be sufficient to ensure that the range of plans among the states would be acceptable. All states did comply.

1. Each state included regular testing of students' mastery of high standards at multiple points in a school career;
2. Each calculated the rate at which students would progress toward complete control of the curriculum and penalties for schools whose students did not make such progress;
3. Each developed a plan to ensure that classroom teachers were highly qualified,
4. Each was to employ scientifically based instruction methods and materials; and
5. Each submitted its plans for federal approval.[54]

Of course, plans differed among states. I use my state's position to illustrate how the federal tenets have been unfolding within states. With a strong teachers' union in a state with a Republican administration, the Pennsylvania plan demonstrated a modest compromise between the principles of its instructional framework curricula of the early 1990s and the interests of the federal government. In the plan, Pennsylvania teachers were not told what or how to teach, but they were required to accept the federal definitions, to pursue the state standards, and to use the Pennsylvania State Standard Assessments at the end of third, fifth, eighth, and eleventh grades. Baseline quotas for students' scores on these tests were set, and schools whose students did not reach these quotas would be designated as "in need of improvement." Originally, quotas were set at 45 percent proficient or above in mathematics and 35 percent in reading and writing. These quotas would be gradually increased until 2014, when all Pennsylvania students would score proficient or better on all PSSA exams. If a school failed to reach the quota, school administrators would be required to submit a plan to the Pennsylvania Department of Education detailing how the school district intended to raise the students' test scores. Continued failure to meet the continuously raising quotas would bring more prescribed penalties for the district. Districts with failing schools would be required to offer students open enrollment across the district so that students could choose to attend a school with higher average scores and to provide nonproficient students with private individual tutoring from an approved vendor. If scores remained too low for five years, then the Pennsylvania Department of Education (PDE) would reconstitute the school, changing its administration, curricula, and teaching staff.

Before the ink was dry on Pennsylvania's NCLB plan, Pennsylvania governor Tom Ridge invoked a state statute that enabled the PDE to reconstitute failing schools in the Philadelphia school district.[55] Although the school board and the mayor of Philadelphia protested that the schools were improving under its reform plan, Governor Ridge commissioned a $2.7 million study of the Philadelphia City Schools by Edison Education Inc. This for-profit organization concluded that "the School District of Philadelphia is facing grave academic and fiscal crises, with two-thirds of its schools failing and a significant and growing budget deficit."[56] The Edison researchers found the curriculum in disarray, with more than a hundred different reading programs within the district and often several programs within the same school. The report argued that the public school administration was too large, wasteful, and even fiscally irresponsible. None of the school district's attempts to alter its programs had improved students' performance satisfactorily In fact, Edison predicted that only a public-private combination of efforts could save the schools, children, and city. With a $430,000 media campaign, Edison managed to wrestle control over forty-three schools away from the school district. After three years, however, all these reconstituted schools were still designated as in need of improvement because too many students remained below proficiency on the PSSA reading tests. Public funds continue to support these private-public schools despite students' lack of success. However, the reconstitution of Philadelphia schools did send a message to all Pennsylvania school superintendents. Meet the NCLB goals or face private takeover.

Direct Alignment of Federal and Local Programs

NCLB replaced the Reading Excellence Act with the Reading First Initiative in order to ensure the quality control of federally funded reading programs. Under the Reading Excellence Act, many states and local school districts continued to employ their successful plans for the reform of reading education instead of implementing the federally sanctioned programs of scientifically based instruction. Although the Reading Excellence Act was in place for only two years, federal officials deemed it a failure because it did not bring immediate alignment with federal guidelines.[57] The Reading First Initiative of NCLB would guarantee state and local compliance. States would submit scientifically based plans for using Reading First funds to federal officials for review and allow federal regulators into the state periodically to inspect funded programs. In this way, the Reading First Initiative would allow the appearance of local flexibility in implementing the federally approved programs based on the definitions of science and reading from the Reading Excellence Act. For some, these efforts at national alignment invoked images of scientific management on the grand scale that Frederick Taylor originally envisioned.

As reports from New York, California, Florida, and Texas demonstrate, the implementation of the Reading First Initiative has not been uniform or smooth.[58] For example, in Pennsylvania, local school districts submitted detailed proposals to the PDE in order to qualify for funding.[59] Districts were approved for funding if they selected a core basal reading program, purchased standardized achievement tests, and hired private companies to train teachers. Districts that did not follow these guidelines explicitly were invited to Harrisburg for remedial help in preparing a successful proposal. Some districts, however, found it difficult to comply. For example, one district had made steady progress under America Reads and the Reading Excellence Act by working to implement the Reading Recovery and Guided Reading and Writing curricula of the Ohio State University framework. Although the district suffered double-digit unemployment and a rapidly falling tax base, students in the district had raised their PSSA scores in reading until they nearly matched the state average. The PDE denied the district's plan because state officials deemed the twenty-year-old Ohio State model unscientific. While district administrators contemplated making the changes in order to comply with the federally approved model and to qualify for much-needed Reading First funding, Pennsylvanians elected a new Democratic governor, who changed the administration of the PDE. The new officials approved the district proposal without any modifications. Apparently, Republicans and Democrats have differing interpretations of the official definition of scientifically based research and instruction.

Highly Qualified Teachers

In many states across the country, teachers are in short supply.[60] In some districts, administrators must hire unlicensed teachers or shift teachers beyond their certification in order to find teachers of physics, chemistry, calculus, and some areas of special education. In many urban areas, certified teachers of any type are difficult to find. In these districts, administrators hire people who are willing to teach and apply for emergency certification from the state. Although these practices are associated with lower student achievement, many administrators reason that any teacher is better than no teacher in a classroom full of students. In order to address this problem, NCLB simply mandated that states fill every classroom with a highly qualified teacher by 2006. The law offered modest financial support for districts to comply and threatened penalties for those districts that did not. NCLB defines a highly qualified teacher as anyone who holds a minimum of a bachelor's degree, has full state certification, and has demonstrated competence in each of the academic subjects that she teaches. On its surface, the highly qualified teacher statute seems to support teachers and confirm their worth. But without proper funding and incentives to attract and keep good teachers for all subjects, "highly qualified teachers" mocks good teaching.

As of January 1, 2003, the Pennsylvania Department of Education allows teachers to acquire other areas of certification simply by passing the state's specialist exam for that discipline. A call to the PDE seeking a rationale for the new policy met with this reply: If we are to meet the NCLB standards for appropriately certified teachers in each classroom, then we must provide teachers with access to more than one certification. If certified teachers have the knowledge for the certification, then we can issue another certificate to them. Highly qualified in Pennsylvania, therefore, means that a teacher has passed a paper-and-pencil content test. If you are a teacher and also wish to teach art, biology, chemistry, communications, earth science, English, French, German, mathematics, music, physics, reading, citizenship, Spanish, or any combination of them, then all you need to do is pay the Educational Testing Service in order to take the appropriate test, achieve the score set by the PDE, and then pay the state to issue the new certificate. The state qualifying score in reading is below the median score on the test. In this way, "highly qualified" is not a label that you earn through intellectual and pedagogical efforts in university and public school classrooms. Rather, it is something that you buy from ETS and the state. And for Pennsylvania teachers, ETS offers a special rate and a volume discount: one exam costs $80, two cost $145, three cost $130, and four cost $145. Like that huge tub of popcorn at the movie theatre, four certifications for $145 is your best value.

Teacher Education Is Next

Tucked into a fiscal appropriations bill in 2004 was the legislative beginning of the real rationalization of teacher education. Congress has asked the Institute of Education Sciences to conduct a study concerning the consistency of required course work in teacher preparation, how reading and math are taught, and the degree to which programs are aligned with scientific evidence on the subjects. Grover Whitehurst, the director of the institute, will oversee the federal study of teacher education. His comments at the March 2002 White House Conference on Preparing Tomorrow's Teachers suggest the direction for the study.[61] After defining good teaching as having a positive effect on students' achievement test scores and poor teaching as not increasing those scores, Whitehurst described studies that demonstrated no differences in effect on student achievement between graduates of colleges of education and alternative teacher preparation programs. So according to Whitehurst, good teachers mattered, because test score productivity was high, but it didn't really matter how they were educated. What mattered most (that is, correlated most with test scores) were teacher's IQ and specific training to teach to the test. What mattered least were certifications and master's degrees. In fact, years in colleges of education appeared to have no impact on test scores, Whitehurst reported.

To set the parameters for the study of teacher education, Whitehurst invited participation from the Kennedy Kreiger Institute on special education, the American Enterprise Institute, the Thomas B. Fordham Foundation, the Teaching Commission, and the National Council of Teacher Quality. These groups are a who's who of conservative think tanks on education—all favor alternative routes to teacher certification. Representing universities were two deans, one of whom is the dean of Penn State University, where I work. Dean Monk was to represent the American Association of Colleges of Teacher Education. He is not a teacher educator; rather, his specialty is school finance and economics. He has completed studies on the effects of certification in mathematics at the secondary level. Faculty in our college were a bit nervous that he was their representative. Upon his return from the first meeting (September 20, 2004), he reported:

> There was much discussion at the meeting about what counts as "scientific research." The panel is a diverse group with different views about what counts as evidence. There seems to be a willingness to embrace a broad conception of evidence, but there is no denying that experimental and quasi-experimental designs are favored. There is some irony here since the earlier Flexner Study of medical education (which is the supposed prototype for this study) was anything but an experimental type of study.[62]

Irony is an understatement to say the least. In 1910, the Carnegie Foundation hired Alexander Flexner, a former school principal who wrote a book critical of the regular college curricula, to conduct a nationwide study of medical schools.[63] By his own admission, Flexner knew little about medical education or procedures of laboratory sciences. To complete the study, he allegedly visited 175 medical schools across the country in a little more than eight months. While that may seem a fast pace by today's standards, it would be an impossible pace by train, the fastest means available to Flexner. Eight months to visit 175 schools allowed a little more than one and a half days to travel to and examine each medical school. His conclusion that American medical education was disgraceful and unscientific was made before he started the study. His recommendations that admission standards should be raised and the medical curriculum should be changed to two years of laboratory work followed by two years of apprenticeship in clinical practice could not be based on his knowledge of medical education or careful observation of programs. His exemplar programs were at John Hopkins, his alma mater, and Vanderbilt (whose medical dean was Flexner's neighbor). Backed by Carnegie and Rockefeller money, however, Flexner's suggestions led to the closings of one-third of all medical schools in the country and four-fifths of the schools that educated black doctors. Flexner's curriculum directed medical schooling for nearly seventy years and still influences all medical school organizations. Although only the weather service can predict the future, it appears that the director of reading research at the National Institute for Child Health and Human Development will have his wish to "blow up colleges of education" granted as the federal authorities work to bring teacher education in line with the official definitions of reading and science first published in the Reading Excellence Act.

The State's Role in the One Best Method

Since 1980, reading education has faced three competing political ideologies. Reagan's conservatism stressed authority during reading instruction, proposing a return to traditional practices in which texts and teachers were in complete charge of meaning. Reagan and his administration worked diligently to undermine the authority of public schools because they believed that schools imparted the liberal principles of the 1960s. Clinton's neoliberalism highjacked Reagan's agenda during the aftermath of the *Nation at Risk* report, which pushed school reform beyond the conservative fundamentalist Christians. Clinton sought world-class standards and testing programs in reading that would "make sure that our children are ready for the twenty-first century" (Clinton's Wyandotte speech). Clinton's educational policies were designed to remake schools in a form that he understood to be the organization of the future—open, mercurial, and aimed at serving business. As a neoconservative, George W. Bush brokered policy requiring states and schools to take responsibility for students' achievement, admonishing teachers to deliver test scores or lose their jobs to private enterprises. Wielding the only club available to the federal government, Bush sought to achieve alignment among schools, teacher education programs, and federal officials through financial incentives for those who complied and sanctions against those who resisted.

Although these ideological differences should have afforded schools, teachers, and students different opportunities and constraints within reading programs, they did not. All three positions rejected the liberal principles that government is responsible for the development and well-being of its citizens and, therefore, should provide services for all citizens equally. Since schooling is one of the last large-scale, liberal social projects in America, it was a target for reorganization and reduction. Each administration in its own way attempted to undermine the liberal notion that schools are a public good worthy of continued government attention and funding. Reading education served as a primary lever in these efforts to create doubt about the purpose and worth of American public schools. Within twenty-five years, the administrations moved reading education from a model based on well-educated teachers who were able to make decisions about curriculum and student learning to a highly rationalized system for reading instruction based on commercially scripted lessons and standardized assessments.

A Nation at Risk, America Reads, the Reading Excellence Act, and No Child Left Behind assume that American teachers are not teaching children and youth to read. The rhetoric surrounding these documents states that reading levels are plummeting, with more than forty million Americans unable to read. Although there are certainly problems with reading programs in American schools, it is not true that schools are failing to teach reading. Test scores for reading have remained relatively steady over the last thirty years.[64] Moreover, American students read well in comparisons with their peers internationally. The United States ranks second only to Finland at the fourth- and eighth-grade levels on international surveys. There are reading achievement score gaps between rich and poor, minority and white, English-speaking and English-learning, able and disabled students, but those gaps also exist in income, health care, and housing as well. The test scores represent, but do not cause, those social gaps. If lack of success on learning to read caused the social gaps, then the closing of the reading achievement score gap between males and females would have closed the income gap between men and women. But women earn only 73 percent as much as men in similar jobs. The federal government could do something about those social gaps, if citizens held it responsible. Closing those social gaps would close the achievement gaps before the 2014 deadline. It's an ideological battle.

Chapter Six

The Business of Reading

"Paper or plastic?"

Beneath this existential crisis at the end of every contemporary grocery checkout line lies the triumph of scientific management. "Would you like fries with your order?" harkens the same laurels. "Patrick Shannon? You have been preapproved . . ." Each of these statements is scripted in order to control the initiation and responses of service workers across the country and, now thanks to globalization, around the world.[1] The control, as Frederick Taylor explained at the turn of the last century, improves the efficiency and effectiveness of the service to be provided as well as ensures its quality. Because success of service work often hinges on the quality of social interactions between server and served, employers regiment their workers' speech and movements. In *Fast Food, Fast Talk*, Robin Leidner characterized the choreography of working the McDonald's drive-through window.[2]

Greet the Customer—Welcome to McDonalds
Take the order—May I take your order. Would you like . . . with that?
Assemble the order
Receive payment—Four dollars and forty-eight cents please
Present the order
Thank the customer—Thank you, have a nice day, and visit again soon

Within this exchange, the worker follows the script in order to expedite service because, quite simply, time is money. McDonald's statistics suggest that unit sales increase one percent for every six seconds shaved from the drive-through transactions.[3] In order to shave seconds, some McDonald's restaurants now outsource drive-through order taking by using central call centers away from the building rather than cashiers at the restaurant. Starbucks' management has data that suggest that greeting customers within thirty seconds of their entry to the store nearly doubles the likelihood of repeat business. In order to beat their competition, fast-food businesses and retail chains employ efficiency experts to continuously hone their operations. The scripting of talk and movement, which Taylor labeled the instructional card of scientific management, is just one twist to direct service workers in the production of company profits.

This call may be recorded to ensure quality.

Because the speed and precision of workers' words and actions translate into sales and profits within highly competitive businesses, employers monitor the words and actions of their workers. The traditional gaze of the foreman in manufacturing plants of old has been transformed into cameras, digital codes, voice recording, and even fake customers in modern corporations. These sources of surveillance provide employers with a sampling of workers' words and actions, and by reviewing these data, employers can track the performances of each worker on each assignment during each day of work. Such processes enable employers to provide continuous feedback to their employees in order to maximize their productivity. Because employees don't know when they might be "sampled," they stick to the script at all times.[4] In this way, corporate words and actions become their words and actions, and over time, these practices appear normal within the workplace.

Employment statistics suggest that the majority of American workers are subject to these aspects of scientific management within their employment. Although jobs in manufacturing have decreased from 35 percent in 1945 to 12 percent in 2005, 42 percent face demands for scripted speech and actions within their service work.[5] Even physicians working within managed care have remarked on the scientific management of their time, actions, and words with patients in order to maintain the steady flow of bodies through the system. Despite the rhetoric to the contrary about the new high-skill, high-wage jobs emerging within the global economy, the scripting of words and behaviors for employment is likely to increase. According to the U.S. Department of Labor's report *Tomorrow's Jobs—2004 to 2014*, most new jobs will be created within the service sector.[6]

retail sales
registered nurse
postsecondary teachers
customer service
janitor

wait-staff

home health aides

nurses aides

operations managers (not requiring engineering degree)

home care and maintenance

Each of these jobs could be classified as service work, and therefore, each could be subject to scripts for efficiency and effectiveness. While each could involve some specialized training for employees in order to qualify for the position, none requires the world-class academic standards that business leaders have called for since the 1980s.[7] In fact, none of these jobs appears to demand high skill or offer high wages. With few exceptions these jobs seem to make modest literacy demands on workers beyond the ability to follow the contemporary version of instructional cards of the modern scientifically managed workplace.[8] This is not to disparage the jobs or the workers who fill them, but to comment directly upon the rhetoric surrounding business leaders' calls for school reform and their active participation in federal, state, and local district plans for schooling in America. In this chapter, I describe that involvement, focusing on the success of those leaders in defining the problems of education and reestablishing the classroom as a market for basal readers and other commercially prepared materials, the one best system for teaching reading.

The Business of Schooling

At the turn of the nineteenth century, businessmen sought a school system that would prepare students to work in an increasingly industrialized society. They proposed that schools be remade in the image of industry, employing time management principles, measuring the effectiveness of teaching and learning, and funding decisions based on productivity and efficiency. Because industry would be based on divisions of labor, separating mental and physical activities, schooling should include academic tracks for students who would enter employment at appropriate levels for their abilities and temperaments. In order to determine which track was best suited for each student, educational psychologists developed tests to sort students scientifically.

Throughout the century, public schools more or less complied with these proposals, developing vocational education, academic tracks, standardized tests, special education, and compensatory schooling laws to ensure universal opportunity. When the curriculum veered too sharply toward either academics or self-awareness, business leaders and political pundits would call for correction, and schools would list back toward the industrial model.[9] When in the 1950s and 1960s, the courts acknowledged that some groups were systematically excluded or poorly served, then the federal government attempted legislative and policy remedies to ensure that all were subject to public education.[10] These educational moves were complemented by civil rights legislation and the War on Poverty to provide political and economic support for disadvantaged groups in order to enable them to participate in educational decisions by voting and in school life because the were adequately fed, housed, and cared for.[11] Although by no means perfect, the American public school system was at least partially responsible for the rise of the American economy across the first two-thirds of the century.[12] Amount of education was directly tied to income level as high school (and then college) graduates filled the ranks of middle managers within the large industrial bureaucracies that planned and supervised American production. Overall, American businessmen were pleased with American schools through the 1960s.

> Many Americans who graduated from the public school system before 1965 feel they received a very adequate education. After all, our education prepared us to hold almost any position in U. S. society. I personally, am a graduate of the Chicago public schools and the University of Illinois. Today, my fellow classmates are architects, judges, bankers, lawyers, engineers, school administrators, teachers, ministers, professors, doctors, business executives, government officials, and social workers. No other country has logged such an impressive record in educating the masses. The education system provided us, the children of working class families, with the opportunity to move into some of the most responsible and exciting positions in our society. We are grateful.[13]

In "The Human Capital Century," Claudia Goldin attributes the U.S. economic advantage over the rest of the world to the American investment in universal secondary education.[14] She notes that many developing nations are now following that model. She characterizes the first half of the twentieth century as a time when "education ran faster than technology," enabling workers to innovate, productivity to rise, and the possibility of full employment. In this way, universal secondary education in the United States closed the income gap between classes and invented a middle class. Goldin argues that since 1970, however, technology has run faster than education, shifting work from humans to machines and quelling the need for universal education. Since that time, Goldin observes, the virtues of universal secondary education in the United States—publicly funded, managed by numerous small fiscally independent districts, open and forgiving, academic yet practical curricula, and secular in control—have now become vices.

The more public display of business leaders' interest in public school during the last two decades should be interpreted within this context. Business leaders have considered schools to be a tool for the production of worker dispositions since the 1880s, and recently, they have recognized the double bind that U.S. corporations face.[15] Until the 1980s, most corporations were organized for an economy that was quickly fading away, and they needed to shed workers as well as train new workers in order to stay competitive with quickly emerging economies on the Pacific Rim and in a united Europe. In order to accomplish this transformation, business leaders sought to reorganize schools along the lines of the corporate organizations that they imagined were needed—small, flexible, private structures that could quickly adapt to the changing markets in a global economy. Business leaders defined schools' primary market as American business. After the *Nation at Risk* report in 1983, many business leaders began direct interventions into schools. These initiatives came in four waves and became more prescriptive in each succeeding one.

- Corporations attempted partnerships with schools and educational agencies to improve preschool programs, science and mathematics achievement, mentoring programs, and high school completion rates in urban areas (e.g., Grand Metropolitan Inc.'s Kids and the Power of Work; Amoco's Science Enrichment; Coopers & Lybrand's mentoring project in Orlando; and Coca-Cola Foundation's Valued Youth Program).

- Increasingly, business leaders began to focus on the loose organizational structures of public schools, which lacked the characteristics of well-run companies: a well-defined mission, a coherent management theory, an organizational plan, and protocols for evaluation (e.g., Rochester Business Education Task Force, Chicago's Corporate/Community Schools of America, and UNUM Corporation's Transformational Outcome-Based System).

- Frustrations mounting with the slow speed of school reform, business leaders began to echo conservative pundits who advocated that the only thing to save public education was to develop systems of competition. This concern manifested itself in corporate promotion of school choice programs (e.g., Wisconsin's public funding for private schools and Minnesota's public choice programs) and calls for world-class standards, which would send ready-made workers to the new high-wage, high-skill jobs to be created among the new international corporations.

- On the heals of this advocacy, business leaders developed action committees that would work strategically with government agencies to ensure that business concerns and solutions would be not only heard but implemented (e.g., Committee for Economic Development's 1985 report *Investing in Our Children: Business and the Public Schools* and the Business Roundtable Ad Hoc Committee on Education's *Role of Business on Education Reform: Blueprint for Action*, 1988).[16]

After three years of continuous media coverage of *A Nation at Risk*'s charge that America had fallen behind other nations economically and public schools were to blame, the Carnegie Forum on Education and Economy polled the "American public" and declared the public and business leaders were ready to outsource manufacturing jobs to other countries and raise the academic standards for school in order to make American youth ready to assume the high-skill, high-wage jobs that would emerge from the new American information economy. Although the forum's sample of the public seemed slight (1,500 polled in a population of 180,000,000), the number of business leaders (202 out of the 1,000 largest American corporations) foretold of the overrepresentation of business leaders in later education policy groups.

It is clear from these sizable majorities that the American people and business leaders are both convinced that the way for this country to become competitive with foreign businesses, especially the Japanese, is not to try to revert back in time and try to compete with unskilled and low skilled labor. But instead, they believe, the U. S. should face up to exporting or automating such lower skill jobs and production activities and turn instead to creating whole new opportunities on a base of a labor pool that is far more sophisticated and far better trained to perform those highly skilled tasks that would once again make the U.S. competitive in the world. Of course, this also means developing a whole array of fully competitive products and services which in turn will allow high wages and salaries and a continued high standard of living. But both groups surveyed are prepared to face this challenge.

In turn, to achieve this objective, big majorities are also convinced a whole new approach to educating and training the American work force must be undertaken. Most are convinced this is the only real answer to the kind of economic competition the country now faces from abroad. By 78–20 percent among the public and 85–13 percent among business leaders, they believe this.[17]

Beginning with the 1989 Education Summit at the National Governors Association in Charlottesville, Virginia, business leaders took a leading role in the school reform movement. In fact, the *Business Roundtable Educational Reform Goals of 1989* preceded the *America 2000 Communiqué* that was negotiated during President Bush's educational summit later that year.[18] Both documents were remarkably similar. Each was directed toward raising academic standards and outcomes with strong testing programs to hold schools accountable for student achievement. Moreover, both emphasized school readiness programs, professional development for teachers, and increased use of technology. The BRT reform goals favored a more explicit business model with rewards and penalties for individual school performances, provisions for social and health care services for low-income students, and decentralization of decisionmaking (based upon a national mandate for improvement). The summit's communiqué left more room for negotiation among stakeholders with vague statements about clear lines of accountability, authority, and readiness for school. The feds also mentioned the conservative agenda of functional literacy and safe, drug-free schools, while omitting the idea of governmental support of increased social and health services altogether. The similarities were not coincidental, as the BRT sent representatives to the NGA Education Summit as the opening act of it's ten-year campaign to reform American public schools.

In 1995, the BRT published its nine essential components of a successful education system: standards, performance assessment, school accountability, school autonomy, professional development, learning readiness, parent involvement, technology, and safety and discipline (note the continued absence of literacy but assimilation of the government's concern for safe schools). And in 1996, the NGA and the BRT sponsored a second educational summit, which was held at the IBM Executive Conference Center in Palisades, New York. "It is hard to overestimate the importance of the simple fact that the Summit was the product of private not public interest."[19] The planning committee included the CEOs from IBM, AT&T, Bell South, Eastman Kodak, Procter & Gamble, and Boeing, but no professional educators. "The constitution of the 1996 Education Summit sent a clear signal, viz., that the 'professional educators,' whatever their individual talents, as a group have failed the nation's public schools and now it's time for someone else to try."[20] The business leaders were clearly frustrated because initial efforts to purchase national standards from professional educational organizations yielded both mixed products and skepticism about a federal interference with state authority.[21]

In order to coordinate their campaign to bring standards, assessment, and accountability to every state, the participants in the second educational summit established Achieve, a nonprofit organization charged to act as an advocate and clearinghouse of data for the summit's agenda. Achieve's board of directors was composed of five governors and six CEOs, and its funding was secured with donations from corporate foundations (e.g., Gates, GE, and Prudential) and corporations (e.g., Boeing, IBM, and Washington Mutual). Achieve became the sponsor of subsequent educational summits in 1999, 2001, and 2005. Acting on its basic charge, Achieve has worked with state education departments in many projects to improve the quality of standards and assessment and to provide the public with means to judge the relative success of state efforts to address the summit's policies for school reform. Part of this work has been to subcontract with university professors and research centers to design the structures and tools necessary to make progress.[22] Since that time, Achieve has written its own sets of standards and benchmarks in mathematics and English language arts, setting minimum parameters for postsecondary education and employment.[23]

After the 1996 Education Summit, BRT asked its members to work state by state, offering their expertise and guidance to state governments in order to develop standards, assessments, and accountability systems. Following *The Business Roundtable Participation Guide: A Primer for Business on Education*, corporate leaders within states would meet with their state officials in order to explain the economic realities of school reform in their jurisdiction. Simply put, these business leaders leveraged their economic importance in the state, describing that if they were unable to find appropriately educated workers within the state, then the corporations would move their headquarters or plants to where they could locate a suitable workforce. By the end of the BRT's ten-year campaign, business leaders could point with pride to success within forty-five states that produced academic standards in reading, writing, science, and history and forty-eight states that tested all students in order to check progress.[24]

Because of that success, the Education Summit of 1999 could focus on setting "rewards and consequences" for teachers, students, and schools based on the student outcomes of state assessments. President Clinton, twenty-four governors, thirty-three business leaders, nineteen state superintendents and education commissioners, and thirty-five invited guests attended the Achieve-sponsored conference held again at IBM's executive conference center. Among the invited guests, for the first time, were heads of teacher unions, state school board officials, and the head of the National Urban League (the only nonwhite participant). Again, no principals, teachers, or students were invited. For the first time, the participants outlined specific methods to improve the quality of teachers: professional development tied directly to standards and testing, alternative certification to bring competition into teacher education, and merit pay based on test scores. Reiterating President Clinton's America Reads goal, the participants affirmed that "virtually all children [could] read well by third grade" if schools would employ methods demonstrated to bring test results. The 1999 action statement set the tone for further discussion concerning the need for there to be teeth in state policies.

> Accountability is the cornerstone of standards-based reform. To date, our education system has operated with few incentives for success and even fewer consequences for failure. The job security and compensation of teachers and administrators have, in large measure, been disconnected from teachers' success in improving student achievement. Students, except for the relative handful seeking admission to highly selective colleges and universities, have had little reason to work hard in high school because access to further education or employment has not depended on their performance in school. This must change.[25]

The 2001 and 2005 National Education Summits are nearly indistinguishable from the Bush administration's No Child Left Behind policy, which employed each of BRT's nine essential components of a successful school system. The 2001 summit was held only a month after the terrorist attacks on the World Trade Center and Pentagon and only months before NCLB became law. Although the participants celebrated the reforms in schools since their 1999 action plan, the leadership expressed continued dismay with the speed at which the changes were progressing. They called for a mechanism that would accelerate the development of accountability systems across states in order that schools would catch up to what they characterized as rapid changes in job requirements in American business. The 2005 National Education Summit marked a turning away from the state-by-state agenda that brought standards and testing to nearly every state even before NCLB. "Improving high schools one school or one state at a time is not moving fast enough," explained Arthur Ryan, CEO of Prudential Financial and cochair of Achieve.[26] The Summit announced its support of Achieve's efforts to provide national guidelines of academics required by colleges and businesses. The American Diploma Project would coordinate the reform efforts in thirteen states in order "to restore the value of the high school diploma" (Bob Taft, governor of Ohio and Achieve cochair).

Hoping to duplicate the successful bridging of schooling to business during the first half of the human-capital century, business leaders took bold steps to enhance federal oversight of the reformation of the American public school system. Blaming schools for not keeping pace with global economics, business leaders set to change the management, raise the academic standards, induce market competition, enforce high-stakes testing, remake teacher training, and introduce technological innovation. At each step after the original *A Nation at Risk* report, business leaders seemed to be better organized and one to several steps ahead of the federal government, leading many to assume that business was the driving force for the changes. To stay steps ahead and in control of the agenda, business leaders used corporate foundations to fund their meetings, Achieve, their reports, and their school initiatives.[27] As the federal government pulled further and further away from social responsibilities to its citizens from the Reagan to the George W. Bush administrations (with only slight relief during the Clinton years), business leaders stepped forward to put their stamp on one of the few remaining governmental social programs.[28] These were not bold new actions; business leaders have directed public schools for at least a century. Rather, the retreat of government from its traditional responsibility made the steps more transparent as business leaders sought to manipulate American social structures in order to control the costs of doing business.

Schools as Markets

Nearly $400 billion dollars are spent on K–12 public school students every year. Those funds support each of fifty million students with approximately $7,500. The funding pays for the buildings, all hardware that's in them and around them, the salary and benefits of all who work in schools, and curriculum supplies. Although the cost of Medicare is beginning to rival its expense in some states, public school education assumes the largest part of most state budgets and more than $50 billion in federal funds each year. Whichever way you examine them, schools are lucrative markets for a variety of businesses—lawyers, architects, construction companies, furniture manufacturers, computer hardware and software industries, and textbook publishers. Since the 1980s, school reforms have expanded considerably the textbook, testing, tutoring, and technology markets, providing financial incentives for businesses to participate in policy development at state and federal levels in order to keep markets open and growing.

Textbooks

The rise of whole language challenged the authority of commercially prepared basal materials in elementary school classrooms. Because those materials separated planning from instruction and reduced reading to skill development, whole language advocates argued that basals and all their components were not helpful for teaching or learning reading. Rather than identifying the one best system through which all children could learn to read, basal materials imposed a system that discouraged children from the natural development of reading that was taking place authentically in children's everyday lives. Teachers' manuals gave the wrong information on teaching, learning, and reading. Children's anthologies provided manipulated texts designed to practice skills rather than inform or engage readers; workbooks diverted children's attention from authentic uses of literacy; and basal tests simply fulfilled the assumptions that the publishers had made about learning and reading. According to many whole language advocates, basal materials should be exchanged for children's literature, magazines, and newspapers as well as paper and pencils, if children were to learn how to read and write.[29] Knowledgeable teachers, then, would respond appropriately to students' approximations in order to help students progress toward sophisticated literacy.

This threat to publishers' dominance of elementary reading programs was met with two responses. First, reading experts worked to refute the whole language claims about basals and basal-directed instruction.[30] For example, basal authors Jim Baumann and Dick Allington criticized the charges against teachers' manuals; Jim Flood and Diane Lapp, also basal authors, challenged the critiques concerning the limited types of text included in basal materials; and basal author Jim Hoffman and others argued skill pages were fewer and isolated decoding was deemphasized in the revised teachers' manuals. Each proclaimed that if the criticism of basals had been valid in the past, then it was no longer valid within the latest editions. To the undecided, Hoffman explained, "to others, who perhaps take a less sinister view of schooling, the new basals may be seen as an enhanced resource for teachers opening a new set of possibilities to help move their students along the path to literacy." In the first volume of the *Handbook of Reading Research* in 1984, basal reading materials were considered indirectly in two chapters—beginning reading instruction and managing classrooms.[31] The second volume, however, devoted a chapter to the publishing industry and textbooks, which affirmed the importance of commercial reading materials but also pointed to the commercial strategy that was already under way:

> Much is known about reading textbooks from historical and educational research, and most of it points to the central importance of reading textbooks in the teaching and learning of reading—from colonial times to the present. Research has played an increasing role in the design, selection and use of reading textbooks in the classroom. However, the large investments and competition among publishers have made the role of marketing of state and local adoption committees and of teacher preferences equally, if not more, influential in the design and content of readers.[32]

Second, in between the two editions of the handbook, the California Reading Initiative took effect, in which California refused to purchase any commercial reading materials for instruction that did not include authentic children's literature appropriate for the multiple cultural backgrounds of California students and did not move away from a decoding-first format in order to enable students to use what they knew about language to learn to read.[33] The threat that California—the largest market for commercial reading materials—would not purchase any of the existing basal programs sent shock waves through the publishing industry. In order to hold on to relative market shares, most basal publishers quickly adopted the language of whole language. Even the titles of the new versions signaled change: Treasury of Literature (Hartcourt, Brace, and Janovich, 1993), The Literature Experience (Houghton Mifflin, 1993), A New View (Macmillan McGraw-Hill, 1993), Celebrate Reading (Scott, Foresman, 1993), and New Dimensions in the World of Reading (Silver Burdett-Ginn, 1993).

The new versions used the terms of whole language, process writing, and literature-based reading as if they were interchangeable and not anchored to particular theories and sets of research. The students' readers became "children's literature anthologies"; seatwork became "workshops" in which students completed their "journals" (workbooks and worksheets). Teachers' directions were labeled "invitations," and correct answers to direct questions were dubbed children's "personal responses to literature." Completed assignments were to be kept in folders marked "portfolios." Following the kindergarten and first-grade lessons were direct representations of "emergent reading." At each turn, basal authors and publishers did their best to rename traditional basal practices with the terms used by their critics. Advocates of whole language responded sharply that the structure of basals had not changed at all.[34] Teachers were still to follow plans that others had prepared for them; students were directed to perform exercises for instructional purposes only; and tests still determined what parts of each lesson mattered for both teachers and students. But for many, and this is a great failing of the whole language movement, these renamed commercial reading materials became whole language instruction across the United States.[35] Although the percent of teachers using basals during this period was said to decline, more than 80 percent of elementary school teachers admitted that they continued to rely heavily on basals while professing to be whole language teachers.

Whole language and literature basals held sway with publishers until the mid-1990s when the California Reading Initiative and the whole language philosophy it promoted was blamed for the continued low NAEP scores in reading.[36] Supported by a swell of religious groups who objected to whole language's decentering of meaning from the text[37] and the Republicans' successful attempts to counter President Clinton's America Reads Initiative, publishing companies put an abrupt end to the whole language terminology in their promotional materials and basal products.[38] A survey of the advertisements in the International Reading Association's journal for elementary school practitioners demonstrates the change in 1998. And with the first mention in the Reading Excellence Act that reading instruction must be scientifically based on experimental research, publishers began their campaign to demonstrate the superior science within their basal materials, leaving the language of whole language on the editors' and layout designers' tables.[39]

As the language of federal policies became more precise about how science would be defined in federal programs, the terminology used to refer to commercial materials changed from "basals" to "core materials." The term *basal* had been compromised in two ways. First, for twenty years, reading experts had criticized publishers' reluctance to incorporate the latest research findings quickly into their pages.[40] Publishers found it difficult to proclaim materials that had been labeled slow to incorporate scientific findings as being the new research-based solutions that the federal government sought. Second, the basal publishers had just promoted their wares as whole language—the target of the new scientifically based policies. The term *core reading program* replaced *basal* in the early parts of the G. W. Bush administration within the language surrounding the No Child Left Behind law. As one of three federally sponsored organizations that were to oversee the dissemination and evaluation of Reading First, the Oregon Reading First Center defined the new term.

> The selection and adoption of an effective, research-based core reading program in the primary grades is a critical step in the development of an effective schoolwide reading initiative. The investment in identifying a core program that aligns with research and fits the needs of learners in your school will reap long-term benefits for children's reading acquisition and development.
>
> Historically, core-reading programs have been referred to as basal reading programs in that they serve as the "base" for reading instruction. Adoption of a core does not imply that other materials and strategies are not used to provide a rich, comprehensive program of instruction. The core program, however, should serve as the primary reading program for the school and the expectation is that all teachers within and between the primary grades will use the core program as the base of reading instruction. Such programs may or may not be commercial textbook series.[41]

The Oregon Reading First Center wrote a consumers' guide to evaluate core reading programs and completed an analysis of nine. The results favored

Reading Mastery, Open Court, and Houghton Mifflin because those programs systematically addressed the same topics as the National Reading Panel's report: phonemic awareness, phonics, fluency, vocabulary, and comprehension. Elaine Garan offered another rationale for these selections.[42] The compilers of the guide were paid consultants of the commercial publishers during the writing of the latest editions of the core reading programs (nee basals). Just as in the past, the publishing companies hired the new reading experts associated with scientifically based reading instruction as defined by the federal government (e.g., Barbara Foorman, Marilyn Adams, Louisa Moats, Linnea Ehri, Joseph Torgesen, Ed Kame'enui, and Deborah Simmons). In this way, people who made decisions about reading instruction nationally were in the employ of publishing companies. The appearance of conflict of interest provoked a congressional investigation in 2005–6 as well as inquiries from the American Association of Publishers. "As an industry, we're not trying to create an un-level playing field."[43]

According to Stephen Metcalf, the near federal endorsement of these three core reading programs caught stockbrokers' attention, making Macmillan McGraw-Hill (publisher of Mastery Reading and Open Court), Houghton Mifflin, and Harcourt General growth stocks.[44] In fact, they were labeled "Bush stocks" because of the G. W. Bush administration's tendency toward crony capitalism in which personal friendships influenced the decisions over the awarding of contracts. For example, members of the McGraw family and employees of their publishing company figured prominently in the Bush family's literacy initiatives (Barbara Bush Foundation, the Texas miracle," Reading First Initiative). Their publishing consultants testify regularly before Congress: their CEOs serve the Business Roundtable educational programs; and Harold McGraw III served on the G. W. Bush presidential transition team.

Tests

The declaration that "results matter" in *A Nation at Risk* was predicated on the assumption that reading ability could be easily and accurately measured. Calls for accountability concerning results assumed that reading ability could be counted objectively. These assumptions were based on nearly one hundred years of psychometric research conducted in order to establish the one best test of reading ability. This work led to diagnostic tests for students who seemed slow to learn to read; norm-referenced achievement tests that would compare reading levels among students; criterion-referenced tests of specific skills that had been taught; and aptitude tests (many of which later were decided to be achievement tests) that could be used to predict success in further schooling. Each of these tests was commercially available to schools at the time of the

"educational crisis." However, none was deemed appropriate to meet the demands for high-stakes tests in order to determine students' proficiency on the
world-class standards in each state. Rather, new tests were to be written that
would be aligned completely with state standards in reading, math, writing, and
eventually science. These new tests would be uniform across an entire state to
afford cross-district comparisons. Business leaders were directly involved in
articulating this need for new tests. And representatives of test publishing companies were present as the U.S. Congress, and then state legislatures worked
their ways toward this decision. According to Bruce Hunter of the American
Association of School Administrators,

> I've been lobbying on education issues since 1982, but the test pub-
> lishers have been active at a level I've never seen before. At every hear-
> ing, every discussion, the big test publishers are always present with at
> least one lobbyist, sometimes more.[45]

This process produced two markets into which established publishers
and new entrepreneurs jumped aggressively—sale of new tests and new test
preparation tools to improve student performance on those new tests. The
demand for new state tests altered a fifty-year-old industry in which publishing companies produced norm-referenced tests that they sold to individual
school districts. With production costs of approximately $4 million and net
sales of $20 million across the five- to eight-year cycle, these tests were profit-
able because a single test form could be used across the entire cycle and
throughout the United States. The new market, however, required criterion-
referenced tests aligned with each state's standards that could be released to the
public after each administration. These new demands force a 30 to 70 percent
decline in the norm-referenced market.[46] However, the testing requirements
of NCLB—annual testing in reading in grades 3 through 8 and then again in
high school—more than compensated for this decline. For example, forty-five
million student tests were needed during the 2005 school year. More than
eleven million new tests were required in twenty-three states in order to comply with NCLB by 2006. Conservative estimates of total testing market are
placed as high as $2.3 billion annually (of the $500 billion spent annually on
elementary and secondary schools in the United States).

Five companies occupied 90 percent of the testing market in 2005:
Pearson Education Measurement, ETS, CTB/McGraw-Hill, Harcourt Assessment, and Houghton Mifflin (Riverside). The market shares of each company
vary as they vie periodically for new state contracts. Pearson and ETS are relative newcomers to this group and both provide custom service, writing entirely
new tests that correspond to each set of state standards. The latter three continue to produce tests that can be sold across states with elaborate explanations

of how their tests fit the states' standards. In 2004, ETS found that its custom shop was expensive, as it lost $18 million on its three-year $175 million contract with California. The size of the market and its rapid expansion, however, have brought increased competition from start-up educational testing companies. For example, Pearson was successful in 2004, winning the Michigan contract with a bid of $48 million, beating Data Recognition's $84 million and Measurement Inc.'s $114 million bids. The wide range in bids among the large and small companies demonstrates the continued dominance of the large companies within the field.

In order to reduce the risk to profits, however, companies have started to outsource much of the work of test writing. Many small testing companies began as subcontractors that specialized in one aspect of reading test construction. Although the larger companies continue to publish and distribute a high percentage of the reading tests, newer companies have assumed responsibility for many of the other steps in the testing process:

Content creation—Brown Publishing, WestEd, Victory Productions

Standards alignment—McREL, PLATO Learning, Words and Numbers

Psychometric evaluation—Pacific Metrics, Applied Measurement Professionals

Test delivery—Knowledge Analysis Technologies, Questar

Test scoring—Vantage Learning, Measurement Inc. Wireless Generation

Score analysis and reporting—Westat, the Grow Network

The rapid growth in demand and the retooling of the testing industry have caused a number of problems. First, industry, state departments, and local school districts have difficulty finding employees with psychometric expertise to write and evaluate the relative merits of these new tests. The accelerated schedules for testing under NCLB have strained the productive capacities of testing companies, forcing them to compete for expertise, causing knowledgeable state and school employees to accept lucrative employment with testing companies. Although this has been good for the individuals, public schools and state departments have experienced a void of these individuals, who can choose knowledgeably among the alternatives. Thus, the testing industry has little oversight and enjoys a sellers' market. Haste in production and lack of oversight have created problems in test alignment, scoring, and quick reporting. A series of lawsuits have followed each mishap, requiring school districts to build penalty clauses of all types into their testing contracts and testing publishers to seek federal and state protection from accountability lawsuits.[47]

In 2005, Congress began to investigate conflict of interest surrounding test selection. Most of the controversy focused on the Reading First initiative and the Dynamic Indicators of Basic Early Literacy Skills (DIBELS). Many school districts and state departments of education complained that they were forced to include this test within their battery of assessments or their proposal in order to become a Reading First program. Upon inspection, the government found that the same individuals who wrote the test were among the evaluators of its relative utility within the Reading First agenda and were also selected to oversee the deployment of Reading First programs across the country. In *Education Week*, Kathleen Manzo wrote: "the close oversight of the $1 billion-a-year program has allowed a handful of commercial reading programs, assessments, and consultants to reap much of that money, while others have been shut out of the competition, according to documents and confirmation by several state officials."[48]

The market is not limited to the sale and scoring of tests. NCLB included provisions for school districts to provide external tutors for students who did not make adequate yearly progress for two consecutive years. Shortly after the signing of the law, Adam Newman of Eduventures explained the optimism of the supplemental education services industry. "If companies like Sylvan, Kaplan, the Princeton Review, tutor.com and others can improve the performance of those students in greatest need of academic assistance, it will send a strong message regarding the way in which supplemental programs, in complement with traditional instruction, can assist all schools and students in achieving academic goals."[49] With 5 to 20 percent of all Title I funds to be devoted to tutoring, the potential profits were large. For example, Philadelphia schools had one hundred thousand eligible students with more than $23 million to spend on tutoring. Pennsylvania approved more than fifty providers of tutors split among nonprofit, for-profit, faith-based, and school district alternatives. Even the school-based alternatives were open to subcontracting with Princeton Review, Voyager, Kaplan, and Fast ForWord, signing contracts to provide services within the Philadelphia school district's extended-day program. Eugene Wade, a former Edison Schools vice president, reported that his Platform Learning invested "a couple of million" dollars in developing curriculum, recruiting and training teachers, reaching out to parents, computerizing student records, and acquiring sites from which to operate in Boston, New York, Camden, New Jersey, and Newark, New Jersey, as well as Philadelphia.[50] From the business point of view, a hundred thousand students scoring below proficiency on the state reading test is a signal for investors to move their money toward K–12 businesses.

NCLB allowed for considerable variation among the means for providing tutoring. In a press release, Nina Rees, then assistant deputy secretary of education, described the strengths of virtual tutoring programs in which the tutor and student never met face-to-face.[51] After the note that no tutoring program had ever been evaluated independently in order to demonstrate its benefits, Rees stated that virtual tutors were "often certified teachers, retired teachers, professors and graduate school students." Once hired, she explained, all tutors completed a rigorous training and certification program that included technology education, training in online tutoring etiquette, mock tutoring sessions, and professional development seminars. Every tutor passed a full background check. Within some virtual tutoring firms, however, employees need not be on the North American continent. Nancy Van Meter, director of the Center on Accountability and Privatization at the American Federation of Teachers, suggested that the outsourcing of tutors raised questions about the efficacy of virtual tutoring, "even more dramatically than we've seen here in the States."[52] The Education Industry Association, which includes more than six hundred educational business members, agreed that "US taxpayers should not be supporting off-shore educational staff."[53]

Getting the Business for Twenty-five Years

Profit is the goal of business. This fact should not come as a shock to anyone. If business is interested in a project or institution, there is a potential for it to bring profits in the near or distant future. Many lament that American corporations, if there are such things any longer with a global economy, look mostly to the near future for profits in order to remain attractive to new investors. Business leaders' interest in schooling in general and in reading instruction in particular should be understood in this light. Schools and reading instruction must adapt to new historical conditions, business leaders argue, or they will fail to provide effective and efficient workers to business. And if there are enhanced and new marketing opportunities for business to receive more and more of the public funding for schooling and reading instruction, then that's an incentive for business to become intimately involved in both. Although economists like to explain that the good products will drive the bad from the market in education, we know from many examples in the automobile, food, and drug industries that such economic theories do not often materialize. Think of Hummers, Count Chocula, and Vioxx. The definition of what makes a product good is very slippery for each. Buyers beware.

Business leaders are involved because they want workers who are more predictable, efficient, and productive, as these attributes make companies more profitable. They want workers who are interchangeable and adaptable when markets twist and turn and business must head in different directions. Such workers reduce the considerable risks to companies' capital. Without these workers, business leaders fear for their companies, but also for the workers who will not be able to fend for themselves when the creative destruction of capitalism renders their skills obsolete within an economy that does not care for them and with a government that values individual responsibility. Business leaders preach self-interest for companies and workers because they cannot care for workers individually or collectively and remain attractive to Wall Street investors. And business leaders look for the help of government to hide this not so little secret by allocating authority to business values through educational policy. NCLB is the latest and to this point most visible artifact of this help. But it is not a change in direction from a different, better relationship between business and government around schooling or reading instruction. Business leaders have always attempted to remake schools in their own image and have used different levels of government and science to do so.

Chapter Seven

The Scientific Solution

(18) SCIENTIFICALLY BASED RESEARCH STANDARDS—(A) the term "scientifically based research standards" means research standards that—

    (i)   apply rigorous, systematic, and objective methodology to obtain reliable and valid knowledge relevant to education activities and programs; and

    (ii) present findings and make claims that are appropriate to and supported by the methods that have been employed.

(B) The term includes, appropriate to the research being conducted—

    (i)   employing systematic, empirical methods that draw on observation or experiment;

    (ii) involving data analyses that are adequate to support the general findings;

    (iii) relying on measurements or observational methods that provide reliable data;

    (iv) making claims of causal relationships only in random assignment experiments or other designs (to the extent such designs substantially eliminate plausible competing explanations for the obtained results);

    (v) ensuring that studies and methods are presented in sufficient detail and clarity to allow for replication or, at a minimum, to offer the opportunity to build systematically on the findings of the research;

    (vi) obtaining acceptance by a peer-reviewed journal or approval by a panel of independent experts through a comparably rigorous, objective, and scientific review; and

    (vii) using research designs and methods appropriate to the research question posed.[1]

These lines define the central term within the Educational Sciences Reform Act of 2002, which was designed to increase and enhance the role of science within public education. The act transformed the Office of Education Research and Improvement into the Institute for Education Science, charged with the development and dissemination of information about schools and learning that adhered to scientifically based research standards. The congressional preludes to the act—Reading Excellence Act, Castle Bill HR 4875, and No Child Left Behind—caused quite a stir among education and reading experts.[2] Some welcomed the emphases on experimentation, statistical significance, and randomized designs because these methods promised to direct education toward more predictable outcomes. Others criticized the Education Science Reform Act because it ignored several decades of concerns regarding a positivist frame for social science. These critics found their interpretivist research to be discredited as prescientific and banned from use in public schools.

The struggle over the definition and practices of science is centuries old. The modern, western version began at the turn of the sixteenth century, when the work of Galileo, Kepler, Brache, and others began to stretch the credulity of Scholastic interpretations of the nature of the heavens. Scholastic knowledge required expert interpretation of God's plans for the world and all that was in it. Scholastic scholars worked from Saint Thomas Aquinas' efforts to blend Aristotle's work with Christian theology. The result was a method of determining the truth through a process that favored the authority of the past: first, scripture or church precedent was interpreted to articulate God's rule for a particular situation; second, deductive reasoning was used to determine how that rule should be manifest in contemporary ideas, actions, and things; and finally, empirical evidence was sought to confirm the rule and its determination within everyday life. According to that system, the world became understandable to all because new information or concerns could be assimilated into existing knowledge. In Western Europe, the Catholic clergy and university professors performed these services for common people. At the turn of the sixteenth century, British politician Francis Bacon did not mince his words concerning his contempt for this approach and the failure of scientific inquiry to that point.

For fruits and work are as it were sponsors and sureties for the truth of philosophies. Now from these systems of the Greek and their ramifications through particular sciences there can hardly after the lapse of so many years be adduced a single experiment which tends to relieve and benefit the conditions of man.[3]

Intellectual historians credit Francis Bacon's work as among the first articulations of the modern mind—a rejection of the authority of custom, confidence in faith, and cyclical view of time in favor of the preeminence of empirical data, the power of inductive reasoning, and a progressive and linear conception of time.[4] Bacon argued that if people would use their senses systematically, then natural and physical laws could be induced without expert interpretation. In this way, Bacon flipped Scholastic methods of determining truth, placing observation of empirical evidence at the top. Through inductive reasoning, patterns within observations could be identified for testing in subsequent investigations. Once patterns were confirmed across time and place, then laws of nature could be induced. Hoping to avoid the fate of Galileo (threat of torture and house arrest for blasphemy), Bacon was careful and quick to explain that these newly discovered laws were God's work. Bacon labeled his suggestions for scientific practice Method, which he always capitalized in his writing, claiming that Method would render nature predictable, allowing it to be harnessed in order to make material improvements in peoples' lives.

Without established limits to what people could know about the world, there were no limits on the engineering of people's lives for the better. As a consequence, the notion of continuous progress over time could be imagined. Bad times would not necessarily follow good times—like one season follows another—because once the laws of nature were known, then improvements could always be made. Method not only changed understandings of truth but also changed conceptions of time, providing a new rationale for inquiry moving away from the search for God's plans toward the discovery of the systems of all things and beings to improve people's lives. Accordingly, methodical inquiry into the nature of things (and people) would bring progress for all. Bacon surmised that this modern mind would eventually tame both nature and society, reducing labor, increasing its productivity, and bringing prosperity to all. In order to ensure this progress, however, the new scientific method would have to be allowed free rein in its employment on all matters.

In his utopian travel narrative, The New Atlantis, Bacon proposed a social organization that would enable the scientific method to direct society.[5] He proposed a centrally organized research and development center (Solomon's House) in which specifically trained technicians would collect sense data and then submit them to analysts, who would table them and discuss their significance. In turn, these analysts would present their interpretations to theorists, who would develop them into greater axioms and, in time, natural laws. This hierarchical division of labor required differing talents and levels of expertise, but Bacon assured that the new hierarchy would not re-create the power structures of old Scholasticism, which relied on the authority of the past to protect the status quo. Rather, in the new Atlantis, the technicians who gathered the empirical data would actually drive the scientific process and therefore society, because without reliable data, the analysts and theorists would be idle, even socially and politically useless. Within his vision of small communities of less than one thousand, Bacon assumed twenty-four technicians would feed twelve analysts, who would defer to three theorists.

If you look carefully at the rhetoric surrounding the so-called reading wars over the last two decades, you can identify Bacon's charges against Scholasticism within the attempts by educational scientists to paint interpretivist and teacher research as unscientific. Although interpretivists and teachers might generate empirical data during their work, champions of experimental science argue those data are not systematically gathered, are not described enough to permit replication, and are not subjected to objective theoretical scrutiny, and therefore, the data cannot help to discover causal relationships in reading instruction. Rather, as characterized, teachers' data are simply testimony to good practice for others to read and interpret. In an article titled "Campaigns for Moving Research into Practice," University of Oregon professor Douglas Carnine criticized:

> Historically, public abhorrence of unpreparedness has triggered a metamorphosis in numerous professions: medicine, pharmacology, accounting, actuarial sciences and seafaring. The premetamorphosis state of an immature profession is characterized by (a) expertise based on the subjective judgments of the individual professional, (b) trust based on personal contact rather than on quantification, and (c) autonomy allowed by reliance on perceived expertise and trust that staves off standardized procedures based on experimental findings. . . .
>
> The metamorphosis results in movement toward a mature profession. This postmetamorphosis stage is characterized by the increasing use of scientific methods for determining efficacy: (a) a shift from judgments of individual experts to judgments constrained by quantified data that can be inspected by a broad audience, (b) less emphasis on personal trust and more emphasis on objectivity, and (c) diminished autonomy by experts and a greater role for standardized measures and procedures informed by scientific investigations. Education is just beginning to go through a metamorphosis from an immature to a mature profession.[6]

Carnine's remarks position educators as faithful followers of tradition (like the Scholastics), seeking authority and deferring to a select few who can translate the mysteries of learning and teaching reading for them. This combination of subjectivity and dependence, Carnine claims, keeps teaching from becoming an effective profession. Just as Bacon had before him, Carnine argues that scientific progress can be made only after the field reaches consensus on one best method for teaching reading. And Carnine calls for campaigns— "systematic aggressive action"—to hasten the metamorphosis within the field. To be more accurate, by 1999, the campaign was well under way to discredit the research base for whole language in order to restore scientific management of reading instruction.

This chapter examines three such campaigns to reinstate experimental science as the primary authority in reading education: standards; NICHD-sponsored studies of reading and reading instruction; and federally sponsored state-of-the-art reports on the teaching of reading. Although participants within these campaigns did not begin with a single goal in mind, their collective actions resulted in the passage of the Education Science Act of 2002, which defined science as experimentation, restricted the distribution of "unscientific" information to schools, and reserved all federal funds for school projects based on scientifically based research standards. It should be clear right from the start of this chapter that these efforts were political in nature rather than objective actions to determine truth because interpretivist epistemologies and ontologies were not and are not addressed in any of the deliberations and negotiations of policies. Rather, experimentation became privileged because it better met the needs of politicians and business leaders. Although science has been foregrounded in the rhetoric of educational reform, science has served as a club to daze the public and to silence educators who have disagreed with the assumptions, goals, and methods of school reform since the 1980s.

National Standards

Business and government calls for school reform in order to improve America's economic competitiveness both threatened and challenged various professional organizations in the education field. In report after report, schools were criticized for a failure to meet the needs of students and society. Business leaders, government officials, and think tank intellectuals wrote these reports without much representation from school personnel or educational experts. In fact, public school officials, teacher educators, and educational experts were considered to be part of the problem that beset American education rather than participants capable of finding solutions to these problems. The drive to Goals 2000 at the 1989 National Governors Association Education Summit appeared to bypass professional educators in the reorganization of public schools and schools of education. Outsiders—business leaders and politicians—were to be included, and traditional school insiders were consulted at best. This threat to the legitimacy and authority of professional organizations in reading and English language arts created the conditions for the use and abuse of professional expertise within the school reform movement.

In her study "The National Council of Teachers of English, Corporate Philanthropy, and the National Education Standards," Kim McCollum Clark wrote that NCTE and the International Reading Association volunteered to write the national standards for English language arts (to include reading) shortly after the 1989 National Governors Association summit.[7] In fact, NCTE had negotiated and renegotiated standards for teaching English language arts in schools periodically since its inception at the turn of the nineteenth century. These sets of standards spanned the spectrum of curricular possibilities and were typically tied to popular educational ideologies of their times. In 1892, the *Report of the Committee of Ten* presented a humanistic focus on traditional classic works to direct the instruction in American elementary and secondary classrooms. The reorganization of English in 1917 fitted well within the parameters of scientific management. During the 1960s, the participants in the Dartmouth Conference set learner-centered tenets for English teachers to employ, and the 1987 English Coalition Conference's *Democracy Through Language* document valorized language and cultural diversity for their contribution to America's past, present, and future. Advocates for each set of standards remained within NCTE and IRA, making for healthy debate about the needed direction of the field.

The National Goals Panel established at the summit in 1989 was not interested in debate. Rather, it was looking for an explicit statement to direct the nation's teachers and students toward practical outcomes that would make all eligible for the high-skill, high-wage jobs that the business leaders promised would become available. Debate with these organizations over definitions of literacy and appropriate ways of teaching children to read and write would dilute the expected standards. Those standards would state explicitly what all children should know and when they should know it. According to the National Goals Panel, the debates should end, and consensus on standards should prevail. None of the existing sets of NCTE standards was considered appropriate, and Diane Ravitch, then assistant secretary of education, offered the job of writing new explicit standards to the Center for the Study of Reading at the University of Illinois, which had produced the *Becoming a Nation of Readers* (1985) report and commissioned the *Beginning to Read* (1991) report. The center authors for both reports had adhered closely to the federal call for proposals in those documents, and the center had a track record of quality work within budget and deadline. P. David Pearson, the director of the center at that time, felt uncomfortable with the idea that the center would speak for the profession on national standards and proposed that the center work in conjunction with the two main professional organizations concerned with reading. The center would oversee the work while the NCTE and IRA leadership would develop a process for producing the standards. On October 13, 1992, a joint press release stated, "The USDE today announced a three-year, $1.8 million project to develop national standards in English, to be carried out jointly by the Center for the Study of Reading, based at the University of Illinois at Urbana-Champaign; the International Reading Association, Newark, Delaware; and the National Council of Teachers of English, Urbana, Illinois."[8]

Although the executive committees for these organizations had been aware of these negotiations, the NCTE and IRA leadership had to justify the project to their memberships. Among other concerns, NCTE and IRA members worried that federal interference in curricular matters set a dangerous precedent, usurping a state's right. The first task was to settle on a definition of standards. Pearson took the lead: "The Standards Project for English Language Arts (SPELA) will not set performance standards for student achievement. Instead it will create what have been called content or curriculum standards; in the national standards lingo, the project will describe what students 'should know and be able to do' at various stages in their school careers."[9] The results of the project would be "national standards, yes, but federal standards, no." NCTE's executive director assured, "we are free to write the standards as we see fit, and if the membership doesn't like the standards, we can reject them."[10] Janet Emig, chair of the SPELA group, wrote, "no federal body can legislate our success or failure."[11] Pearson offered five rationales for the project:

> We could create a national conversation about what we value in teaching and learning English.
>
> We might influence both public and professional investment of time and resources.
>
> We can create a healthy tension—a homeostasis between commonality and diversity in the field.
>
> We could ensure a challenging, supportive and thoughtful curriculum for all students.
>
> We could create a process for "using" the standards.[12]

In the end, Pearson reasoned that if the center or NCTE or IRA opted not to participate, then it was less likely that the standards would "reflect what research has taught us about the teaching and learning of English."

Without a referendum among the membership, the SPELA leadership declared a consensus that the project was worthwhile and at least potentially productive for the field. Under the guidance of the center, three task forces were formed to forge elementary, middle, and secondary school standards. Right from the start, these groups worked in different directions than Pearson had defined for them. A schedule was arranged to summon a selected set of classroom teachers and university professors twice annually to weeklong retreats in order to discuss the parameters of the standards at each level collected from various state affiliates of the two professional organizations. Executive secretaries at each level would then translate these discussions into standards language that "could be shared broadly for review, critique and consensus."[13] The June 1993 *NCTE Council Chronicle* provided some insight into the workings of these task forces that met in Snowbird, Utah.[14] Groups would attempt to reach consensus on what they believed to be the importance of suggestions for standards, to articulate standards they thought had been overlooked, and to write vignettes of classroom practice that would make their intentions for the standards more explicit for school personnel.

The results at Snowbird were packaged as a sampler for review by the network of affiliates. This sampler offered a matrix that positioned five strands (reading/literature, writing, language, real-world literacy, and interconnections) across three levels. The document provided nine examples with short vignettes to provide reviewers with some indication of what was to come from the next meeting of the task forces. Reviewers were not necessarily kind, and the SPELA board met to revise both the process and the document in order to develop standards that were more clearly stated, gave some indication of how teachers should address and meet the standards, and were not prescriptive.[15] A second sampler was developed (without the task forces meeting) and distributed to reviewers. This shorter version had three strands (oral language, reading, and writing), with the promise that each would be introduced with clear definitions of what was meant by each term included. Vignettes were absent from the document. McCollum Clark commented:

> These early drafts are more easily characterized by their differences than by their similarities. The forms the writers take in each draft, from a complexly embedded standard to lists divided by thirds—do not speak of consensus. Indeed, they could easily characterize opposing curriculum groups. The concern for clarity that motivated the refinement of the SPELA project by definition simplified more complicated views of literacy education that resist simple statements.[16]

This controversy did not have a chance to surface among the memberships because on March 20, 1994, the federal government withdrew its funding from SPELA less than halfway through the project because "we find that there has not been substantial progress toward meeting the objectives in any of the approved applications, and there is serious doubt that the University of Illinois will be able to achieve the stated goals within the given time."[17] According to a federal reviewing team, the SPELA documents demonstrated that the writers had "serious" problems in articulating what students should know and be able to perform in the fields of language, literacy, and literature. Calling the SPELA report "a loose assemblage of ideas and opinions" that focused on learning activities that should be available for all students, the reviewers declared the project a failure. This dismissal and withdrawal of funding were unprecedented among the many federal standards projects. Although the history standards were labeled a national disgrace in the popular press,[18] and were denounced in the *Congressional Record* (1995), the National Center for History in Schools received all its funding and was allowed to complete its project.

SPELA immediately disbanded as a result of the federal retreat. According to its leadership, the federal officials had failed to understand the SPELA documents and misinterpreted the relationship. By seeking specific language for standards too early, the government was discounting SPELA's unique "grassroots" approach to the development of the standards. In the *Education Week* article announcing the government's decision, Pearson was quoted, "I thought we were developing these standards for kids, their parents, and their teachers. Apparently, the federal government was the real audience all along."[19] Clearly, the SPELA leadership had misjudged the federal agenda for the English language arts standards. Without a written agreement on SPELA's responsibilities, the organization was free to develop its process; however, the government was free to withdraw its funding as well. After the Center for the Study of Reading and Janet Emig left the project, the leadership of NCTE and IRA held discussions with U.S. Department of Education officials in attempts to renew their involvement in writing national standards. In July 1994, officials from the office of Educational Research and Improvement posted a call for proposals for writing English standards, ending IRA's and NCTE's involvement in the federal project. The federal officials withdrew their call for proposals for national standards in December 1994, deciding that they would monitor the development of state standards for reading and language arts.

NCTE and IRA continued to write what they now called professional standards for English language arts outside the federal framework. Over the course of two years, they merged separate documents into a series of drafts that were discussed in public forums when the organizations met for their annual conventions. Joining with the Council of Chief State School Officers, they decided to work with state governments as they began to develop standards.

The drafts of the standards began to move toward Pearson's original charge—content and performance standards, informing the public what students should know and be able to do at various times in their schooling. As the scope of the standards became more limited, the authorship of the standards became cloudy. An executive committee revised the version the federal government rejected. A committee of four reworked that draft after it received severe criticism during the fall 1994 NCTE convention. After a working party at the spring NCTE 1995 convention wrote that the draft could have been written in 1965, one representative from the IRA and one from NCTE wrote a completely new draft, which in turn was edited in house once again after criticism. In the end, the IRA/NCTE professional standards for English language arts are twelve statements about what students should have the opportunity to do in classrooms that are elaborated into a sequence of activities across the school years.

Although the final product, meant to be an IRA-NCTE consensus document, might be a useful resource for teachers, administrators, and state officials, helping them to grasp the complexities of students' language use, the official rationales for the project and the process used in its preparation had some unfortunate consequences for the professional organizations and the field. From the beginning, the professional organizations let the government set the agenda for the project, accepting the government's rejection of the existing professional documents and the century-long negotiation among professionals over the definition and purpose of English language arts in the United States. By accepting the government's funding for the project, the professional organizations forfeited their autonomy and authority over the field. That point was emphasized dramatically when SPELA was fired from the federal project and discredited in Congress and by the popular press.

Second, the constant readjustments of the process for writing the standards projected a leadership without confidence in the project or its membership. The number of participants decreased from scores to two and then one across the two years of work. Although feedback was sought, it was eventually bypassed for the final form, which was presented to the membership as a completed document. Although the memberships might be proud of the standards, they cannot be proud of a process that at first assumed their assent and then often ignored their opinion. Finally, the process and product demonstrated what P. David Pearson feared from the beginning when providing rationales for the importance of SPELA's participation: "If we rely equally on best practice and research for our ideas about standards, then they will reflect research to the degree that best practices also reflect research."[20] Virtually all of the theory and research used to substantiate the IRA/NCTE standards fell outside of the government's then working definition of science (later encoded in the Education Science Act of 2002), and the professional organizations did not recognize the need to defend their position, ultimately undercutting their ability to advocate for broader definitions of the science of teaching and learning to read.

NICHD Research on Reading

When IRA and NCTE delivered their standards to the state officials, they met a rival document intended to direct state efforts to produce standards for reading. Bonita Grossen's *30 Years of Research: What We Now Know About How Children Learn to Read* was already circulating among the states.[21] It quickly captured the imagination of the state officials in California and Texas.[22] The Grossen report provided a summary of research studies sponsored by the National Institute of Child Health and Human Development. According to Grossen, NICHD initiated a program of research on reading difficulties with the advent of the Elementary and Secondary Education Act of 1965. However, since the 1985 Health Research Extension Act, NICHD had rededicated itself to improving the quality of reading research by conducting long-term, prospective, longitudinal and multidisciplinary investigations. Toward that end, NICHD established research centers across the United States to harness the work of more than 100 researchers in medicine, psychology, and education.

Although the Grossen report was soundly criticized, it represented two important elements in the campaign to make teaching a profession.[23] First, it positioned reading difficulties as medical issues, implying that personal cures were required. Second, it sanctioned heavily financed, large-scale studies as the only legitimate means in order to establish the one best method of teaching reading. The medical metaphor has a long history in reading education, dating back to the turn of the nineteenth century when psychology was separating from philosophy and medical schools were undergoing a thorough restructuring in the hands of philanthropic organizations. Throughout the century, reading experts adopted the terminology of medicine to describe their work—*clinic, treatment,* even *basal* come from medicine. Beyond this historical association, however, the new emphasis on medicine sought to subsume the reading field within the project to understand the biology, chemistry, and physics of reading. The NICHD project was to approach reading as pathology—to study its problems in order to infer its norms. This approach positioned the study of reading as the investigation of a disease for which an inoculation was necessary in order for normal growth to occur. Acceptable reading research would look within "unhealthy" individuals in order to determine the causes of problems and to develop the appropriate course of treatment. "Using modern neuroimaging technology, medical researchers have identified a unique signature on the brain scans of persons with reading problems."[24]

Of course, pathology isn't the only approach available to medical or reading researchers. In fact, the federal Office of Educational Research and Improvement funded the Center for the Improvement of Early Reading Achievement from 1997 to 2002, which employed a sociocultural rather than medical framework in order to explore what worked, linguistic and cultural diversity, preparation of teachers, and accountability.

> CIERA looked at all contexts that influenced children's acquisition of reading (family, community, school, state policy and federal policy). The breadth of its vision is seen in the collaboration of researchers from cognitive and sociocultural perspectives. This reflected the need to understand the workings of the child's mind, but not divorced from the contexts in which that mind was learning.[25]

Rather than pursuing NICHD's reading pathology, CIERA took a public health approach that studied the conditions under which normal growth took place and identified environmental factors that were conducive to such development. The public health model did not reject the findings of pathology or its calls for interventions when problems arose, but it did place and orient reading research within decidedly broader contexts, ones more likely to produce sustainable solutions in schools. For example, a public health approach examined the economic circumstances of developing readers and how nutrition, shelter, and health care factored in; it looked at political history to determine the impact of legal exclusions on current reading development; and it considered cultural practices of how texts have been approached in different ways by different groups. In Grossen's summary of NICHD research, social, historical, cultural, even developmental psychological explanations of reading were eliminated from consideration because all eyes were fixed on the blood flow to the "appropriate" areas of the brain.

The need for a pathological approach was captured in Grossen's epidemic rhetoric: "about 40 percent of the population have reading problems severe enough to hinder their enjoyment of reading."[26] Because NICHD defined reading as a health problem in 1985, funding medical researchers and special education professors to lead investigations, the federal government could boast that it had identified treatments that would ensure that 95 percent of all American students would learn to read by third grade. According to Grossen, the causes of all reading problems were primarily phonological—poor readers did not process phonemes easily and quickly. Of course, previous generations of educators and researchers had drawn similar conclusions and others had found fault with them, but Grossen proposed that the debate ended with the NICHD studies because of their size and rigor. All that remained was for schools to implement the medical solutions.

Reid Lyons coordinates the parallel investigation of similar questions across several centers. Under Lyon's leadership, the researchers determine that the questions have been answered only when the findings replicate across researchers and settings. Findings with a high degree of replicability are finally considered incontrovertible findings and then form the basis for additional research questions. Funding is awarded the research centers [*sic*] through competitive peer review preprocess. A panel of researchers, who are not competing for the research funds, award the funds after evaluating competing proposals according to specific criteria.[27]

According to Grossen, the NICHD studies used rigorous scientific procedures following medical models, while previous studies on reading were theory driven, short in duration, and confounded by sampling bias. NICHD researchers were unbiased, able to extend their investigations for years at a time, and careful to avoid overrepresentation of traits within populations to be studied. To make her point explicitly, Grossen contrasted the research studies that whole language advocates cited to support their claims promoting meaning-based processing in reading against the sound-based studies from NICHD.[28] Her criteria of length and size favored the NICHD studies dramatically. In order to engage in studies of three years in length and more than two hundred randomly assigned subjects, reading researchers required sizeable grants from federal or philanthropic agencies. None of the whole language studies enjoyed such funding, suggesting that the funding sources favored pathological approaches to reading research.

The Grossen report argued that the NICHD studies offered seven major implications for early reading instruction, each stemming from the general conclusion that sound processing was the primary route to learning to read.

Begin with direct instruction in phonemic awareness in kindergarten,

Teach spelling correspondence for each sound directly,

Teach spelling relationships directly,

Demonstrate methods to sound out words,

Employ only decodable texts,

Read interesting texts aloud, and

Keep decoding and comprehension instruction separate, but in balance.[29]

If these NICHD implications would be encoded in educational policy and executed faithfully in classrooms, then 95 percent of American students would learn to read efficiently.

In order to disseminate these research findings to school personnel, NICHD turned to the American Federation of Teachers (AFT). Its *Teaching Reading Is Rocket Science* report was written by Louisa Moats, a professor of pediatrics at the University of Texas Health Center in Houston, who held an NICHD contract when she wrote the report in 1998. "Only recently has basic research allowed the community of reading scientists and educators to agree on what needs to be done."[30] Extending well beyond experimental results, Moats presented the strategy for achieving NICHD's promised results: research should guide the field, set the standards and curricula for teacher education accordingly, align state certifications with these standards, create institutes for professors and inservice teachers to master these standards, press textbook publishers to improve their products, promote professional development according to a physician's model, and raise teacher pay. None of these policy guidelines was based on research of any type. Certainly none of the recommendations had been tested experimentally. Rather, these were simply logical steps that would appear to work in bureaucratic institutions.

The impact of the Grossen and Moats reports and the NICHD studies each summarized were remarkably influential within state legislatures and among state education department officials. *Education Week* named NICHD as the driving force behind this back-to-basics movement.

> State lawmakers around the country, citing poor reading scores and what they see as the failure of schools to find a sure formula for improving literacy, have decided to take on the task themselves. As a result, educators from New York to California have been faced with increasingly prescriptive mandates designed to change the way children are taught to read.[31]

CIERA studies placed NICHD and AFT as the two most influential organizations in reading reform.[32] "NICHD's efforts were enticing to policymakers because of their quantitative and easy to understand findings, their successful dissemination of their research findings, and their medical approach."[33] NICHD officials were cited for their aggressive and effective efforts to translate their research findings into educational policy. Parts of NICHD's campaign drew criticism from many within the reading research field. For example, Barbara Taylor and colleagues challenged NICHD for making research findings public before the studies had passed through peer review, a traditional measure of quality control.[34] Selecting one study as an example, Taylor demonstrated how peer review of the work before its circulation among policymakers and the press could have contextualized its findings, informing the public of their limitations as well as advantages. This challenge and subsequent responses from NICHD researchers demonstrated clearly the differences not only among research metaphors and methodologies but also in expected relationships between research and policy. Although NICHD's and Taylor's expected relationships both could easily be classified as policy-driven research in which researchers followed policymakers' lead,[35] the CIERA researchers appeared distressed by what they considered to be the overt politicization of reading research within the NICHD agenda.

> Policymakers and educators feel the urgency of finding an easy answer and producing results. Foorman and her colleagues appear to present just such an easy answer in the last line of their article by suggesting that widespread reading failure might be prevented through explicit teaching of the alphabetic principle. Further, when the authors of this widely publicized study use their results as the basis for highlighting specific commercial programs such as Open Court and SRA Reading Mastery, they contribute to the impression that students' reading problems will be solved if a school simply buys the right program.[36]

Physician and medical researcher Steven Strauss attacked NICHD claims of a medical research model, the scope of the research, and the politicization of the findings.[37] To begin, Strauss found the NICHD focus too narrow, excluding the social underpinnings of reading outside the research laboratory. NICHD-funded researchers examined only some parts of reading—phonological processing—but not the act itself. "We are still awaiting NICHD research on how competent readers coordinate 'the elementary components' of reading."[38] NICHD researchers focused only on what could be easily controlled, manipulated, and measured, rather than on complex acts of reading for everyday purposes. Strauss implied that this narrow focus became most apparent in the agency's funding choices. Virtually all its grants were devoted to either neurological or cognitive studies, without any attention to influences outside of readers' heads because reviewers of the grant proposals and consequent research reports were conducted by other NICHD-funded researchers. For Strauss, this pattern of review was a clear violation of protocols in medical research. Moreover, Strauss questioned the government advocacy of the NICHD findings without careful research on the likely consequences for students. He cautioned that the NICHD research and policy agenda appeared to be politically useful in the federal government's and corporations' project for the construction of high-stakes testing and accountability.[39]

Federal Reports on Reading and Reading Instruction

> Mr. President, this amendment has been cleared on both sides. It simply follows up on last year's report of the Commission on Read-

ing, *Becoming a Nation of Readers*. . . . It recommended that "well designed phonics instruction be used through the second grade," but it did not indicate specifically which beginning reading programs provide such instruction.[40]

One year after the Office of Educational Research and Improvement commissioned a state-of-the-art report on reading and reading instruction, Senator Paul Zorinsky proposed that the Department of Education compile a table that named the commercial programs that met the Commission on Reading's standards for being well designed. In keeping with other *What Works* documents that the Department published,[41] Zorinsky reasoned that this table would supply schools with the necessary information they needed to teach 95 percent of all students to read. The Department of Education packaged the Zorinsky bill within its call for proposals for a national center for reading research. Associate director of the existing center P. David Pearson was candid in his acknowledgment that the center's reauthorization was contingent on engaging further in the study of phonics beyond the *Becoming Nation of Readers* report. "We could not ignore the issues." [42] The center subcontracted the study to educational psychologist Marilyn Adams, who wrote the *Beginning to Read* report.

The Adams report provided an encyclopedic treatment of phonics, its place in reading, and its teaching. The report was scholarly, highly technical, and lengthy, and before it was released, the center decided to prepare an executive summary of the report for public consumption. Because Adams declined the offer, the center hired Steven Stahl, Jean Osborn, and Fran Lehr to write the summary.[43] The federal government produced fifty thousand copies of the summary for distribution and offered the full report to MIT Press for publication. According to all reviewers, the summary reduced Adams' argument considerably, promoting phonics instruction more stridently.

> To make the summary more readable, Stahl, Osborn, and Lehr recast my prose in shorter words and simpler sentences. . . . The summarizers also threw out the technical jargon and reduced the citation burden, occasionally replacing great lists of primary references with a single review.
>
> I guess I agree that it is more firmly centered on the knowledge and processes directly supporting word recognition than the book. However, I am equally sure that this was an accident of the summarization process. Specifically in shortening, it was typically the topic that was kept and the qualification that was tossed.[44]

Depending on reading experts' position on reading, Adams had either captured the essence of the behavior or reduced the social complexity to a visual process. The International Reading Association devoted a special issue of *The Reading Teacher* to a discussion of the merits of the reports. Adams was allowed the first and last words in that discussion, explaining that she had simply reviewed the research evidence and reported its findings that phonics was necessary, but not sufficient, for learning to read and most of the existing methods and programs were "a waste of time."[45] Most of the critics were complimentary about the thorough nature of the review but worried about its scope, claiming that the content of the subtitle—*Thinking and Learning About Print*—did not capture the social, cognitive, and emotional nature of *Beginning to Read*. Moreover, they worried that the summary would direct state and local officials to mandate phonics instruction for all students during the primary grades, despite Adams' qualifications. Among the six *Reading Teacher* reviewers, one thought the summary was a necessary addition. In my contribution to the issue, I commented on the politics of the event:

> To make a long story short, the Center received its funding and the government received its report on phonics—not necessarily in the Adams full report, but certainly with its summary. This short lesson in the politics of reading research should make us reconsider reading researchers' complacent claims of objectivity and neutrality in their work. It should cause reading researchers to wonder who sets our agenda for reading.

Adams replied to my remarks without acknowledging how the government would use her work.

> Meanwhile, the profession is threatened with out and out dismissal from the decision making process. If we, as reading professionals, refuse to address these issues on the basis of research, then—as should be abundantly clear from events of the last few years—our state and local governments are prepared to do so on the basis of politics.[46]

In her response, Adams displayed a functionalist understanding of reading education policy and politics, assuming that policymaking was a rational process in means-ends analyses that relied on empirical or analytic science to make decisions. Without her report and the evidence she considered, she believed, policymakers would be unable to make rational policy decisions concerning the problems that they had identified and would be influenced by special interests. According to this logic, reading research should accept policymakers' representation of reading education and search for the solutions to those problems on their terms alone. All other research is moot.

Five years later, Congress authorized yet another state-of-the-art report on reading and reading education. The report was funded by the Office of Special Education, OERI, and NICHD in order to develop a consensus of what could be done to prevent the rising number of students assigned to special education classes for reading problems. The prestigious National Academy of Science would supervise the report through its National Research Council, which would, according to its historic duty, advise the federal government on this matter. Seventeen preeminent experts on reading, language, and child development met seven times for three-day seminars over a three-year period in order to sort through the research on language and reading development of children from ages three through eight. According to the committee chair, Harvard University language scholar Catherine Snow, the committee "presupposed a componential view of literacy" that reading was composed of hierarchically arranged cognitive sub-skills. With this presupposition, the committee drew essentially the same conclusions as the Adams report:

> The Committee built on the research findings of the last 20 years, which have converged on the conclusion that mastering specific cognitive subskills (letter recognition, grapheme-phonic mapping, rapid lexical access as well as skills with various forms of discourse privileged in the classroom and some world knowledge) to a high degree provokes literacy participation.[47]

With the moral authority of approval from the National Academy of Science, federal funding, and a panel of experts, *Preventing Reading Difficulties in Young Children* confirmed the NICHD-sponsored research on the phonological nature of reading, the pathological view of reading, and the secondary status of social contexts on learning to read. In its final chapter, the committee listed its advice to the federal government: all children required excellent reading instruction to prevent difficulties, including the alphabetic principle, reading sight words, reading words by mapping speech sounds to parts of words, achieving fluency, and comprehension. To begin this sequence, all primary-grade teachers should start with phonological awareness, phonics, and frequent assessment of fluency. Only the report's recommendation for English learners was out of step with the contemporary government position on literacy. The committee recommended that English learners be taught in their native language until they had acquired sufficient English to learn to read. Although the committee sought to embed its recommendations within activities of language development, content discussion, and writing, even supportive reviewers of the report worried about the consequences of its recommendations.

> However, if the recommendations get picked up by policy makers and transformed into legislative mandates that tell schools and teachers to teach in particular ways because of their presumed evidential

superiority, then I fear all of that energy which could go into new research and development initiatives, will be channeled into new policy battles over curriculum control.[48]

Other critics were not so sanguine. For example, James Gee challenged the presupposition that subskills predominated in reading and wondered how the report would differ if the committee assumed reading were sets of social practices within contexts rather than a hierarchical cognitive process.[49] He leveled two charges. First, the Committee limited itself to discussions of school reading, assuming reading to be a single universal behavior, and second, it failed to recognize that this assumption positioned many students as deficient without recognizing multiple ways in which these students used language and symbols effectively in some environments. According to Gee, the committee misunderstood that reading at school required many students to learn a different set of activities, attitudes, and values than the ones they had acquired at home. Reading difficulties, he argued, could arise from problems with any classroom requirement, and not just with the particular phonological tasks. By neglecting this possibility, Gee charged, the committee's recommendations could produce more reading difficulties than they would meliorate. Gee supported his concerns by identifying apparent contradictions within the report and with reference to New Literacy Studies that "do not see young children learning to read, but rather young children getting scaffolded socialization (enculturation) into different and multiple literacy practices, each connected to specific forms of language, specific activities, and specific identities."[50]

Snow's reply to Gee on behalf of the committee was measured. If Gee believed his charges to be correct, then he should conduct experiments that would demonstrate the existence of multiple readings, their social rather than cognitive foundation, and the effects of societal interventions on the reading of individuals. Snow retorted that without such evidence, the reading research community could not evaluate Gee's claims and policymakers would not pay any heed. She concluded that seventeen committee members and fourteen independent reviewers stood behind the report, hoping "to improve the welfare of children, in particular the children most likely to fail in school."[51] In effect just as Adams had responded to me, Snow called Gee irrational and told him to join her in conducting functionalist policy-driven research in service to the government's agenda.

National Reading Panel

Before the *Preventing Reading Difficulties in Young Children* report was published, Congress directed the head of NICHD and secretary of education to convene a national reading panel to review and assess again the research on teaching reading with implications for classroom practice. In the wake of a Republican Congress' successful conversion of President Clinton's America Reads Initiative into the Reading Excellence Act, the congressional mandate set empirical evidence as the criterion for judging the value of reading research. The House and Senate definitions of scientific research of reading differed slightly, with the Senate version allowing more than experimental results;[52] however, both required experimental certainty in determining causality. The panel began its work with this criterion for causality as the deciding factor of whether or not published research would be included in its analyses.

In order to get this a priori assumption, the panel members were personally selected for the panel. Panel member S. Jay Samuels acknowledged this fact during a discussion of the consequences of the panel's report.

> The areas of focus and the methods of analyses were decided by who was selected to the panel. The five areas of emphasis in the report do not capture all there is to reading. Rather they are the specialties of the panel members. Tom Trabasso in comprehension, Linnea Ehri in phonics, me for fluency. I fought for my topic as did the others. The outcome could not have been otherwise. That does not compromise the report. It simply demonstrates its limits.[53]

The members represented only a narrow spectrum of the reading field, decidedly slanted toward the NICHD medical point of view. Six members were cognitive scientists in addition to Professor Shaywitz, an NICHD grant recipient and member of the National Research Council's panel for the *Preventing* report. The remaining seven members were split among university and public school administrators, a CPA, a public school teacher, and a reading education faculty member. As Professor Samuels stated, the direction of the report was determined with the selection of the members. And the members did not disappoint. They began by excluding most of the work that reading experts had labeled reading research because it did not adhere to the experimentalist criterion circulating in Congress at that time. Their position ignored the loud and active debates concerning the definition of science among philosophers.[54]

Panel members believed that their experimentalist criterion set their report apart from the *Preventing Reading Difficulties* report because it focused exclusively on causal findings and statistical evaluations of those findings rather than a consensus among the committee members. The panel positioned the previous report as subjective, learned opinion, and not an objective process by which the real science of reading and reading instruction could be determined. The panel's feeling of superiority, however, required that it narrow the scope of its work to only those questions for which there were sufficient numbers of experimental studies to conduct the statistical meta-analyses. For example, despite direct advocacy within all the other state-of-the-art reading reports of the previous fifteen years, the panel members excluded the importance of reading independently as a scientifically based instructional technique because they could not locate studies that met their criteria. Such omission led some school districts to require that teachers eliminate independent reading from their instructional schedules.[55] Jim Cunningham put the panel's decisions in perspective:

> I contend that education, including the teaching of reading, is more like fostering healthy human development, building a successful business, maintaining an effective military and providing good parenting than it is like administering medical or psychological interventions. American business and the American military are each the envy of the world, yet imagine how little of their cumulative wisdom and common practice is supported by the kind of research the NRP would insist upon for investigating claims about reading instruction. For instance, what would happen if parents began to feel doubts about any practice that does not have enough experimental support to conduct a meta-analysis?[55]

As panel member S. J. Samuels acknowledged, the findings of the NRP report could be predicted from those members convened. Direct instruction was mandated in alphabetics (phonemic awareness and phonics instruction), fluency, vocabulary, and comprehension because the panel found incontrovertible evidence for each. Recommendations for teacher education and technology were also made, although the panel admitted that these remarks were speculative because there were not enough good studies to conduct meta-analyses on either. As the *Preventing Reading Difficulties* report did, the NRP report added little to the *Beginning to Read* report and *Becoming a Nation of Readers*. In fact, the panel dropped any discussion of second language learning; it neglected most of the studies that the reading education field considered scientific; and it failed to consider the actual practices of reading instruction in school classrooms. In the executive summary of the panel's report (which does not name authorship), subtleties and qualifications for their interpretations and implications are removed completely in order to make the clearest statements of how the scientific evidence should direct classroom instruction.[57] Much of the criticism of the report's findings is directed toward the recommendations in the summary, emphasizing its double reduction of the complexities of reading and reading instruction and the dangers of using it to write federal, state, and local school policy for reading education.[58]

The Perfect Storm: State, Business, and Science in Reading Education

The *perfect storm* is the name given to the 1991 northeaster off the coast of Massachusetts that ruined hundreds of homes and took several lives. As a metaphor, it is the confluence of specific events, which singly would not be consequential, but when combined magnify the effects and spin out of control. Reading education in the United States experienced the perfect storm just after the turn of the twenty-first century, and it is still experiencing the consequences as I write this book. If the Education Science Reform Act of 2002, the Reading First Initiative, or the No Child Left Behind legislation were enacted on its own or without the combined support of government officials, business leaders, and many reading experts, then the impact on teachers would not be so great. But together, the narrowing of education science to experimentation with notification that only experimental work will be considered for federal funding; the requirement to use a commercially prepared core reading program in Reading First schools; the grip of adequate yearly progress among disaggregated student scores; and businesses poised to leap into these markets to supply new testing, instructional, test preparation, and required tutoring services keep even the best schools in America in continuous triage activities to keep themselves afloat. The schools that have not been successful in the past are already submerged below the surface, leaking funds to private businesses, which lurk in the surrounding waters, protected from the same requirements that the schools must now follow. Some test scores rise for some groups, some fall for others while the tempest blows public schools toward private markets.

Chapter Eight

Teachers as Targets

In 1992, Francis Fukuyama penned *The End of History and the Last Man*, a book in which he argued that the end of the cold war signaled the end of the linear progression of human history.[1] His premise was that the collapse of the Soviet Union (under the economic weight of the arms race) represented the victory of western liberal democracy over all other forms of government. His theoretical point of origin for this argument was that the antagonisms within the Master and Slave dialectic that Hegel posed at the beginning of the nineteenth century had been substantially resolved in the triumph of the world's democracies over the world's dictatorships. The spirit of freedom had finally been realized in the 1990s.[2] Fukuyama based this claim upon what he considered to be irrefutable evidence—the governments in the majority of countries around the world characterized themselves as democracies, governments by the people. Because, at least in theory, democracies provide all individuals the freedom to vote for whom they hope will represent their interests in government, the Master and Slave can coexist, if not live in complete harmony. In Fukuyama's view, a society's winners could lie down with its losers in order to form a citizenry secure in the knowledge that they participated in the system that brought about their government. In Hegelian terms, the purpose of history had been realized, and therefore, history had ended.

Fukuyama acknowledged that this end of history would not be the conclusion of the world and its events—it was not Armageddon. Rather, the end of history meant that the centuries-old struggle over which form of political, social, and economic governance was best had concluded. Although some conflicts within and among nations might continue over perceived slights in recognition or distribution, these conflicts would not reopen the fundamental debate over political ideologies because antidemocracies in their many forms (e.g., dictatorships, monarchies, and one-party systems) had been discredited as unproductive in meeting the basic physical, political, and emotional needs of their citizens. In Fukuyama's end of history, the world's citizens now agreed that history had found its one best system—western liberal democracy—and it was only a matter of time before all people would be politically equal and accept this state of being.[3] Fukuyama, however, was not particularly sanguine about the potential effects of this sense of satisfaction on the fate of individuals. The Last Man in his title was a direct reference to Nietzsche's fear that consensus made individuals apathetic, weak willed, unable to dream. He is a comfort seeker "who merely earns his living and keeps warm."[4] Fukuyama worried that personal and social agency would dissipate within this complacent state of being at the end of history. And as a result, corporate and technological power would replace individual human agency.

Whether or not Fukuyama is correct about the end of history, his use of Hegelian notions of history fits well the unfolding of the perfect storm within American reading education. For example, the official history of reading education, Nila Banton Smith's *American Reading Instruction*, provides a chronology of continuous progress from colonial times to her present.[5] Its "story" tells of American educators' search for the one best method that would bring universal literacy within the United States. The International Reading Association has kept this story in print since the 1960s, with most recent editions being updated by contemporary scholars.[6] Perhaps without explicit intention, Smith followed Hegel's notion of history as the continued progression toward the realization of the spirit. In Smith's version, government, science, and business worked in rational coordination to make the spirit of universal literacy a reality. Reading scientists discovered the laws of reading, learning, and teaching; industry provided the technology based on those laws; and governments supplied the system for delivery of literacy to its populace. Although Smith and her subsequent editors did not foresee the end of this history for reading education, many current reading experts, the federal government, and publishers proclaim that we now have reached consensus within the field concerning how people learn to read and how reading should be taught.[7] The reading wars are over, they declare, and all sides must harness their efforts behind the one best system. According to this logic, No Child Left Behind legislation is the proper mechanism to coordinate all parties in these efforts by setting a timetable of 2014 for universal literacy to be achieved. For reading education, then, history has ended. President George W. Bush reports that this end should be celebrated.

> It so happens this is the fourth anniversary of when I signed the No Child Left Behind Act. I think the No Child Left Behind Act is one of

the most significant accomplishments in education in a long, long time. I want to thank both the Republicans and Democrats who worked together back then to get this piece of legislation passed. It is a really important piece of legislation that is working. And I'm here today to talk about the spirit of the No Child Left Behind Act, the evidence that says it's working and my deep desire to work with Congress to make sure it continues to have the desired effect on children all across the country. . . .

I remember when I was the governor of Texas, there was a lot of debate about different types of curriculum, different ways to teach reading. You might remember those debates. They were full of all kinds of politics. The best way to cut through political debate is to measure. The best way to say, the program I'm using is working is because you're able to measure to determine whether or not it's working. . . .

The system is working. That's what's important for people to understand. And by the way, any attempt to roll back accountability in Washington, DC, will be—I'll fight any attempt to do that. I'm just not going to let it happen. We're making too much progress.[8]

President Bush considers NCLB to be working according to plan. In this chapter, I explore what "it's working" means for classroom teachers across the country. In four words, NCLB means the *discrediting, reduction, deskilling,* and *reskilling* of teachers to extents unimaginable in 1988 when I wrote the first edition of this book. Then, many reading educators found it hard to accept my evidence for the deskilling and reskilling of teachers under teacher and school effectiveness models. Now, Richard Allington, James Baumann, Robert Calfee, James Hoffman, Robert Tierney, and others use these terms to describe the current plight of teachers and soon-to-be fate of teacher educators.[9] I begin this chapter with the statute on teacher qualifications that requires that schools ensure that a "highly qualified teacher" will direct every school lesson by the end of the 2006 school year. Although a lofty goal, the requirement has had unfortunate consequences for teachers and the concepts of reading and teaching in general. Next, I examine the provisions within the law concerning teachers' professional development, and the federal (and consequently state) government's attempt to control the types of information allowed within professional development programs. Unless recommended methods are deemed to be scientifically based according to the Education Science Reform Act of 2002, they cannot be included within professional development programs using state or federal funds. Consequently, certain words cannot be spoken and some reading strategies with years of practical evidence cannot be discussed during many professional development sessions. This action could be the most direct sign of deskilling possible. Finally, I address the impact of the instructional requirements of the Reading First Initiative, which forces schools to adopt core reading programs and teachers to follow them faithfully. These commercial programs supply the new skills that teachers must apply in order to bring about the promised universal literacy; each of the official core programs has explicit scripts for teachers and students to follow.

Highly Qualified Teachers

Since the publication of *A Nation at Risk*, business and government officials have charged that teachers and schools must change in order for the United States to successfully compete in the world economy. Annually since the mid-1980s, news media have reported comparisons of students' test scores among local school districts, regions, states, and nations in order to chastise public schools and teachers. In each comparison, lower scores have been associated with faulty curricular goals and instruction. Reporters argued that if schools would adopt higher standards and teachers would work toward those standards according to scientifically based methods, then each student would become proficient, succeed academically, find employment, and keep American advantages in global markets. The bottom line of these reports is that schools—that is, teachers—are not performing adequately. If teachers and schools were not understood as the problem, then President Clinton's solution in America Reads would not have rested on the influx of volunteer tutors and President George W. Bush's fix would not ultimately rest on private tutors for those students who do not reach proficiency. Absent from these charges or solutions is any recognition of historical, social, and economic factors that have influenced the outcomes of academic testing for its nearly one-hundred-year history—socially marginalized groups that receive grossly lower amounts of social and economic support in the United States score lower (significantly lower) than mainstream students.[10] As groups become less socially and economically marginalized, the average scores of their children become indistinguishable from other mainstream groups. Clearly, more than teachers and schools are involved, but business, government, and many reading experts keep the public gaze primarily on public school teachers.

Just as with the name No Child Left Behind, the section of the law titled Highly Qualified Teachers is a rhetorical triumph. The title frames the argument so that no rational person could object. *Highly qualified teacher* invokes images of the best teacher from anyone who reads or hears the phrase. Who could possibly oppose someone similar to the best teacher in her memory being assigned to every classroom across the nation? Every objection appears irrational. The reality of the statute, however, is much different than its rhetorical promise.

The official rationale behind the calls for highly qualified teachers is a reaction to the increasing tendency of school administrators to hire unlicensed teachers and to assign licensed teachers to responsibilities outside the parameters of their teaching specialties in order to fill vacancies. Although these practices are statistically associated with lower student achievement, many administrators reason that any teacher is better than no teacher in a classroom full of students. Without careful study of why these teaching shortages occur—particularly in urban and rural settings—NCLB simply mandated that all states fill each classroom with a highly qualified teacher by the end of the 2005–2006 school year or face significant government sanctions. According to the law, a highly qualified teacher must (1) hold at least a bachelor's degree; (2) have full state teacher certification or have passed the state licensure exam and hold a license to teach; and (3) demonstrate competence in each academic subject in which he teaches. These seem to be modest, even minimal requirements, and Congress offered school districts financial support in order to help school administrators attract such teachers to all vacant positions by 2006.

On Friday, May 12, 2006, however, the federal Department of Education announced a one-year extension for every state.[11] None had complied completely by finding a highly qualified teacher for every subject, although some states had made more progress than others. The federal DOE threatened nine states, the District of Columbia, and Puerto Rico with loss of all federal education funding because they had apparently made little effort toward meeting the old goal. Their chief executive officers for education were called to Washington, DC, to explain. The other forty-one states must mail an explanation of how they will—not intend to—meet the standard within the next year. "The day of reckoning is here, and it's not going to pass."[12]

In order to comply with the highly qualified requirement, many states have permitted already certified teachers to acquire additional certifications through examination only. This quick alternative bypasses traditional teacher certification programs at universities. The rationale for the alternative is the notion that content knowledge is all that is necessary to qualify someone to teach any subject. For example, in Pennsylvania, the department of education (PDE) allows certified teachers to acquire other areas of certification by surpassing a set score on the state's specialist test for that subject. According to officials at the PDE, the policy is necessary particularly in rural schools because insufficient numbers of students enroll in specialized natural and social science courses to warrant hiring one teacher for each subject. The option is available, however, to all certified teachers, and a sliding scale of cost has been established for teachers who seek multiple certifications through examinations during one sitting. This alternative has made it easier for school districts to comply, although Pennsylvania did not meet the federal 2006 timetable.

The certification-by-examination-only policy does much more than simply establish a quicker way to determine who is highly qualified. It reduces each subject area, teaching in general, and the term *qualified* in particular to the items on the test in each subject. In this way, the policy of becoming highly qualified through examination positions the teacher as well. For example, to be certified in reading in Pennsylvania, an already certified teacher must receive an acceptable score on the Praxis exam. That test has 120 multiple-choice items spread across four content categories: theoretical knowledge (22 questions), application of theory into practice (54 questions), assessment (32 questions), and leadership (12 questions). According to the PRAXIS website, the content categories are based upon the National Reading Panel report and the Professional Standards and Ethics Committee of the International Reading Association.[13] Within the theory and practice categories, alphabetics, phonics, fluency, vocabulary, and comprehension are covered, with an emphasis placed upon the recommendations from the panel's summary.[14] The questions reduce important points for discussion to simple facts. For example, item 2 asks:

> According to research, which of the following is the single most important home-based activity for preschool children in building the knowledge required for children's eventual success in reading?
>
> A. Children memorizing nursery rhymes
> B. Children and parents talking about school
> C. Parents teaching children the alphabet
> D. Parents reading aloud to children
> E. Parents identifying unfamiliar words

A test taker could make an argument for any of these alternatives. Of course, the objective of a test writer is to confuse the unsure test taker and to distract her attention. D is correct according to the answer key, but its correctness is confounded by the Education Science Reform Act requirement for implying causality. That is, the research in support of reading aloud is correlational and, therefore, has not been experimentally confirmed as "working." If a test taker reads too much into the question after NCLB or is thinking too deeply about advice for parents, then he will be in a quandary. The distracters are not all equally compelling. The memorization of nursery rhymes would attract the attention of core knowledge advocates—fans of E. D. Hirsch or William Bennett. Direct instruction of the alphabet is recommended in the National Reading Panel report, although parents might do it improperly. Certainly parents identifying unfamiliar words cannot hurt their children, but it might not guarantee later success in learning to read either. Option B is a true spoiler for this item. Parents talking to their children thoughtfully about any issue provides their children with a broad vocabulary and information about the purposes and uses of language. Talk in the home and classroom has been correlated with reading achievement as well.[15] Both B and D are appropriate answers based on research. Both experiences in listening to books and talking with adults are essential in learning to read. I'd flip a coin to decide which I would recommend first to parents. But having to flip the coin on too many items because I know too much about actually teaching children to read could be fatal in acquiring reading certification and becoming highly qualified in Pennsylvania.

Perhaps officials in the Pennsylvania Department of Education recognized this hazard, because they set the passing score to receive certification in reading below the state mean for the test. If the test taker exceeds this cutoff score, then she becomes immediately highly qualified to teach reading in any Pennsylvania classroom, ranging from kindergarten through high school. This makes a mockery of both certification and *highly qualified*. The social and pragmatic dynamics of making good decisions regularly become discredited—in fact, ignored—for the sake of expedience. Yet making good decisions regularly is what a teacher must do to be effective. Those decisions vary according to a multitude of social and practical factors. For instance, a reading teacher faced with making recommendations to parents should know the personal and community resources available to parents and gauge his recommendations accordingly. Working parents with apparently little print in their lives might become discouraged or take offense when told to read to their children because they often find ways to use the texts available to them in order to read and talk to and with their children.[16] A highly qualified teacher should have this cultural knowledge and these social skills as well as the theoretical knowledge about reading aloud and conversation. Requiring the latter without the former discredits the daily lives of teachers and teaching.

Legitimate conceptions of reading print have varied across time and place, from profound interest in literal translation of scripture to open-ended semiotic interpretations of representational text.[17] Writers have devoted their lives to the careful exploration of these types of reading and find them purposeful and useful among different groups and individuals within and across social settings. All are still in play in contemporary American life. Teachers find these sometimes competing conceptions within the expectations of their students and parents. Consider, for example, the classroom teacher who has students from religious fundamentalist groups, nonprint cultures, or politically active communities. Which conception of reading should the teacher adopt? The Praxis test does not even consider these questions; rather it locks teachers, students, and families into a single definition.

If the highly qualified requirement were to work for teachers and students instead of against them, then it would entertain the intellectual and performative aspects of teaching reading as well as a broader knowledge base.[18] Intellectuals are judged by the quality and rigor of the questions that they ask and the sophistication of the methods in which they pursue answers. Teachers face profound questions each day that they work: Who are these students? What are the relationships among them? What do they know? How might I further what they know? How might what they learn affect their lives individually and collectively? What can I hope for? What is possible? While these questions might seem grand and abstract, they are, in fact, embedded in the small and practical aspects of classroom life. For example, consider the decisions about book selection for students who are struggling with issues of culture and diversity. Teachers must address these questions if they intend to demonstrate the power of reading in people's social development.[19] Teachers of reading, highly qualified ones, ponder and act on such questions regularly. If given time and permission to think about them, good teachers engage in inquiries that can lead to transformative pedagogy in and out of their classrooms. But NCLB works against good teaching within its simplistic conception of highly qualified without careful investigations of the conditions that led to the current staffing in public schools across the country.

Approved Professional Development

NCLB addresses reading instruction through the Reading First Initiative, which offered $5 billion over a six-year period to local districts to help every child learn to read by the end of third grade. The funds were delivered through state departments of education, which awarded funding to school districts that met basic requirements concerning the relative economic needs of their students and their willingness to comply with federal suggestions for essential elements of successful reading programs. These incentives were intended to bring school reading programs into compliance with federal regulations and to ensure the fidelity of the districts' commitment to recommended programs. In order to help schools districts and states develop successful proposals for funding, the federal Department of Education established regional centers for the dissemination and evaluation of Reading First information and programs. The officials at these centers judged the relative merits of district proposals against federal standards. Working from the summary of the National Reading Panel report and the Education Science Reform Act of 2002, all states eventually produced acceptable proposals and received funding. Although the federal officials would later deny that they promoted any particular form of reading instruction, most states recognized quickly that every district was expected to adopt a core reading program and to implement a structure for professional development to ensure that teachers would implement that program properly.[20]

To leave little to chance, the federal government provided a list of core reading programs that it argued fit its specifications of scientifically based reading research (e.g., Open Court Reading, Mastery Reading, Harcourt, Houghton Mifflin, and Scott Foresman).[21] Along with the core reading programs, the federal government provided guidelines for professional development in reading instruction that would be worthy of Reading First funding. In fact, the federal government prohibited the use of federal funds for any professional development activities that could not be directly related to scientifically based reading research (SBRR). Funded professional development programs were to focus solely on reading instruction, to help teachers work from diagnostic data derived from students' class work, and to extend over enough time to ensure that teachers were applying the suggestions appropriately. While federal statutes permitted consideration of the principles of differing instructional programs, they limited local professional development to the effective delivery of one such program. In these ways, federal officials were confident that teachers would receive their official message about reading instruction without contradiction.

The allure of the Reading First financial incentives created moral dilemmas for some district administrators.

> "The [Reading First Initiative] grant is extremely program-driven. You have to choose from a very small list of programs, and then you have to implement with fidelity. You can't buy the program and then massage it into what works in your school. I understand that it's an attempt to bring consistency to a school's reading program, but for us, it didn't make sense.
>
> If we had been invited to develop a proposal without being required to purchase a prescriptive program, we would have definitely applied. We would have relied on the research that individualized instruction increases student achievement, and we would have put our dollars into professional development, additional staff, and more resources that meet the unique needs of our learners.
>
> I think there has been an attempt to kind of teacher-proof our classrooms. If you just follow a certain program with fidelity, then your kids are going to succeed. I think that is diminishing to the professionalism of our teachers. There is really no substitute for having highly skilled teachers in the classroom.[22]

Because of budgetary concerns, officials in other school districts believed that they did not have the option to decline the financial incentives of Reading First. In Pennsylvania, the application process required district officials to apply to the state department of education with specific plans on how the funds would lead to higher reading test scores on state examinations.[23] The state offered a seminar in Harrisburg for those eligible districts that were not successful with their initial proposal. Each unsuccessful district was assigned a technical adviser to help district officials redraft its proposal along more acceptable lines. These advisers made clear what the state and federal governments would accept. Following is a memo of instructions to a school official who had applied for Reading First funding in order to continue a five-year Reading Excellence grant program that had been consistently successful in raising students' tests scores in the district. The memo states that in order for this district to receive Reading First funding, it would have to scrap its current program for a core reading program, use specified commercial achievement tests, and use a single provider of professional development to help the district's teachers be successful.

1. Number the pages of the grant.

2. On the first page, the first paragraph indicates success with the current approach to reading, but the data show otherwise. The district was selected on the basis of the need to improve reading performance. You need to identify the gaps in performance and practice.

3. Ohio State Literacy Framework is not research based, scientific, systematic, direct, explicit [*sic*] improving the instruction of large numbers of students.

4. Under the instructional assessment, page 2, all reading first [sic] must be used to support outcomes. You will need to put in another outcome assessment, such as the Terra Nova. For instructional assessments, you will need to select from the grid that was distributed at the December inservice and actually name the tests for screening, progress monitoring and diagnostic at the grade levels and then provide for purchase in the budget page. Use the matrix provided.

5. Page 3—instructional strategies—Reading First monies should be spent very soon on actually purchasing a scientifically based reading series from the 5–6 that are available, not to study the situation for a long period of time.

6. Page 4—no mention of the PaTTAN to provide the professional development. Work, provided in the IU should be done in concert with PaTTAN trainers. Link all professional development to state, regional, and local.

7. Page 6—use this limited time to select and purchase a reading series so that you can use this year's monies to pay for it.

8. Page 7—district leadership team. Does this district have reading supervisors and reading specialists? If so, they should [be] considered for the team.

9. Page 9—it is only the schools identified for reading first [*sic*] for the grant. Persons from other schools can [not] attend professional development.

10. Page 10—the [school's current literacy program] is mentioned repeatedly, but it is not scientifically based research reading instruction. It is not to be found in the literature with a research base. Furthermore, the purpose of reading first [*sic*] is to implement new structures because the current ones are not successful enough. In the full paragraph on page 10, there needs to be mention of how the district will institute a new approach to reading, rather than just trying to enhance its current one.

11. Page 10—you need to specifically mention how the scientifically based areas of reading instruction will be implemented, rather than just mention the term.

12. Page 12—Evaluation strategies. Too general. Need to describe how the different selected assessments will be implemented and used to guide instruction. The actual assessment grid from the December training should be evident.

13. Budget page 18—are the five full time literacy coaches new positions? Or are they being used to fund already existing positions? This must be clear. For example, do you already have reading specialists and are you proposing five additional coaches?

14. Core reading materials—how did you arrive at the figure?? There is no mention in the grant that you have selected a reading series, and that is acceptable for the very short term, but there should be some basis for the figure, such as 80.00—100.00 per student that it costs to purchase a series.

15. Budget does not include payment of substitutes or of teachers to attend inservice? How will you arrive at this point?

The technical adviser who wrote this memo represented the state's position on what should transpire in classrooms across the Commonwealth of Pennsylvania. Ignoring the district's and teachers' past successes, the state placed its complete faith in science, the market, and centralized authority to help this district. Science is mentioned in three different points, twice asserting that the Ohio State framework is not scientific and once as a curricular suggestion (points 3, 10, and 11). The market is mentioned in six points, all based upon the district consuming private goods and services. Three times the district is told to buy a basal reading series from an authorized selection (points 5, 7, and 14). Two points require the district to purchase commercial tests (points 4 and 12). Point 6 informs the district to obtain the services of the authorized trainer in order to qualify for Reading First funding.

The memo's tone conveyed the sense of absolute authority. The technical adviser lectured the district official, who had assumed higher scores indicated that the district's program had been successful. Her original grant proposal sought the state to acknowledge its progress over the last five years. Although the district is among the poorest in the state, its previously state-funded program based on the Ohio State framework raised its third graders' test scores within two points of the state average. The district accomplished this by trusting its teachers to employ the components of a balanced reading program—reading aloud, shared reading and writing, guided reading and writing, and independent reading and writing—without the assistance of a private professional development program or a core reading program. Similar to the Montana district described in the quote on page 174, the officials in the Pennsylvania district sought to make decisions about their program. The technical adviser, however, scoffed at the suggestion that their current program was working and told district officials to implement a core program that would supplant teachers' authority with the expertise of basal authors, test designers, and commercial trainers. At best in such an approved program, district teachers would become assistants to the officially sanctioned technologies of Reading First; at worst, they would continue to be portrayed as the cause of the "crisis" in reading when the federal one best program failed.

Scripted Lessons

NCLB requires perfection from teachers. By 2014, all students must be proficient in reading, writing, math, and science. Every student, or the school will be reconstituted! Although the school administrators can help, teachers carry the load of this requirement. NCLB's expectation of perfection puts enormous pressure on school systems to ensure that human error will not creep into their classroom. Since to err is human, the quest for perfection must lead away from human activity. For even with constant rehearsal, humans will make mistakes—bakers' cakes will fall, virtuosos' solos will miss a note, batters will swing and miss, even surgeons will nick a vein.[24] These human errors happen despite bakers' years of practice, violinists' hours of replaying a piece, ball players' lifetimes of swings, and surgeons' performance of a hundred similar procedures. No one expects all cakes to be perfect each time, all solos to reach the identical quality, or a hit for every pitch. Although people might expect perfection of surgeons, every hospital conducts a weekly morbidity and mortality conference during which physicians meet to review the mistakes made. The point of these meetings appears to be the sentiment that doctors can learn from their mistakes and can be trusted to police themselves, yet another M and M conference will be held the following week because the science of medicine is not perfect and neither are the people who perform that science in everyday, and sometimes unique, circumstances.

Since the sixteenth century, the solution for human error has been to convert process from human labor to technology.[25] The oven routinizes more of the baking process so that the baker has fewer decisions to make. The soloist has the metronome and digital recorders; the batter has a batting tee and cage for her swings; and the surgeon has the laser to pinpoint the cuts. Each uses technology to eliminate error, but as the scientific management movement in the early 1900s found, none can eliminate the human factor completely. According to the Reading First Initiative, the core reading program is the technology of reading instruction. In order to reduce error and increase productivity in reading instruction, NCLB expects teachers to apply that latest technology. School districts qualify for Reading First funding if and only if they adopt a scientifically based reading program and implement it with fidelity. As the Pennsylvania technical adviser made clear, federal officials believe that only core reading programs are sufficiently scientifically based to direct classroom activities during reading instruction. Once this proper technology is selected, teachers are expected to follow the directions in the teachers' manuals religiously.

In the first edition of *Broken Promises*, I reviewed the language of the teachers' manuals in order to demonstrate that publishers set the parameters of reading instruction in most classrooms across the United States. The accountability systems within those earlier programs tied teachers' actions to student performance through explicitly directed lessons and criterion-referenced tests written to program specifications. Although the publishers of these earlier programs claimed that their materials were the realization of the science of reading and instruction at that time, they failed to lead to universal literacy in America. More precisely, teachers employing those basal programs in the social conditions of the latter half of twentieth-century America produced higher test scores among the upper- and middle-class students but failed to produce acceptable scores among the poor, minorities, English language learners, and disabled. In that first edition, I argued that these results were not due to teachers' human error; rather the differing outcomes were a reflection of historical biases in America against these social groups that were systematically encoded in the materials and procedures of reading instruction at the time. In order to resist that tradition, I proposed a critical approach in which teachers acted on this new knowledge by identifying the biases within the basals and their practice. Such action would create new understandings of the power of literacy in a democratic society and lead to new methods of teaching toward an equal distribution of that power.

Business, the federal government, and many reading experts pushed in the opposition direction of such recommendations, claiming that teachers alone caused the achievement gaps because they did not properly understand reading itself or how to teach reading accordingly.[26] Their recommendations for the commercial production of the one best method within core reading programs were, of course, simply an echo of the theory of scientific management from the turn of the last century. In order to overcome the achievement gap, they argued, teachers must be held accountable for their deployment of the appropriate technology, tightening the connections between classroom lessons and test scores according to the needs of different social groups. Consider the categories that McGraw-Hill uses to explain its materials to potential customers.[27] First, recognize that currently McGraw-Hill publishes eight core reading programs, many of which were originally published by independent companies that McGraw-Hill acquired since the first edition of *Broken Promises*. Second, note that those eight are distributed across literacy based, balanced basal, and skills based categories, defined according to the populations to be served. Third, pay attention to the terms used to describe those populations.

> *Literacy Based*—Wright Group Core Reading; or Breakthrough to Literacy: These programs work well in districts where students begin formal schooling with basic skills acquired at home or in academic preschools. Reading programs in this category develop language through literature.
>
> *Balanced Basal*—Glencoe Literature; MacMillian Reading; Glencoe Reading; or Jamestown Signature Reading. The traditional basal program is effective with most students.
>
> *Skills Based*—Open Court; Jamestown Intervention; or Direct Instruction. These programs have proven to be especially effective with students who come from disadvantaged backgrounds, have limited proficiency in English, or have special needs. Lesson plans are highly structured.[28]

In this categorization scheme, students from more prosperous homes listen to and read literature in order to develop their language. Students from disadvantaged backgrounds (poor and minority students) need more structure during their lessons in order to overcome the deficits of their inadequate understandings of basic skills. Curt Dudley-Marling and Pat Paugh characterized this scheme as a direct continuation of unequal reading instruction.[29] Students from advantaged backgrounds are taught the social and cognitive practices of reading literature, sophisticated prose, and nonfiction, while students from disadvantage backgrounds are presented structured opportunities to read decodable text written only to help children practice the skills being taught. Dudley-Marling and Paugh did not mince words in their critique.

> Students in more affluent schools are given opportunities to draw on their language and experience as means for infusing their cultural and linguistic identities in to the official curriculum, what Dyson (1993) calls "staking a claim." Students in poor and working class schools, places overpopulated by students of color, are the object of a methods fetish (Bartholome, 1994) that makes no room for their linguistic and cultural identities. The languages and experiences of students in poor and working class schools are problems. Poor and working class students learn skills that can be used in the marketplace; students from privileged homes learn the skills they need to use the marketplace for their own ends. To students in middle and upper middle class schools, we declare, "Your ways with words, your ways of being in the world are welcome here." To students already disadvantaged by poverty and discrimination, we proclaim, "Let them eat skills" (Noble, 1994). The rich get richer; the poor get direct instruction.[30]

Publishers, business, federal government, and reading experts who back such core reading programs position teachers to deepen and maintain the literacy gaps between the haves and the have-nots in America. For teachers, the proof of this positioning can be found in the teachers' manuals from literacy-based, balanced basals, and skills-based core reading programs. In order to test this hypothesis, I visited area schools to examine the commercial core programs in use. The school district in which I live does not use a commercial program as the core to its reading instruction; rather it supplies teachers with a combined social studies and English language arts curriculum for kindergarten through sixth grade. Some teachers supplement their instruction with Wright Group materials. Committees of teachers and subject curricular specialists originally composed this format in the 1970s, and the district has developed and maintained the approach since that time to considerable success.[31] For special education students, however, the district has selected Reading Mastery, a marked contrast to its classroom program. McGraw-Hill would label this district as splitting its program between literacy-based and skills-based programs. A second area school district purchased and employs Harcourt Trophies, a balanced basal, for all students. A more urban district in the area has selected Open Court materials. All the programs in the districts were published or edited after 2003, with NCLB, Reading First, and the Education Science Reform Act in place. For my analyses, I examined lessons from the first- and third-grade teachers' manuals.

Literacy-Based Programs

Wright Group's Sunshine program does not look like basals of old.[32] Its roots are in New Zealand starting in the1960s with an experimental attempt to establish a reading curriculum based on students' reading of specific texts of ever increasing difficulty. The process was called leveling of text, and the originators believed that developing readers required multiple texts at each level in order to progress toward more sophisticated reading. In time the curriculum began to take pedagogical shape as well with a regular pattern of demonstrated reading, assisted reading, and independent reading becoming the foundation of the guided approach to reading instruction. Fluency, accuracy, and self-monitoring were the primary measures of students' early development, with comprehension being developed through discussion. The program (texts, pedagogy, and assessments) became commercially available in New Zealand as the Sunshine curriculum, and arguably, the guided reading approach began in the United States when Thomas Wright acquired its American publishing rights.

The program is now assembled in boxes, folders, and small books by McGraw-Hill. The teachers' manuals are presented differently as well, with directions spread among the various parts of the program and one coordinating manual that lists the relevant materials and skills for each book lesson in a yearlong instructional program. Teachers are asked to choose among the big books, student books, cassettes, plays, and chapter books or the option of the "carefully designed grade-level kit" with the coordinating manual. The five components from the National Reading Panel report—alphabetics, phonics, fluency, vocabulary, and comprehension—are not mentioned in the introduction to the materials. Rather, teachers using the program are expected to "lead students through the literacy learning process from phonics to chapter books, building confidence and important language access tools along the way." Because the grade-level kit is optional, Sunshine affords teachers considerable control over the curriculum and instruction within its program structure. The authors assume that teachers will determine the pace for each student through the reading of the leveled texts.

A first-grade Sunshine story lesson follows a directed reading activity format, providing teachers with suggestions for what to do before, during, and after the story reading. The lesson focus is set with a simple list—"silent guided reading, 168 words, and genre fiction." Teachers are told to establish prior knowledge, build background, introduce the book, and consider the skills bank before reading. The language register is imperative. "Ask questions to help you determine what the students know about robots." The authors provide two questions. The language of the directions becomes more directive during the skills-bank activity. "Explain that when the letters c and r 'crash together,' they make the /cr/ sound. Turn to page 4 and have the students find another cr word." The target word is supplied for the teacher to determine the correct answer. The after-reading activities, while directive, are much less didactic. For example, "Reflect on Reading Strategies. Discuss with students the strategies they used to solve print problems." The authors offer no suggestions on what the children should say or which strategies the teacher should emphasize. Apparently, the Sunshine authors believe that teachers know these strategies well and that the students should demonstrate their self-awareness without prompting. The assessment of the lesson asks teachers to concentrate on students' oral fluency, particularly the students' negotiation of the text's punctuation and its impact on the reader's expression. A worksheet is expected to be assigned in order to begin first-grade students' understanding of story grammar as a summarization tool.

One size fits all students in the Sunshine program. The only accommodations for English language learners are made in marginal notation. In the lesson just described, these notes remind teachers to spend more time on vocabulary and the Americanism contractions. Only students who do not reach level H books successfully during the school year or students who demonstrate sufficient fluency and accuracy to pass to level I books will miss this lesson. Teacher judgments are to determine these possibilities. When a teacher or school opts for the grade-level kits, these degrees of responsibility begin to evaporate. That is, the carefully designed nature of this option moves control of the curriculum and lessons further away from the classroom teacher. In the grade-level kits, stories are coordinated around skill sequences, which all teachers must deliver to each student regardless of her performance on the oral reading assessment (benchmark) books. McGraw-Hill demonstrates its sensitivity toward tighter control within its other K–3 literacy-based program Breakthrough to Literacy. "Backed by over twenty years of scientific research conducted initially at the University of Iowa, the *Breakthrough to Literacy* model clearly supports the recommendations of the National Reading Panel Report and No Child Left Behind legislation."

Balanced Reading Programs

Harcourt Trophies was published in 2005 under a tiered system of authorship.[33] Isabel Beck, Roger Farr, and Dorothy Strickland are senior authors, and Alma

Flor Ada, Marcia Brechtel, Margaret McKeown, Nancy Roser, and Hallie Kay Yopp are authors. The program is bright and colorful with a remarkable set of components—anthologies, teachers' manuals, at least three sets of workbooks and worksheets, sets of books for independent reading (also available on audiotape), CD-ROMs, DVDs, and other computer software, and an elaborate assessment program. All the texts are well constructed with great care taken to ensure that the labels can be easily interpreted in order that they can be found and employed when needed. In short, Trophies is an excellent representation of a balanced program.

The curriculum is based on the five components of the National Reading Panel report, with special attention given to alphabetics, phonics, fluency, vocabulary, and comprehension, housed in a daily lesson format of oral language, skills and strategies, reading, and language arts. The emphases within the format change appropriately between the first and third grades. For example, phonics, spelling, and high-frequency words occupy the skills section (labeled word work in first grade) while comprehension and vocabulary are the skills for third grade. Within these broad categories specific topics are listed across a daily schedule for a lesson. In first grade, each lesson is stretched across seven school days; in third it's a five-day cycle. Specific topics are addressed repeatedly within a lesson cycle. For example, fact and opinion within the third-grade comprehension strand is considered on three successive days—first, with a single example and explanation, second, with repeated probes across an entire story within the assigned text in the anthology, and finally, in a two-page test preparation assignment. In order to help teachers navigate through the curriculum, the teachers' manuals include a two-page matrix that presents the structure of the program at a glance, with strands and topics on the y-axis and days of the lesson cycle on the x-axis. The visual effect is both impressive and overwhelming as the responsibilities of teaching appear to be complete and too numerous for a single day or cycle.

To help teachers make decisions about which aspects of the listed topics to cover, the authors provide a *T* after the entries that will appear on the tests. For example, in the first-grade lesson, the digraph *ch*, the high-frequency words *how, many, air, animals, around, fly, live, soon,* and *turns*, and the nouns of animal names will be tested. Each has a *T* after its listing. Listening and responding to the big book reading, reading a decodable book, and writing something special about an animal will not be tested. Here alphabetics, phonics, and grammar trump reading and writing within the seven-day lesson cycle. In this scheme, the *T* marks the hierarchy of importance without any explanation. In order to help teachers plan instruction for individuals within a classroom, the authors provide another matrix for pretests, progress checks, and posttests of the lesson elements marked with a *T*. This matrix is less complex than the first.

The pre- and post-test matrices contrast if performance is below level, on level, and advanced against contingency conditions. If a student's performance is below the cutoff criterion for an element, then the teacher should employ the authors' suggestions for reteaching that component of the lesson. For below-level performers, teachers are directed to redeploy the materials already considered, including all of the special directions for below-level performers, to add supplemental practice with worksheets on the same topic, and to break out the "intervention resource kit" with further workbook and worksheet solutions. For on-level students, teachers are directed to keep to the core instruction, offer the cross-curricular centers, and provide a practice book. The advanced performers get more challenging worksheets and more books to read. Harcourt supplies all three types of tests, the correct answers, and the cutoff criteria. With the assessment matrices, the curricular decision points are established and the curricular decisions are made for teachers. The labels for the materials make the location of each assigned form readily available.

These separate routes through the lessons do not contain the same amount or type of information. Consider the decision directions after the progress check on vocabulary in the third-grade lesson. Students who do not reach criterion on the six assigned vocabulary words are presented with the extra support worksheet that requires, for example, that they fill in the word *clenched* to the sentence "I _____ the reins when my pony jumped." On-level students are asked to find synonyms for the vocabulary words and then write new sentences. Advanced students are challenged with the opportunity to imagine that they are at an auction with fantastic things to sell for millions of dollars and then to make a list and representations of those objects for sale. Each student, regardless of his performance on the progress assessment, reconsiders the six vocabulary words. The trajectories of their literacies are altered by the demands of the added work. The ones who score below level simply repeat the past. Students on level extend to more sophisticated labels for the practice of word substitution and are asked to compose, albeit in a modest way. Wouldn't the composed sentences of the below-level students provide more information about their thinking while validating their potential to make sense of these words? Students with high scores are asked to imagine and play with language. Does it seem unlikely that the students who score below and on level could benefit from and enjoy playing with language in order to come to grips with auctions and the language that surrounds them? With these decisions, the authors lay the groundwork for the reading achievement gaps to increase rather than close.

During the late 1980s, commercially prepared basal reading programs set the goals, curriculum, materials, and assessment procedures for teachers. They left only the time variable open for teachers to control. While the assessment program and reporting procedures ensured that administrators monitored the rates with which teachers and schools proceeded through the materials, there was little direct attention to time. Within the new Harcourt Trophies balanced core reading program, however, authors set the times for each lesson and each part of the lesson. First, the goals of the program are apportioned over the grade levels. Within those levels, goals are named directly and situated within the lesson strands. Each strand is given time parameters in which teachers are expected to present the materials. For example, at the third-grade level, reading instruction is allotted 90 minutes, with 5 to 15 for oral language, 15 for skill and strategy lessons, 15 allotted for reading, and 45 designed for language arts. Each strand has multiple skills assigned to it, which should be accomplished within the specified time in order to complete the day's assignment and to be ready for the next day's work. To meet the time requirements, some parts of the strand often need to be deleted (untested portions are the most likely candidates) or different days' responsibilities begin to bleed into one another. At the first-grade level, another layer of time constraints is added concerning classroom management. Each 120- or 150-minute period assigned to language arts is to begin with 40 minutes of whole-group instruction with morning message, text sharing, and skill and strategy demonstration; followed by a 60- to 90-minute small-group period in which students are grouped for special attention and teachers rotate through groups to support their reading of assigned text and to monitor independent seatwork assignments; and conclude with 30 minutes of closure with the entire class, in which writing and grammar work take place. Although the time frames are intended to help teachers keep lessons quickly paced and varied, they in fact turn time into teachers' enemy, forcing them to watch the clock as well as pay attention to the children's performances on assignments.

Within each lesson, the directions to teachers are straightforward and unambiguous. Two types of statements are made. At times, the authors address teachers in order to inform them about the basal components or to provide some factual information needed for a particular lesson or story. These statements are infrequent but noticeable and distinct in tone and register. For example, the first-grade lesson includes the following section:

THEME CONNECTION

From Head to Toe shows animals moving different parts of their bodies in various ways and asking, "Can you do it?" Children imitate each movement, replying, "I can do it!" As the title suggests, the movement begins at the head, moving down to the neck and shoulders, and so on, ending with a child challenging a parrot to wiggle its toes. Children can use their imaginations as they explore creative movements.

The third-grade lesson offers this tidbit:

HISTORICAL FICTION

Historical fiction is a story that is set in the past and portrays people, places, and events that did happen or could have happened.

Both of these statements present teachers with information that is not remarkable but helps focus the work to come on what the authors believe to be important. The declarative statements convey authority of knowledge but do not impose a frame of mind upon or require specific action from teachers. Tone is respectful, if not a bit condescending. The quotations are representative of this type of statement and often are presented in list formats.

By far, the majority of statements to teachers are in the form of commands that direct teachers to take some action in order to command students' attention and behavior. These sentences are written in the imperative with a tone that not only conveys authority but projects a sense that teachers must comply. These statements are not choices offered, but rather directions on how to employ the materials properly or to lead students to particular learning of predetermined content. For example, the first-grade reading of "From Head to Toe," referenced earlier, continues in these directions:

CHORAL RECITING

Organize children into two groups. As you reread From Head to Toe, have one group recite the question *Can you do it?* and the other group recite the reply *I can do it!*

The third-grade example also turns quickly to the imperative:

PREVIEW AND PREDICT

Have students read the genre information on page 148. Then have them preview the selection. Ask them what they think the selection is about, based on their preview and the characteristics of historical fiction. Then have them make predictions about what will happen to Leah's family. Students can begin a fact-opinion chart. See Transparency F on page T 54.

Such language sets teachers in motion in order to fulfill the basal authors' plans. It also establishes a hierarchy of authority with basal authors on top and students at the bottom. In between these strata, teachers are to follow directions. Harcourt offers different language when directing teachers to consider the three groups of students formed according to their scores on the lesson pretest. Just the first sentence for the separated instructions for the groups demonstrates these differences.

Below Level—Have students read the title and tell what they see on the
first two pages.

On Level—Students can take turns with a partner as they read aloud
each page of the selection.

Advanced—Students may read independently at their own pace.

The imperative disappears for higher-scoring students, and the verb
changes among the levels of success. On-level students are able (*can*) and the
advanced students are permitted (*may*). Perhaps this distinction seems slight,
but when coupled with the instructions for how to manage this portion of the
lesson, the differences seem important. Below-level children must meet in a
small group to be led by the teacher. On-level students are to work in pairs. Advanced students read independently. The language of the teachers' manual
imparts a different level of trust that affects the relationships between teacher
and students and between students and their reading instruction. Again the
gaps in reading achievement are extended by the balanced core reading program through the language directing teachers' instruction.

Skills-Based Programs

True to their label, skills-based core reading programs feature alphabetics,
phonics, fluency, and vocabulary over comprehension during early reading
instruction. Authors assume that mastery of the elemental parts of reading
is necessary before the act of reading is possible. Accordingly, teachers begin
with letters, work through sound blending toward words, and then consider
what those words might mean singly and in sentences and longer contexts.
The assumption for the sequence is based on the notion that students already
possess the meanings for thousands of words before they enter school and
that cracking the alphabetic code is the primary task of reading. Because of
the code's primacy, the skills of cracking it must be taught directly and systematically in order that all students become master decoders. Skills-based
core reading programs are distinguished by the order of elements within
lessons at the lower levels, with pronounced emphasis on letters, sounds, and
blending within tightly structured lessons to be presented to all students.
Letter- and word-level practice activities and assessment predominate. Publishers contend that all students will learn to read if teachers follow explicitly all the directions in the teachers' manuals. They base contentions over
skills-based superiority on statistical evidence that demonstrates that a skills
approach does improve early readers' scores on various decoding tests. Results are mixed when comparing skills-based and balanced programs
through measures of comprehension.[34]

For example, McGraw-Hill's SRA Open Court Reading represents a skills-based core reading program that appears on the approved list for Reading First funding.[35] It offers a comprehensive language arts program and includes a plethora of materials for instruction, practice, assessment, and reteaching. Its appearance is indistinguishable from that of balanced programs—colorful, well made, and expensive. It shares the multiple-day format, the single-book and anthology approach, and the directed reading activity framework. The teachers' manuals include similar tone and register in directions to teachers. In the edition I examined (2003 was used in area schools), the authors include a greater percentage of descriptive and informative language within the majority of imperative discourse. For example, a first-grade unit overview has several paragraphs on the theme topic of imagination.

> Students, along with many adults, commonly think of imagination as "making things up"—especially things of a bizarre or fanciful nature. Making things up is one aspect of imagination, but there are many other aspects as well. It takes imagination to plan wisely, anticipate outcomes, and identify people's feelings.

The section continues to explain how addressing imagination might affect students' capabilities for divergent thinking. These descriptions are more elaborate than any similar uses of language in the balanced Harcourt core reading program. Perhaps the length and depth in Open Court can be attributed to the authors' position that teachers cannot assume any prior knowledge of skills or information among students and, therefore, must teach explicitly and systematically. Perhaps this position includes teachers as well as students.

Imperative statements direct teachers throughout every aspect of each lesson. Often Open Court is labeled a scripted core reading program because it provides teachers with exact language to use in every situation in order to ensure the maximum fidelity of their work. Authors report that they do not intend the teachers' manuals to be scripts for lessons and contend that the language of their teachers' manuals resembles that of the balanced programs. This claim seems accurate in terms of tone and number. For example, the Open Court directive "Have students read the title and author's and illustrator's names aloud" could appear in Harcourt Trophies' first-grade lesson as well as the Open Court teachers' manuals. This language is quite distinct from an actual script provided in McGraw-Hill's SRA Reading Mastery program.[36]

READING VOCABULARY

Task 13 Children say the sounds, then sound out the word

a. Touch the first ball of the arrow for **am. You're going to sound it out.** Point to the ball for **a. What sound are you going to say first?**

Touch the ball. *aaa.* **Yes, aaa.** Point to the ball for **m. What sound are you going to say next?** Touch the ball. *mmm.* **Yes, mmm.** Lesson 34

At the bottom of this page, a large black dot (labeled a ball) begins a continuous line that ends with a direction arrow. This line is a graphic representation of left-to-right progression in reading. A smaller dot appears on each letter. The regular print in the previous quote directs teachers' fingers as the bolded print directs their exact words to students. The sounds in italics present the students' utterances that must be made for the lesson to proceed. All children must respond in unison. The lesson labeled reading vocabulary has five steps with similar didactic wording, commanding both teachers' and students' actions to read the word *am.* Although also a skills-based program, Reading Mastery uses a different tone and register than Open Court in its scripts. Regardless of how effective Reading Mastery might or might not be as a core reading program, it clearly controls each aspect of every reading lesson without regard for teacher, student, or situation. Open Court does not follow this scripted design. It might be true, however, that Open Court redefines the term *scripted.*

> In every district wide adoption of Open Court we know of in California, teachers are required to complete every activity described in the teachers manual with the entire class and to do it at a prescribed pace (i.e., so many lessons within so many days), whether it is appropriate for the particular students in their classes or not. . . . We see Open Court as a new form of scripted instruction, not one where the teacher's words are scripted verbatim, but one in which what, when and how teachers teach is controlled by people outside the classroom, not amenable to classroom teachers' judgment based on their knowledge of their students.[37]

In this way, the skills-based core reading programs position teachers to treat all students as if they lacked any knowledge of print or reading. Every teacher provides every student with the same lesson, sometimes repeating the directions verbatim and other times mimicking the directives supplied in the manuals. Although this assumption appears to remedy the achievement gaps by offering all students the same experiences, it simply masks the existing gaps during reading lessons. No student gets richer, to use Dudley-Marling and Paugh's phrase, during school, but that does not compensate for the out-of-school experiences where the rich continue their advantaged access to more sophisticated literacy experiences. At the same time, teachers are lumped together as well. None knows more than any other. None can reason or experiment in productive ways. None of their interests, words, or actions can be spontaneous. None can develop herself as a teacher outside the parameters of the skills-based core reading programs or develop as a human being during the reading lessons.

The End of History

The future is not bright for teachers, if the government's, businesses', and reading experts' end of history for reading instruction is allowed to stand. The expeditious moves to create highly qualified teachers of reading substitute quick credentials and testing for teachers' knowledge and experiences. The intellectual and performative core of teaching is denigrated without achieving the desired goal of providing a good teacher in every classroom for every subject taught. Moreover, this highly qualified solution does not address the causes of the problem that led to the shortage in the first place. What are the incentive structures that would bring the right people to the schools that lack capable teachers? Those studies are pushed aside by the ultimatums and deadlines of NCLB and the business market to prepare teachers for the certification tests.

The rationale for the imposition of limits on teachers' professional development in reading also rests on the end-of-history metaphor. Because reading experts believe that they have discovered the neural essence of reading, established the one best system of teaching reading, and declared a consensus on these matters, it only makes sense to limit discussion on alternatives. "Why waste time and money?" government officials ask, distribute the knowledge behind the consensus as quickly as possible by targeting professional development funds toward that end. Through this act, teachers' curiosity is honed by the scientifically based approach, leaving all other possibilities for instruction outside official boundaries. As the principal from Montana explained, if states and school districts take the federal money, then they must follow the federal lead and stop asking some questions. Again businesses are happy to be able to direct their products toward these goals as well, eliminating the need to tailor their products to specific contexts and sets of issues. Only the illusion of variety is needed because the solution is not teachers' knowledge or capacity to pose and address questions. According to federal regulations, professional development means only the increased precision with which teachers can employ a core reading program.

At the end of history for reading instruction, teachers are tethered to the teachers' manuals of approximately five core reading programs. From the federal government's, businesses', and many reading experts' point of view (and it appears to be singular), this connection is necessary because teachers cannot teach reading based on their own understandings of reading or instruction, even after they complete many hours of professional development. In fact, the best teachers, that is the ones whose students score the highest on state reading tests, are said to be the ones who follow the teachers' manual scripts most closely. The scripts and the materials that support them supply the goals, curriculum, instruction, means of assessment, interpretations of that assessment, and the directions for reteaching, leaving teachers to manage the students as they move through the commercially prepared system according to publishers' plans. This sacrifice of teachers' intellect and development is deemed necessary in order to close the reading achievement gaps among various social groups of students. Yet as designed, core reading programs position teachers to maintain those gaps, leading some groups toward sophisticated reading through a great variety of texts and tasks and others to functional ends by directing students' attention primarily toward tested skills and impoverished texts.

Chapter Nine

A Process of Elimination

During the third week of April 2006, the Associated Press distributed a series of articles on No Child Left Behind.[1] The articles appeared in papers across the country amid other items that seemed to question the George W. Bush administration's War on Terror, health policies, border closings, environmental programs, and tax cuts during a time of growing budget deficits. The crux of the NCLB articles was the discovery that schools and teachers were excluding students' scores from adequate yearly progress reports that required disaggregation by race, class, English proficiency, and physical and mental ability. The tone of the articles implied that public educators feared that these students would depress the schools' average test scores below the state thresholds, causing schools to be labeled "needs improvement" and triggering expensive supplemental service efforts. It appeared that in order to preserve their jobs, teachers and administrators subverted the lofty NCLB goals of literacy proficiency for all. The articles noted that although parents believe that all students can reach this goal, many schoolteachers have their doubts. As evidence that teachers and parents are not aligned on NCLB, one article quoted a seventy-five-year-old kindergarten teacher from Florida who stated that not all students come from "fine families."

Unlike the other articles on the Bush Administration's policies, which raised questions, the NCLB stories promoted the federal point of view that public school teachers are not working to benefit individuals or for a strong and equitable America. This juxtaposition of articles attests to the power of the Bush administrations' No Child Left Behind framing of educational policy and the strength of the business community behind it. Although the rhetorical frames for other social issues are questioned openly on the front page of many newspapers across the country,[2] the title No Child Left Behind is not. It still captures the imagination of both pundits and the public, who accept at face value NCLB's commitment that all children can learn, that what they are taught is necessary for their futures in an increasingly uncertain world, and that schools should be institutions that render predictable results to enable equal opportunities within the American version of democracy. Personal learning with social consequences for the national economy and democracy are indeed worthy goals. American schools, however, have never offered equal opportunities to all students, and the American government has never offered equal opportunities to its citizens.[3] NCLB is not an attempt to distrupt this history; rather it is a meeting place for several of America's most cherished biases.

No Child Left Behind is the most recent iteration of the century-old project to find the one best method of reading instruction in order to render the outcomes more predictable, equipping American workers to meet the literacy demands of the contemporary economy. Throughout the twentieth century, American reading instruction has prepared groups of students differently to meet those demands. Although NCLB pretends to address these differences through market ideology, it portends to deepen the differences among groups in an economy that no longer has a need for all people. In this chapter, I argue that Americans have not and do not act as if they value equal opportunity for children or citizens and that schools are designed to provide scientific evidence that the historical inequalities in America are legitimate, justified, and natural. In the second part of the chapter, I present a case study of how the current structures of reading instruction will eventually provide the data to reorganize public schools according to high-stakes tests that purposely exclude some social groups from higher levels of schooling. In this way, the biases of the past are furthered by NCLB, which provides scientific justifications for American history.

Continued Inequalities

In the August 2005 issue of the *Teachers College Record*, David Berliner surveyed the impact of economic inequality in America upon school achievement.[4] He began with the fact that Americans accept the highest level of child poverty of any industrialized country in the world. Scandinavian countries have 2 or 3 percent of their children living in poverty; Germany permits 10 percent; but in the United States, nearly 22 percent of children live in poverty. More than one out of five children live in a family below the poverty line. The American poverty line for a family of four is just over $19,000. Living below the poverty line means that these children have inadequate housing, lack nutritional meals, and receive spotty health care. Berliner links each of these factors with lower achievement scores. Tired, hungry, and ill students do not score as high on standardized tests as their rested, regularly fed, and healthy peers regardless of what the school programs might include. At least abstractly, Americans accept these scores as indicative of what children have learned and what they are capable of learning in the future. That is, schools and society believe that schools reward merit: students who score higher on tests are given more opportunities and students who score lower are made to repeat the past opportunities until they jump over the proficiency bar. These incentives are intended to close the achievement gap as poor children work harder in order to earn new opportunities.

In *Meritocracy, Inc.*, Lani Guinier argued, however, that achievement test scores have less to do with merit and more to do with social class status.[5] The science of testing hides this bias because the tests appear to make objective, mathematical decisions based solely on who is worthy of greater opportunity. Guinier offered a different way of reading the achievement gap between various groups. Although NCLB holds the individual student and teacher accountable for the score, assuming the test validity and objectivity, Guinier charged that both the test content and the decision to use the score for prediction are skewed toward class and cultural elites, allocating further opportunities in order to maintain social, economic, and political gaps under scientific pretense.

> I am arguing that many of the criteria we associate with individual talent and effort do not measure the individual in isolation but rather parallel the phenomena associated with aristocracy; what we're calling individual talent is actually a function of that individual's social position or opportunities gained by virtue of family and ancestry. So although the system we call meritocracy is presumed to be more democratic and egalitarian than aristocracy, it is in fact reproducing that which it was intended to dislodge.[6]

Over half a century ago, the U.S. Supreme Court ruled that southern schools' segregation was unconstitutional and inherently unequal. Between the mid-1960s and the 1980s, school segregation was in decline; however, during the last two decades, resegregation of schools has been occurring across America despite an increase in diversity within the student population. Over the last thirty years, the black student population has increased by nearly six million; four million more Latino students and three million more Asian students attend public schools. Six million fewer white students are enrolled. Although schools should be more racially diverse, Jonathan Kozol refers to schools as the shame of a nation because of racial segregation and unequal conditions.[7] Gary Orfield and others attribute the resegregation in schools directly to a continued segregation of housing in America, in which minorities inhabit and are steered toward inner cities and rings of older suburbs, and white families isolate themselves in suburbs and exburbs or send their children to private schools if they remain in cities.[8] Orfield argues that racially resegregated schools offer vastly unequal educational opportunities. In fact, he found that the gaps in achievement and graduations rates, which had been closing between the 1960s and the mid-1980s, began to expand in concert with this resegregation.

Continued and growing poverty and segregation make a mockery of the NCLB commitment that all children will learn. Of course, all children can and do learn daily, but what are poor and minority children learning when American adults stand by silently, witnessing these inequalities? Despite the hard work of some researchers and teachers who struggle diligently to lessen the blows of poverty and segregation, the primary lesson for these groups is clear. In America, equal opportunity means that middle- and upper-class white students are born with advantages, believe that they have earned them, and work to maintain them through social and economic policies and institutions. This is not pessimistic talk or "the subtle bias of low expectations," as President George W. Bush often repeats. Rather it is a logical conclusion based on one hundred years of test results that continue to offer class and race as the best predictors of achievement test scores. In this way, the academic consequences of poverty and segregation are not problems for science to solve through experimentation and technology that isolate the individual as the unit of learning. Rather, these consequences are political issues to be decided by moral commitment to a democracy based on social, economic, and political equalities.

Federal officials and business leaders demonstrate little interest in actually securing the future of all American children. If they were interested, then poverty rates would be shrinking instead of growing each year during the Bush administration.[9] In fact in 2004, 37 million Americans, more than 12 million of them children, were poor. If government and business leaders worried about racial inequality, then they would not rest while 33 percent of all black children lived in poverty. Instead of direct assistance, the government reduced aid to the poor.[10] For example, the formula for determining the poverty rates was established in 1963 by simply tripling the cost of food required to keep an individual healthy. In 1963, food consumed one-third of a household budget. Today, however, food is relatively less expensive, occupying only one-tenth of the budget. The federal government has not made corresponding adjustments in the poverty rate and, therefore, provides inadequate funding for those who fall below the poverty line and hides the fact that many more Americans are impoverished. If the original one-third ratio of food cost were preserved, then the current U.S. poverty rate would be at least three times higher than currently reported (the 14 percent of Americans living in poverty in 2005 would increase to more than 40 percent of Americans below the adjusted poverty line). Nor has the government or business helped workers to keep pace with rising costs. Two full-time jobs at minimum wage will not enable a family of four to move above the current poverty line. The George W. Bush administration rejected any increase toward a living wage as inflationary and likely to cause job loss. Nor is the government willing to provide for the health or nutrition of poor citizens. According to the 2005 census, 45.8 million Americans do not have health insurance, an increase of nearly a million citizens from 2004; 38 percent of the uninsured are children.[11] According to the Children's Defense Fund, food and shelter insecurity are rising also. More families were unsure of where and how they would find a meal or where they would sleep at some time during the previous year.[12] Clearly federal government and businesses have not committed fully to securing the well-being of children in America. Rather they shirk responsibility and push it toward teachers and the individuals in need. For many children (and many adult Americans), the slogan No Child Left Behind rings hollow.

How the Process Works

Rather than deliver on its rhetoric, NCLB is organized to induce school "failure" and promote reorganization around market designs.[13] It is a nightmare for schools and teachers, but it has even darker social consequences for groups of children—the "scientific" identification of human waste in America. NCLB is expected to identify the "many" in Richard Herrnstein and Charles Murry's statement "for many people, there is nothing they can learn that will repay the cost of the teaching."[14] When I first read that sentence in *The Bell Curve* during 1994, I considered it to be among the coldest remarks on human potential ever written in a democracy. Up to that point, I imagined everyone shared, at least rhetorically, the liberal optimism of American schooling—the notion that it's never too late to learn and everyone deserves a second, and even third, chance. Such sentiment was a motivation behind the GI Bill after World War II, the desegregation of schools in the 1960s, and inclusion of exceptional students during the 1970s. Given a chance, everyone could learn more at school, and it was worth it socially, economically, and politically to fund him to do so. This commitment to universal schooling for all ages distinguished the United States from all other countries. But the tenets of NCLB demonstrate that some representatives in the federal government have lost that vision, despite their rhetoric to the contrary.

I began to see this intention while reading the quarterly *Bulletin* from our son's school. The photograph on the first page of the fall edition presented three children of different races—Asian, Latino, and white—mugging for the camera. Page 3 offered verbal "snapshots" of the school curriculum. Kindergartners began their schooling by studying the school environment. Sixth graders were beating on African drums during the Passports to Understanding unit. High school biology and journalism students were using new wireless laptops in their workrooms. Between pages 4 and 13 of the *Bulletin*, parents and community members could read about a Japanese educational exchange, a peace garden, clubs and organizations during and after school, nutrition advice, community fund-raising, a diversity banner, special ceremonies for retired teachers, and homeowner tax relief. The *Bulletin* represented our public schools as vital parts of our community, worthy of our continued emotional, political, and financial support. These pages were meant to convey the district values of caring, diversity, inquiry, civic involvement, and respect. On pages 14 and 15, however, the focus of the *Bulletin* changed sharply with the district report card.

> We are pleased to present the 2003–2004 Academic Achievement report. As required by federal No Child Left Behind legislation, this report is designed to communicate our performance on key indicators: achievement in reading and mathematics, attendance, graduation rate, the performance of subgroups, and teacher qualifications. The report is based on 2004 Adequate Yearly Progress (AYP) reports, as measured by the Pennsylvania System of School Assessment tests, recently released by the Pennsylvania Department of Education. By 2014, all students are expected to achieve at the proficient or advanced level. Our report card contains good news for our community about the overall performance of our students and schools. As before, we will use standardized test results such as these in our continuous effort to improve the academic success of our students.

The district was pleased to report its results to the community because its only visible blemish was that one school did not reach the 95 percent plateau for taking the test (only 94.4 percent took the tests when scheduled). The district's graduation rate was 97.9 percent; its attendance rate was 95.9 percent; and 79 percent of the seniors planned to attend four-year colleges. The high school averaged fourteen National Merit finalists annually over the last six years. Out of 613 teachers, only 4 had emergency credentials from the state (a high school gym teacher, middle school Spanish and reading teachers, and an elementary reading teacher). Four hundred and thirty-eight teachers had graduate degrees. A national business magazine had named the school district "the best in the country." The district personnel were justifiably proud of these accomplishments. Most school districts around the United States can only envy such descriptive statistics.

The numbers, however, did not bode well for the future of our celebrated school district over the next decade. At the time of that issue of the *Bulletin*, district students were 15 to 25 percentage points ahead of the state requirements for AYP. Within the decade, however, the state requirements must match NCLB requirements of perfection—all students must be proficient in tested subjects. Although Pennsylvania allowed districts to set the pace within which they would achieve that goal, all districts must have 100 percent proficiency by 2014. In 2004, the minimum state thresholds were set at 45 percent of all students in math and 35 percent in reading. At all levels and in all subjects, three-quarters of the general population of students in this district were considered proficient or advanced after testing. Only 25 percent were found to be basic or below basic in their reading practices on the state test. As the years progress toward 2014, however, this 25 percent must shrink to zero. The district's first graders in 2004 are the students who all must be proficient by the end of their school careers or the school district will face sanctions. During that decade, those first graders will be tested annually between third and eighth grades and then once in high school. As they move toward that high school test (in reading, writing, math, and science), the pressure will mount to ensure that they pass the tests and maintain that proficient score as the tests become more difficult. Not one slip is allowed. Think about the social relationships among the teachers and the students who remain at basic or below basic levels on all or any one of the tests. What types of pressures face those who teeter above the proficiency line?

The demographic makeup of the "failing" 25 percent on 2004 tests complicates matters for the school district. Although the students in the district are predominantly white (more than 90 percent), able (more than 93 percent), native English speaking (more than 98 percent), and not officially poor (84 percent), the students in the bottom 25 percent are disproportionately nonwhite, disabled, English learners, and/or poor. Using the category labels of the school district, African Americans' proficient or above rates ranged from 47 percent to 62 percent depending on the subject and grade level; special education students (IEP) were successful 27 to 50 percent of the time; English language learners (LEP) passed the tests between 30 percent on third-grade reading tests and 78 percent on the eleventh-grade math test; and poor students (low SES) ranged from 42 to 63 percent proficiency or above. At the third-grade level, 74 percent of the basic and below-basic students were from one of these groups; by eleventh grade that number was 81 percent. NCLB positions members of these groups as objects of concern who will determine if our school will be considered successful.

These local test results confirm America's not so well-guarded secret—not every student is successful in our schools (for all types of reasons) and some social groups are served less well than others, even among the "successful" school districts. NCLB, AYP, and disaggregation policies demand that schools address these inequalities by raising the test scores of failing students. Translating this rhetoric into reality, however, is not easy or perhaps even reasonable. The *Bulletin* offered examples of these problems in a microcosm. For example, progress has not been linear. Two-year trends among the scores suggested uneven progress toward full proficiency, and even some regression among some groups. Fifth-grade trends were mixed, with student scores up 2.6 percent in math but down .7 percent in reading. Eighth grade enjoyed a boom year, with students' scores increasing 7.7 percent in math and 4.2 percent in reading. However, eleventh graders slipped in both math and reading—down 3.1 and 1.8 percent, respectively. More distressing, the number of students scoring in the lowest rank, below basic, actually grew for fifth-grade math scores and for high school students in both subjects on the 2004 test.

A closer look at the disaggregated scores indicates these problems are not spread equally across demographic groups. Apparently, the performances of some groups threaten more than others the district's overall chances of ever reaching complete proficiency. Special education students failed to reach the state's cutoff score in reading; English language learners failed in both subjects; and poor students' scores declined (but did not fall enough below the cutoff to warrant official sanctions). Despite these declines, the district was able to use loopholes in the state's regular provisions of NCLB in order to stave off violation of adequate yearly progress for this year. The future, however, does not look as promising. For example, the modal scores for special education students and English language learners were in the below-basic categories across grade levels in both years reported. More special education students, English language learners, poor, and African American high school students were in the below-basic category in 2004 than in 2003. These students, and therefore the school district, are headed in the wrong direction. Punctuating this point, the elementary school with the greatest racial and linguistic diversity had the lowest average scores in the district.[15]

In a local newspaper editorial, the school district's superintendent announced that four hundred Pennsylvania school superintendents signed a petition to have special education students and English language learners exempt from NCLB testing. Our superintendent reasoned that the state examinations are not fair assessments of what these students know and have learned.

She argued that the NCLB system ignores the fact that previous diagnostic tests were used to classify special education students as exceptions to typical school practices, exceptions who needed assistance in order to make any academic progress. Some of these students, she argued, are severally hindered in their learning, yet NCLB requires them to take the same tests at the same time as students who do not need extra academic support. The superintendent questioned the logic of holding special education students to the same standards after already determining that they would not make the same progress in the same ways. In a parallel argument, the superintendent sought to withhold English language learners from testing unless they had been in the country for four years—the time that experts estimate is necessary for children to learn a language sufficiently well to compete equally with native speakers on academic tests. The superintendent concluded her argument with the prediction that the continued testing of special education students and English language learners would certainly ensure that eventually all schools in the Commonwealth would be sanctioned for not making adequate yearly progress. Echoing the position of many critics of NCLB, she maintained that both special education and English language learners could be better served outside the NCLB system and that their inclusion threatened the good results the districts were accomplishing for other groups.

In their appeal, the Pennsylvania superintendents implied that the NCLB law forces school failure by design. By requiring all students to reach a score that some students by definition cannot be reasonably expected to reach, the law causes school failure in the way it defines success. In order to correct this problem, the superintendents implored the federal government to exempt special education students and English language learners from yearly testing. With this request, the superintendents admitted that it will be impossible for schools to ensure that all their students succeed, regardless of how low or high the Pennsylvania Department of Education might set the threshold. According to the superintendents, this admission is a logical consequence given that educational science created these deficit categories in the first place. But their admission sprang the trap of NCLB, which simply states that tested proficiency of high standards is the only acceptable outcome of schooling. Although not a single public school in the country has ever met this goal, every school must now be perfect or be considered a failure. The Pennsylvania superintendents believe that they are being set up for failure.[16]

If successful, the exemption will remove special education students and English language learners from testing, arguably to keep them out of harm's way. However, it will also identify them as groups who are incapable of learning what the government has deemed necessary and valuable skills for all school graduates. Perhaps, then, a likely conclusion is obvious: If schools cannot teach special education students and English language learners to be proficient on what the government values, then why should taxpayers continue to fund the educations of such students beyond a certain elemental level? In this way, the superintendents play in the hands of Herrnstein and Murray by identifying these groups as some of the "many people" who can't learn enough to compensate for the expense. Although it might seem hard-hearted to think this way, who can argue with the facts given the NCLB definition of success? Their test scores demonstrate empirically that these groups are not successful, arguing loudly in favor of the discontinuation of special education students and English language learners from school rolls when they first begin to falter. After that point, the amount they could learn cannot justify the expense given the cost-benefit analysis. Such high-stakes testing and exiting strategy parallel the educational policies of many competing countries in the global economy. In those countries—most based on European models—tests determine which types of schooling or training are open to which types of students.

Further, their petition cannot solve the superintendents' problem; it simply sets a precedent for excluding individuals from other groups as well. Without special education and English language learners being tested, district proficiency rates would undoubtedly rise. However, if our district can serve as an example, these exemptions will not ensure that the districts will ultimately be considered successful by 2014, because the special education students and English language learners do not constitute the entire corps of students who currently are considered basic or below basic. Students of all sorts have received scores of basic and below. If the special education and English language learners can be excluded for their own good, then why shouldn't the members of poor and minority groups be channeled into other opportunities than further schooling? Their test scores also demonstrate a lack of promise, and therefore, further funding of their education appears wasteful.

I admit that this likely outcome runs contrary to the government's official framing for disaggregated scores in NCLB. Federal officials state that the separation of scores by race, class, ability and English proficiency is necessary to monitor schools' treatment of these underserved groups in order to improve their service. However, the official rationale is not convincing. If every student were expected to become proficient on schedule, then an aggregated score would suffice to demonstrate progress. For example, in our school district, the *Bulletin* acknowledged that the district is not perfect according to the state test scores and NCLB's basic premise. The school officials know, and so does the community, that every student in the district does not test at proficient or advanced levels. If every child is to be held to the same standards, then why separate them into demographic groups for reporting? The inevitability of every district's ultimate failure might be postponed without disaggregation, but as the *Bulletin* demonstrated, eventually the number of basic and below-basic students will exceed the "needs improvement" threshold, even in the currently "successful" districts. When school districts fail to surpass the aggregated threshold, the putative recovery processes will begin and students' educational needs will be met. So, it cannot be argued successfully that the disaggregated scores are necessary for the NCLB accountability system to work, just as it cannot be argued successfully that the framers of NCLB have the best interests of all children at heart. Both are rhetorical sleights of hand intended to confuse the public.

Originally, I interpreted NCLB as a neoliberal policy, designed to force competition into the public education system by demonstrating the inability of schools in their current forms to meet the needs of individuals and business. In that reading of NCLB, I focused on the authoritative allocation of neoliberal values within the policy—competition, markets, and human capital development in order to help individuals and American businesses thrive in a global economy.[17] In that analysis, adequate yearly progress and disaggregated test scores were tools to force innovation in schools either through self-reform or reconstitution. They would be the forces of creative destruction that ended schools as we knew them. From those ruins, neoliberals would fashion a hybrid public and private education system, which would mirror the practices of successful multinational corporations by being focused on results, flexible to market demands, and remarkably efficient. I felt secure with that initial interpretation because the neoliberal Clinton administration had proposed all of the components of NCLB in its 1998 version of the Elementary and Secondary Education Act, which it failed to push through Congress. I think the Clinton administration assumed that under would-be president Gore's control, AYP and disaggregated test scores would end public education in a manner similar to how workfare eliminated economic welfare. Through such moves, neoliberals would save American democracy as they define it.

When President George W. Bush cobbled together neoconservative values (discipline for students and teachers through accountability), neoliberal values (world-class standards, results, and efficiency), and liberal values (more money to ensure equal opportunity) in order to pass NCLB in 2002, I considered the law to be an anomaly. The law's name stole the liberal thunder concerning the powers of schooling to bring about equality through opportunity—leave no child behind. Moreover, the law increased the federal presence in public school decision making by tying compliance with continued federal funding. On its face, NCLB neglected the educational values of Bush's conservative political base—state and local control, traditional patriotic and

Christian curricula, individualism, and hierarchies of authority. I wondered why President Bush and his advisers would push a neoliberal policy that would apparently employ liberal means to reach its stated objective. NCLB was a paradox to me until I read and analyzed the local school *Bulletin* and focused on the trends in disaggregated scores.

Those scores and the expectations that all students will reach proficiency in reading, writing, math, and science by 2014 are meant to identify groups— the poor, minorities, immigrants, and physically and mentally disabled— whom conservatives have historically found to be drains on American prosperity.[18] Through AYP and disaggregation, conservatives will gain the empirical evidence to confirm what they have believed for decades: the liberal experiments to educate these groups are doomed to failure because the groups are inferior and incapable of learning what should be taught at higher levels of schooling. If they cannot learn, then there is no point in the public funding their instruction. NCLB is designed to make that point emphatically. According to the rhetoric, even when teachers' attention and school resources have been directed toward these groups' education, many have still failed. By framing public schooling solely through this means-ends analysis based on test scores, no one can claim systemic bias when the pool of failing students is composed primarily of poor, minority, ELL, and special education students. According to conservative logic clearly expressed in *The Bell Curve*, the individuals in these groups have had their chance to prove themselves and have made the most of their abilities.[19] However, because their scores on tests demonstrate that they fall short of the educational standards, they should be excluded from further academic support. Rather than frustrate themselves and waste taxpayers' money, these groups should be happy to find service jobs that the global economy is so good at generating and leave further schooling and the high-skill, high-wage jobs for those who are more capable.

A survey of recent conservative literature on public schooling provides evidence of this dark project. Consider Jay Green and Marcus Winters' study of the Florida program to end social promotion.[20] They argue that their evidence demonstrates flunking a grade is an advantage to an individual if the individual did not score at the proficient level on the state exams. More, but not all, failed students pass the test when taking it after repeating a year of instruction, than the students who were permitted social promotion. Backed by the Manhattan Institute's Educational Research Office, their summary of their study appeared nationally under Green and Winters' byline in the *New York Post*, *Chicago Sun Times*, *San Diego Union Tribune*, and *Washington Times* within three days after the report's release. In *Education Next*, Alan Russo described Chicago's complex experiment in ending social promotion by reporting the paradox that although individuals might be hurt by grade retention, the school and district are helped in the reporting of AYP.[21] Quoting G. Alfred Hess, Russo opined that sacrificing some individual students for the greater district good is warranted and justified by the results. In a Brooking Institution publication, Martin West and Paul Peterson lauded the European educational model with its high-stakes exit examinations because they facilitate meritocracy, directing the most able toward more education and the less able to apprenticeships and work.[22] Finally, Texas public school teacher Paul Zook claimed that NCLB does not go far enough to convey to students and their parents that they are solely and ultimately responsible for their learning, and that students will get what they earn from their efforts at school despite any advantages or limitations of their teaching.[23] In each of these and other conservative arguments, advocates acknowledged that some children will and should be left behind socially and economically—it's good for them and the country.

Claudia Goldin argued that American universal secondary schooling is responsible for the U.S. economic advantage over the rest of the world.[24] She characterized the first half of the twentieth century as a time when "education ran faster than technology," enabling workers to innovate and the possibility of full employment. In this way, universal secondary education in the United States closed the income gap between classes and invented a middle class. Goldin suggested that since 1970, however, technology has run faster than education, shifting work from humans to machines and quelling the need for universal education. Since that time, Goldin observed, the virtues of universal secondary education in the United States—publicly funded, managed by numerous small fiscally independent districts, open and forgiving, academic, yet practical curricula, and secular in control—have now become vices, and that under NCLB, American education will mirror a European model: quasipublic and privately funded, tiered and directed by national standards in an unforgiving system, with a unity of church and state.

Previously when education ran ahead of technology, labor markets sorted students into different life tracks as working-class, minority, and immigrant children drifted toward work or were directed to technical training, allowing only a few to continue an academic focus. Now as technology runs ahead of education and all parts of the world are modernizing, students cut from the academic tracks have fewer options. Fewer workers are needed for businesses to be productive, and there are few, if any, new worlds to which the academically unproficient could emigrate in order to seek economic and social mobility. In *Wasted Lives: Modernity and Its Outcasts*, Zygmunt Bauman concluded that these citizens are now considered superfluous in the current economy— they are unnecessary for work to continue, and moreover, their support soon becomes a drain on the wealth of any nation.[25] Globalization has positioned them as the ones who have not and cannot learn enough to be considered productive, and therefore, they become the waste within the social and economic systems. Because globalization requires efficiency in government as well as business, Bauman understood school reforms across the postindustrial world as the "perfect" design to identify this waste and make the process appear beneficial for the individual and society.

Although it is unlikely that officials will use Bauman's terms, once identified, the waste must be removed from the system. The beginning of this movement can be seen in the AP newspaper articles about two million students across the country whom school administrators have not included in their AYP statistics. Some districts in Pennsylvania have already started to consider and act on such plans. Many technical secondary schools work outside of single school districts, being administered by the state through intermediate regional units. School superintendents contract services, sending students who seek vocational skills training to technical school campuses. In most cases, these students complete required academic subjects in their home schools and then attend skill classes away from home. The technical schools are highly successful in helping students learn those work skills. The majority score within the advanced range on their national and state technical certification examinations. According to technical high school administrators, a high percentage of these students struggle with required academic classes at the home school. Recently some school principals proposed to change the status of the technical schools to comprehensive schools, allowing students to attend such schools for both technical and academic course work. The potential of this proposal has not been lost on local technical school administrators.

> Principals in our area are trying to export their problems to us. In the past, they sent us behavior problems. But now it's the academics that count. At the moment, superintendents are lukewarm about the possibilities because it will cost more per student, but as their scores fall below the adequate yearly progress standard and the expensive penalties kick in, then they will see what the principals already see. These students won't pass because the skills are embedded in poetry and not plumbing or cosmetology. We can probably do a better job with some, but some of our best welding students struggle with reading comprehension of essays and abstract geometry. We are not going to change that easily, and the tests don't seem to value reading blueprints, chemistry of hair gels or figuring angles for bending pipe. So the districts want to make decisions about kids' futures based on

eighth grade state tests. That's not right! I can't imagine what I'd be doing now, if schools had made decisions about my future based on my performance in eighth grade.[26]

This is a remarkably savvy statement. Although this technical school administrator believed that his teachers could help some academically struggling high school students by embedding the academics within vocational interests, he acknowledged that not all his students would climb over the AYP threshold even with the assistance of his teachers. With his personal confession, he implied that some freshmen would be sent to new comprehensive/technical schools against their will. Of course, the decision whether or not to transform the school's status is not his alone to make. The school advisory board, intermediate advisers, and state officials will have the final word on the decision. However, his assessment of the prospect was clear; "it's not right" to make decisions for students that will limit their life choices and chances. What this administrator understands as personal problems for individuals becomes a social issue within the NCLB framework.

Although we did not have the opportunity to discuss the issue, the technical school administrator and I seem to agree that it is the reliance on conservative values in a globalized world that is wrong. We do not accept Herrnstein and Murray's conclusion that there are students who cannot be helped through education. Each might not ever pass the proficiency thresholds in all subjects, but everyone can be helped through continued education. To make this statement, we reject both the neoliberal premise for NCLB and the conservative possibilities of NCLB scientifically sanctioning social hierarchies in a democracy. Although the administrator stated he could not imagine what he would be doing if his potential had been determined at age fourteen, he implied that he would not be an educator or person in authority. Note that he could not bring himself to speculate on what would happen to those students who cannot pass the state exams in eleventh grade after being identified as academically superfluous after eighth grade and assigned to the newly projected comprehensive school after a battery of exams. Those who failed in this new environment would slide beneath the social and economic radar, if they were lucky, and into prison if they were not.[27]

Children as Waste

The public language of NCLB implies a caring educational system that will have all children reading on grade level by the end of their fourth year in public school. The law will accomplish this feat by holding teachers and students accountable for students' learning. Toward that end, school districts are invited to employ highly qualified teachers who will implement core reading programs according to directions in the teachers' manuals in order to ensure that students pass the state reading exams each year of their school careers. To assist teachers in this pursuit, schools employ reading coaches and professional development personnel to ensure fidelity in the use of the core system. Persistent failure for schools means a growth plan, and then reconstitution. For those individuals who fail repeatedly, the government requires school districts to fund private tutoring until a proficient score is made. If allowed to continue, NCLB means a dim future for public schooling and bleak consequences for students because NCLB

> freezes reading as tested skills
>
> alienates students from their learning
>
> assigns academic identities
>
> positions some identities as problems
>
> validates privilege

NCLB freezes all students' reading as the skills tested on state exams. Critics charge that NCLB has reduced reading instruction to "teaching to the test."[28] President Bush acknowledged this fact when he responded that "teaching to the test is the point," and said, "We want the students to pass the tests." The tests are of questionable quality, however. Under NCLB, each state developed its set of tests of reading and determined the threshold scores for proficiency across the grades. Although this act suggests state control, federal authorities approved each state's testing program. Because all state plans eventually passed, some ardent enthusiasts for NCLB suggest that the current program waters down world-class standards so that states may protect themselves from federal government intrusions.[29] To answer this criticism, the federal government included a provision in the Reading First Initiative that required each state to participate in the National Assessment of Educational Progress, which samples students' performance in reading and other subjects biannually. In effect, NAEP serves as a national test against which to measure the relative successes among the states.

Simply by taking this step, the federal government has provided a national set of reading skills.[30] Eventually these skills will supplant the state skills because low scores on NAEP tests (even with high state proficiency rates) will demonstrate the relative successes and failures of state reading education programs. NAEP reading skills leave much to be desired because they neglect the resources children need to direct reading as a powerful force in their lives. NAEP includes items that test general understanding, developing interpretation, making connections among texts, and examining content and structure. Such skills encourage students to make sense of text, but not necessarily to use text in order to pose and answer their own questions or to determine how the text positions them within the world. Freebody and Luke suggest that at best NAEP encourages comprehension and assumes competence in decoding. While not without merit, these skills limit students' understanding of how to use text for multiple purposes or how text can work for and against students' interests.[31] If not tested, these latter pratices will not be taught, leaving students with the ability to follow but not employ and evaluate directions. Freebody and Luke seek reading pedagogy that will enable readers to use conventions of print, create meaning according to their knowledge of the world and others, but also to understand cultural and social functions of texts and how texts convey values and position readers accordingly.[32]

NCLB and Reading First alienate students from their learning. Designed to raise test scores, core reading programs do not permit students to pursue their questions about the world. As entertaining as some of the lessons might be, the essence of the core program is to direct students' attention to the skills to be tested and the practice of those skills within controlled environments reminiscent of Thorndike's laws of learning from the turn of the nineteenth century. Skills are taught separately, practiced in texts that are constructed only for that task, and then tested in isolation first, to ensure identical elements between the skill as taught and tested. The transfer of this training to school reading is accomplished imperfectly as the discrepancies among core reading lesson tests, state tests, and NAEP scores demonstrate. Although superficially it can be argued that students are ultimately in control of their learning even in this environment, the opportunities afforded them are clearly within the publishers' domain. During core reading instruction, the text, topic, questions, and answers are determined outside the relationship of teacher and pupil. What is taught is conformity to direction and what remains in students' control is their behavior within this environment. Those who won't sit, attentive to the core reading lessons, have their behavior managed in successively more severe ways.[33]

In study after study that do not begin with the narrow focus of how to make students master set reading skills, students are described as active learners who seek to know about their world in order to have some sort of impact upon it.[34] They use texts in ways that they have observed to be effective for older individuals whom they value. They approximate those ways to varying levels of success until they become members of communities who are able to ask questions and answer them in order to make their way. Each student brings these adaptive practices with her to school with the expectation that she is a learner who matters in some environment, to be taught that only some learning practices are valid and she is not involved in decisions about which practices will be employed and how and to what ends. For all students, core reading instruction alienates students from their learning practices.

NCLB assigns students academic identities. Even within its goal statement—all children will read on grade level—NCLB develops categories to which students will be assigned: on grade level or below grade level. Since grade level is an arbitrary construct that has changed its definition over time, these identities are illusory. Certainly science cannot establish what the third-grade level is or any other grade level. If statistics were used, then a normal curve of results would be expected under which students would be spread. Which point under the curve should be designated to be the true grade level? And whose scores should be assigned to which curve? Grade level could be defined as years in school, but students do not begin school with the same advantages to tackle school expectations. Grade level is established by decisions made by some criteria that are not scientific or even statistical. Rather the criteria are based on some groups' judgment, making it a political choice to set students' identities.

NCLB positions some categories as normal and other categories as problems. The politics of grade level are a struggle over what will be considered acceptable approximations of sophisticated reading. At any age, students' reading performances represent a range of practices, all of which are successful in some contexts and not in others. The determination of what will be labeled as on grade level, proficient, or passing establishes the parameters of what will be considered normal, exceptional, or problematic. Just through the designation of categories for disaggregation, NCLB sets the terms of normality. White, able, middle-class, English speakers are the norm.[35] Everyone else—minority, poor, English language learners, and physically, emotionally, or mentally disabled students—becomes abnormal, worthy of special attention. As such, the learning and language practices of the normal group become the skills against which all students will be judged and those skills become the curriculum for each grade. The practices of disaggregated groups become problems to be overcome through standardized core reading lessons that will bring "needed structure" to these children's lives.

In this way, NCLB continues the one-best-system-of-reading-instruction project of the twenieth century according to a market ideology, validating economic, cultural, and social privilege among students. Skills, curricula, and structures are still set politically along historical American biases. Classroom well-being is secured by norms based on existing advantages, and merit is rewarded as if it were earned. Schools' success is established by the aggregate expression of these normalized skills. The success of state educational systems can be demonstrated only when students match their state-sponsored work against the national norms of NAEP. It is assumed that once all students meet these norms, then the market will take over and America will be ready to lead the global economy. Anyone or any group that deviates from these norms threatens that potential leadership and must be corrected. In the public rhetoric, NCLB seeks the correction of the "abnormal" through standards and standardization of core reading programs, the private supplemental services provided to individuals, and the programs that reach into the homes of those students to adjust their learning and language practices. Each of these solutions seeks to standardize private customs, language, values, and hopes for the sake of economic gain. In effect, like the one best system of the past, NCLB fails to recognize and value diversity, continues a maldistribution of benefits, and cheats most Americans of the types of reading necessary for them to participate actively in a democracy. In the end, NCLB provides more "scientific" justifications that the existing social, economic, and political hierarchies in America are valid, legitimate, and normal.

Chapter Ten

Then, Now, and Tomorrow

In honor of the centennial celebration of the publication of Edmond Burke Huey's *The Psychology and Pedagogy of Reading*, the Reading Hall of Fame proposed a series of lectures at each of the major professional conferences. In the opening message, Tom Sticht paraphrased George Miller's comments from the foreword of the 1968 MIT republication of the book—all reading research during the twentieth century is simply a rehash and slight articulation of what Huey already knew. At least in one respect, Sticht's point is indisputable. Most reading researchers have sought the complete rationalization of reading and instruction. American teachers face the results of that research every day. Remember your place. Locate the goal. Follow directions. Test for results. Accept full responsibility (except for success). Begin again. Students feel its effects on their bodies as well as in their reading practices. Narrow attention. Accept recommended purposes. Pick up speed. Note the text message. Complete the assignment. Start over. Stripped of its content, this is the reality of reading instruction under the one best method of reading instruction in which teachers and students have struggled for a century to meet on human levels in order to make lessons tolerable, and at times, even pleasurable.

We're told that it must be this way, if teachers are to earn their tax-based salaries by preparing students for the realities of the American economy. At the beginning of the century, that economy was industrial and teachers were to prepare students to fit into various roles in and around the factory. Since the 1980s, Americans have faced a global economy, and teachers have needed to prepare students to meet world-class standards so that all could continuously remake themselves in order to keep up with the unceasing creative destruction of the global capitalism. Although Huey did not anticipate that this economic

211

rationale would be the primary force behind the rationalization of reading instruction, he did recognize that standardized tests would be the criterion by which success would be determined. The social work of a test, then as now, is to sort, and tests of reading abilities are not an exception. In this way, tests become political, as the criteria on which a passing score is set determine who will and who will not be considered acceptable.

Within the debates about the criteria—and these debates were and are continuous—the future of individuals and social groups are determined. Huey seemed oblivious to this fact, but after one hundred years of constant testing, we cannot ignore it. Officials behind NCLB used this fact to their advantage, tying needed funding to 100 percent proficiency, while neglecting economic and social conditions that negate the possibility of reaching that goal. The limits of this rationalization of reading instruction should be apparent to anyone who can cut through the rhetoric of No Child Left Behind and the Reading First Initiative. Schools and reading instruction do not lead society; rather they reflect society and its biases. If the gaps continue to exist outside of schools and reading, they will continue at school as well. NCLB as the current, and reportedly final, one best system is designed to put an end to public schools, teaching as we know it, and higher levels of schooling for members of minorities, the poor, immigrants, and the disabled.

Huey called for reading experts (psychologists) to lead the rationalization of reading and instruction in the twentieth century. On the surface, it might appear that reading researchers have directed reading instruction to our current point. As I have argued throughout this book, however, first business, and now government and business use researchers' scientific findings in order to achieve their goals. Science is the weakest force within the NCLB perfect storm that swirls within and around American reading education. As in Huey's time, publishers continue to direct reading instruction, maintaining and expanding their sizable markets. Federal officials fund research and disseminate project results according to political goals, writing and setting policies that contradict much existing research in order to create new markets for businesses. Business leaders laud the policies of NCLB for the markets that it has created anew. Perhaps most damaging to Huey's dream at present is the fact that there is no scientific basis to the structure of NCLB or the Reading First Initiative— no research that suggests that higher standards create a totally literate populace, that annual testing raises reading test scores, or that quotas for gains in achievement scores will improve teachers' reading instruction or students' test scores. Teachers and students are the unfortunate subjects in the federal political experiment. NCLB structures are extrapolations of business practices, many of which are currently contested by research in industry.[1]

Appropriations from business are nothing new in schooling and reading instruction. During Huey's lifetime, educators followed Frederick Winslow Taylor's designs for scientific management in order to improve reading instruction, and recently reading experts, government officials, and publishers declared that the one best method has been discovered and encoded within the teachers' manuals of core reading programs—the contemporary equivalent of Taylor's instructional card. If enforced properly by the policies of the Reading First Initiative, then (1) all teachers will successfully produce a nation of readers, (2) each citizen of that nation will be productive in the global economy, retooling himself when the economic necessity dictates, (3) U.S. businesses will dominate world markets, and (4) all Americans will prosper. These promises have proved persuasive with school personnel and government officials for more than one hundred years, wavering only during the Great Depression when too many literate citizens found too few places of employment. During the last thirty years, with the rise of market ideology in government, the economic promise of reading instruction has nearly silenced the other original promise of reading and schooling—the development of active and able citizenship. Now reading instruction prepares human capital, and not citizens, for a democracy of consumers and consuming. The consequences of this displacement are evident in the decline in civic participation, the erosion of civil rights, the rise of Christian fundamentalism in public institutions, and the controversies within formal elections.[2]

Americans seem willing to accept the sacrifice of their political selves for the sake of their economic selves because manufacturing plants have closed, moving south and then overseas; companies have cut middle management to the bone; and wages have stagnated for nearly all Americans.[3] The tale that reading instruction and schooling will bring economic prosperity is comforting to most. Even the current chairman of the Federal Reserve fell under its spell when he suggested in his first testimony before Congress that the most important factor in increasing disparity in income was "the rising skill premium, the increased return on education."[4] Economists Ian Becker and Robert Gordon, however, lay waste to this myth. Between 1972 and 2001 the wages and incomes at the 90th percentile rose on average only 1 percent each year. Certainly the wage earners at this level were successful in learning to read at school, but their incomes did not increase. All wage earners below the 90th percentile—most of whom were literate—saw their incomes stall or even fall during that time. Individuals at the 99th percentile for income experienced a nearly 3 percent increase each year, those at the 99.9th percentile welcomed more than a 6 percent annual increase, and the true winners in the global economy at the 99.99th percent income level enjoyed an increase of nearly 17 percent each year.[5] Reading ability, therefore, has little aggregate economic effect when examined closely. Moreover, the promise of high-skill, high-wage jobs for those who become literate is empty as well. Accountants, software designers, and engineers are beginning to experience similar job decimation as workers in manufacturing as outsourcing creeps up the income ladder.[6]

In short, the global economy as currently organized works for very few in the United States and cannot fulfill its promise to those students who must all be proficient in reading when tested in 2014. In a sense, basing the rationale for reforming reading instruction on the market ideology—the myth of the global economy—positions teachers as complicit in the cover-up of the true inequalities in America. By following NCLB without larger critique beyond its inefficiencies or its harsh regulations, teachers spin the myth for their students, encouraging them to develop reading skills now as capital that they can exchange later for high wages. In reality, the benefits of students' (and teachers') work now and later will profit the very few. That larger critique of NCLB and its connections to the global economy can take place on many levels, from analyses of relationships between education and the economy to identification of corruption within materials and subcontractor selection processes to studies of who brokered these policies that created and maintain the current system.[7] Each of these critiques contributes to stories that contradict the economic myth and its consequences. Teachers of reading can contribute to this larger critique simply by shifting the emphasis of their teaching from economic to civic rationales for their work. As most teachers know, however, that shift is not so simple to enact.

In this chapter, I present a definition of civic reading designed to enable all citizens to participate in the political and economic decisions that affect their lives. My understanding of civic reading has changed since the first edition of *Broken Promises*, being informed by remarkable recent research on literacy, much of which has been subsequently discounted as unscientific in the National Reading Panel report, NCLB, and the Education Science Reform Act of 2002. That work has stimulated and is stimulated by the writing and teaching of educators who seek to re-create the civic rationale for teaching reading in public schools. These educators attempt to redirect the stories surrounding reading instruction, emphasizing roles for reading within active civic engagement. In order to tell these stories and to retell them along with their students, the educators have elevated their responsibilities as citizens in a democracy to the same plane as their responsibilities as teachers of reading. That is, they see their work in reading education as the demonstration of the civic power of reading in order to build a just democracy. Moreover, they have done so while avoiding the trap of equating citizenship with simple patriotism.[8] My favorites among these stories connect the work of teachers and students with the lives of other groups struggling to push democracy to its edge.[9]

Civic Life

Teachers interested in reasserting civic development as the rationale for schooling cannot accept the notion that the National Reading Panel report, No Child Left Behind, or Education Science Reform Act of 2002 has brought the end of history for reading education. They cannot envision themselves as the last man, who is powerless and content to follow, earn a living, and keep warm. They cannot fall prey to the culture of fear that argues that teachers are lucky to have jobs and must cling to them at all costs or be replaced. They cannot close their classroom doors and hope that the perfect storm of government, business, and reading experts will pass them by without harm. The culmination of a century-long project, NCLB's penalties for schools demonstrate that teachers cannot run and hide. As others and I have argued, teachers and schools cannot meet the unreasonable demands of NCLB, closing reading achievement gaps within a nation based on historic inequalities. Neither the global economy nor the federal government is currently organized to solve those inequalities. Neither is meant to, and NCLB is the mechanism to bring about the end of public schools and to eliminate scientifically members of the poor, minority, immigrant, and disabled groups from higher levels of schooling. Reordering reading education toward civic reading is in the interests of teachers, students, and all but the members of the 99.99 percent income bracket.

To come to this realization is to understand oneself as a historical being—someone responsible for the development of history through the work of our everyday lives. That responsibility is not simply self-sacrifice, because our participation in the construction of the present and future (and the reconstruction of the past) includes the creation and maintenance of structures to ensure our well-being as well as that of our students'. Over the past thirty years, members of the federal government and business have acted vigorously to limit our understanding of civic responsibilities to the preservation of our immediate families and ourselves. Acts beyond private spheres have been framed as annoyances at best and impediments to our freedom and that of others at worst. Think about Reagan's tax cuts, G. H. W. Bush's thousand points of light, Clinton's end of welfare as we know it, and G. W. Bush's gutting of government regulation of businesses. To varying degrees, each told Americans to mind their personal business and not to worry about others. Each move championed our economic selves over our civic selves while allowing the experts to make decisions about the country's and schools' priorities. As I have argued over the last several chapters, teachers, students, and nearly all Americans are not better off for these acts. And if we do not act soon, public schools, and perhaps the public sphere, will disappear. Without public schools to bolster the public sphere, democracy is in further jeopardy.

Although they are not often in public view, other groups of Americans have already started this work to reclaim a civic center for our lives. In *Democracy's Edge: Choosing to Save Our Country by Bringing Democracy to Life*, Frances Moore Lappe presents a fifty-page list of groups that provide what she calls entry points for a living democracy.[10] These groups populate every state in the union; they address many aspects of public life from agriculture to water distribution and from a more just economy to reclaiming media to promoting security through connections. Recognizing people's anxiety in taking such steps, Lappe offers readers multiple ways to participate in the reordering of priorities. For example, she explains six economic relationships in a living democracy—consumer, worker, voter influencing policy, investor or saver, economic policymaker, and employer—and begins her explanation with statements about the relative power of citizens in each relationship, noting that the number of citizens participating decreases markedly across her categories. Through explicit examples describing civic groups, she explains how more citizens could become involved and effective in the latter categories in order to supplant "thin democracy" with "living democracy." Her comparison is instructive:

> Thin democracy begins on the premise that democracy is a form of government that Americans have been lucky enough to inherit as a completed structure. It works as a republic in which citizens elect a few surrogates to act as public experts in order to make important decisions. Government work and public life involve distasteful choices and activities that are necessary in order to protect the free market which guides the global economy with its invisible hand, enabling our standard of living and private lives. The less government activity the better it is for our individual freedom.
>
> Living democracy is a way of living with others, working actively in order to create, develop and maintain structures based on trust and mutuality. Citizens share responsibility for these structures that should be determined at a level of activity closest to the issue. All citizens, therefore, must develop the "arts of democracy"—active listening and reading, creative and sensitive speaking and writing, negotiation, mediation, conflict use and resolution and mentoring.

Much of the work toward living democracy provides a metaphor for the possibilities of reading education in the United States. Take, for example, the struggle over corporate hog farms in Pennsylvania.[11] As the residents of many other states, Pennsylvanians are told that corporate hog farms will bring new jobs and new tax revenue to impoverished communities. The farms will make the communities players in the global economy as stops in the production of pork for public consumption. As in all production, corporate hog farms seek efficiency and higher profit through scientific research. The implementation of the scientific corporate design has consequences for local communities, however. Fattening three to five thousand piglets from 10 to 250 pounds through the most efficient process requires considerable amounts of grain, antibiotics, and restriction of animal movement. The result is not only pleasantly plump hogs but an ecological disaster. Each hog creates eight times as much waste as one human, placing great strain on communities' ecosystems, eventually contaminating soil, water, and air. After careful study and community organizing, more than eighty townships in Pennsylvania have passed town ordinances to limit the development of corporate hog farms while endorsing the importance of locally owned agriculture.

The state, corporations, and even the Pennsylvania Farm Bureau have responded that these communities do not have the right to ban corporations from farming within their jurisdictions. Moreover, these groups argue that corporations know more about how to farm and about what is good for the economy than do local citizens, and they have data to "prove" their position. Legislators sponsored several bills to repeal these township ordinances and to limit local citizens' capacity to make economic and zoning decisions. Each of these responses stiffened the citizens' resolve. To prepare themselves to take these steps, and then to defend their positions, citizens have used their literacies and pored through a variety of texts in order to learn more about hog farming, economics, citizens' rights, and themselves. These acts of reading and writing have tested their understandings of their histories, cultures, and values. Citizens have related these new scientific, economic, political, and cultural understandings of their lives to the lives of others and the social structures put in place to guide those lives. During their reading, these citizens became aware that they can control their own destinies to certain degrees, and that awareness caused them to act.

Their actions provide important lessons for reading educators, who also face heavily funded, scientifically authorized, and government-sanctioned corporate interests. First, the townspeople questioned science and the market as the primary logics on which to base local decisions. They did not reject science or capitalism, but they questioned the tendency to use generalizations to trump local logic and facts. Although they hoped to use science to improve their lives and recognized that all must sell their labor to live, the townspeople would not elevate scientific and economic facts above the ones that they discovered about how they wanted to live together. Scientists from outside the community could establish levels of contamination and smell that they declared safe for the locals to endure. Economists could demonstrate that giant farms were more efficient. But in the end, the townspeople chose to pay more for pork in exchange for more control over their lives—they recognized that scientists and economists don't always have their best interest at heart.

Second, the townspeople identified a connection between the science of corporate hog farming and the corporations that would profit from the farms. That is, the townspeople soon recognized that corporations could fund and secure science to support their position and that the townspeople could do the same. Some science was for sale. Their recognition of this fact defeated the corporations' and legislators' calls for the townspeople to be objective and rational in their deliberations. Every party had interests that it was pursuing actively in this struggle. Finally, the townspeople expanded the notion of their freedom through their actions. Rather than choose among the solutions that scientists, businessmen, or legislators offered them, the townspeople chose to develop their own criteria for how to conduct their lives and to structure their communities.

Citizen groups such as these demonstrate the tenets of democracy and civic reading for us. "What we share and what makes us fellow citizens in a liberal democratic regime is not a substantive idea of the good, but a set of political principles specific to such a tradition—principles of freedom and equality for all." [12] The struggle to define what's good for communities and the people within them continues even within the groups that work for living democracy. There was and is not a brokered consensus on all issues that might constitute any one group's definition of *good*. There was and is, however, within American democracy, a commitment to the freedom of all citizens to participate equally in some way. [13] Contrary to contemporary efforts to enforce thin democracy as a finished product and to characterize differences as problems, groups' various interests concerning the definitions of these terms—*good, freedom,* and *equality*—are the dynamic forces that keep a democracy alive and vital. Claudia Moufee captured this well.

> It is the tension between consensus—on the values—and dissensus— on interpretation—that makes possible the agonistic dynamics of pluralist democracy. This is why its survival depends on the possibility of forming collective political identities around clearly differentiated positions and the choices among real alternatives. [14]

For living democracy to work, then, individuals must recognize that their identities are multiple and fluid. [15] For example, the individuals in the Pennsylvania townships are workers, parts of church congregations, farmers, volunteers, voters, and members of other social groups that influence their thoughts, actions, and values in substantial ways. All people are members of such groups and more that influence our lives, and we vary our hierarchical arrangements of those influences according to circumstances and intentions. The Pennsylvania townspeople became aware of this power in order to form coalitions that had to be recognized as active forces that could be used to develop clear articulations of positions on this shared concern. They were willing to prioritize their civic identity over all others for the sake of this matter. Some of these coalitions limited their work to fighting corporate hog farms, while others sought new members (and lost some old) in their efforts to address other community issues (Wal-Mart, public works, reelection of incumbents, etc.). Living democracy, then, begins with the development of individuals' identities that are committed to the values of freedom and equality that blend with the values of their other group memberships to instantiate meanings for those terms. At times, the meanings overlap significantly, enabling coalitions to form in order to address local, state, national, and even international issues. This is what it means to be active in civic life—to seek, inform, and work for public issues to improve life for yourself and others. Although this identity of democratic citizenship cannot be fully specified outside of particular contexts, it requires at least three practices: reflexive agency, the will to act, and the ability to make room for adversaries.

Reflexive agency invites citizens to evaluate the world in terms of their intentions and values and, at the same time, to evaluate those intentions and to reflect upon those values. (Should I value economic prosperity over the quality of life in this community?) In this way, citizens take inventory of their identities, their values, their motives, and their actions, investigate the sources of those parts of themselves, and make choices about which ones they hope to enhance and which they hope to diminish.

The will to act, which for many has been diverted from public life to private matters, must be redirected through the recognition that their apparently private matters (objection to the smell and pollution of corporate hog farms) are really connected to public issues because the concerns are shared by many. As individuals become aware of the political possibilities of their multiple and fluid identities and the real opportunities to form larger, more effective coalitions for accomplishing goals shared across social groups, the will to act in civic life increases in likelihood. Reflexive agency ensures that coalitions will not become fixed power blocks as basic and secondary assumptions for action are consistently scrutinized.

Because those identities are not fixed and future intersections of values and interests cannot be predetermined, citizens begin to recognize the need to *respect the positions of their adversaries*—not to the point of agreement, certainly, but enough to recognize commitment to the shared principles of freedom and equality. (Does my legislator's vote against local zoning authority mean that he can't be trusted to represent any of our interests?) The limits on this respect are set by individuals' and groups' commitment to those principles. Anyone rejecting freedom and equality outright stands outside the democratic process and, therefore, becomes the legitimate object of democratic scorn. "Adversaries will fight about the interpretation and the ranking of values, but their common allegiance to the values that constitute the liberal democratic form of life creates a bond of solidarity that expresses their belonging to the common 'we.'"[16]

Throughout the twentieth century, the people behind the governance, business, and science of reading instruction have been committed to these basic democratic values and the role that reading can play in securing those conditions. Their articulations of the one best system were sincere attempts to find means to meet the increasing task demands on reading and the distribution of reading among citizens. The tools that they chose (bureaucracy, commodification, and standardization), however, could not and cannot lead schools and teachers to instructional practices that would or could fulfill the goals of either freedom or equality. NCLB stands as a culmination of their efforts, making visible the normalizing practices that valorize white, middle- and upper-class, able English speakers at the expense of all other identities.[17] Most educators who work within that policy are hopeful that their actions can realize the liberal goals encoded in the rhetoric surrounding NCLB. Most have worked and continue to work earnestly, if unproductively, within the predominant industrial and market ideologies of twentieth-century reading instruction. All are potential coalition allies for those educators who seek to reorder the priorities of reading instruction from development of human capital to civic responsibility. Within the Bush administration, however, the architects of foreign, economic, and domestic policies, including NCLB, do appear to devalue freedom and equality fundamentally, attempting to roll back civic, consumer, environmental, and worker rights in order to enhance and protect the privileges of a few. They have designed policies that channel public funds into the private pockets of a few, and they have set their sights on the destruction of public identities among citizens. These individuals deserve democratic scorn.

The concern for living democracy takes several forms, but most find hope in reinvigorated literacies of citizens.[18] In *Democracies in Flux*, Robert Putnam aligns social capital (his term for civic participation) with an enhanced notion of communication among citizens. Cornell West, in *Democracy Matters*, supports this position on civic engagement through works of literature, linking reading fundamentally with the development of basic democratic values and the continuous struggle to define what they mean. George Lakoff argues in

Whose Freedom? that those struggles take place on a rhetorical level in which groups use media to frame, articulate, and promote their meanings for these basic values. In *Citizenship Under Fire*, Sigal Ben Porath presents the case for reading against the frame of the War on Terror in order to protect difference in pluralistic democracies. In each argument and others as well, civic reading is positioned as a means, if not the means, through which living democracy can be realized locally and, in time, nationally and internationally. Since the first edition of *Broken Promises*, several educators have advocated a similar connection.[19] Henry Giroux revised his argument for critical literacy in *Schooling and the Struggle for Public Life* because the rights of citizens are disappearing rapidly. Jean Anyon focused that argument on urban schools and Jacqueline Edmondson aimed at rural communities. Rebecca Powell and Carole Edelsky work from reading toward living democracy in order to realize the social nature of reading and how it forms the moral core of democratic citizenship. Advocates for the groups targeted in NCLB make the connection between democracy and reading. James Charlton, Victor Romero, Denny Taylor, and Catherine Prendergast describe how text and forms of reading position the disabled, immigrants, the poor, and minorities. All propose the recognition of new types of reading and the redistribution of those types across all citizens.

Civic Reading

> History teaches us that literacy refers to a malleable set of cultural practices that are shaped and reshaped by different, often competing, social and cultural interests. As a result, we do not view how to teach literacy as a scientific decision, but rather as a moral, political, and cultural decision about the kind of literate practices that are needed to enhance peoples' agency over their life trajectories and to enhance communities' intellectual, cultural, and semiotic resources in print/ multi-mediated economies. Literacy education is ultimately about the kind of society and the kinds of citizen/subjects that could and should be constructed.[20]

Allan Luke and Peter Freebody propose a four-resources model of reading in which teachers recognize the historical construction of the definitions of reading over time and place and seek to inventory the reading practices within particular communities. Rather than a unified psychological process, Luke and Freebody maintain that there are multiple types of reading, defined and redefined by the participants (individuals, groups, and institutions) in specific cultural contexts. For example, as many studies have shown, school reading does not often match community members' reading for purposes of consumption, work, or legal matters across cultures, classes, and regions.[21] These negotiations for the definition of reading demonstrate the relative power of participants in relation to one another, affecting definition, recognition, and distribution. As demonstrated repeatedly over the last century, the insistence of a singular psychological definition of reading contradicts the reading of some social groups, signaling the need for official sanction of reading practices in these particular communities. In this way, definitions of reading become culturally prescriptive, positioning some groups for greater access and opportunity and others with less of both.

Instead of an overarching definition of reading, Luke and Freebody sought and continue to seek an inventory of the range of reading practices that community members use and need to conduct their lives. With that inventory, teachers can make decisions on how they might act in their classrooms to ensure that they address, develop, and maintain full complements of reading practices. These actions would draw upon understandings of existing repertoires of students' linguistic, cultural, and textual practices as well as teachers' senses of the possible futures of their students. Such an approach does not lend itself to standardization or commoditification. Rather it requires knowledgeable teachers who are prepared to accept the intellectual challenge of being a reading teacher in a pluralistic democracy.

Luke and Freebody's inventory suggests that readers' practices can be organized under four general categories: coding, text meaning, pragmatic, and critical. Labeling it the Four Resources Model, they argue that each family of practices is necessary, but not sufficient, for reading in the twenty-first century—"none is in and of itself sufficient for literate citizens." They offer their model in several formats. I prefer the version that describes the elements of reading as social practice because it presents the practices as series of questions.[22]

> Coding practices—developing your resources as a code breaker:
>
> > How do I crack this text? How does it work? What are its patterns and conventions? How do the sounds and the marks relate, singly and in combinations?
>
> Text meaning practices—developing your resources as text participant:
>
> > How do the ideas represented in the text string together? What cultural resources can be brought to bear on this text? What are the cultural meanings and possible readings that can be constructed from this text?
>
> Pragmatic practices—developing your resources as text user:
>
> > How do the uses of this text shape its composition? What do I do with this text, here and now? What will others do with it? What are my options and alternatives?

Critical practices—developing your resources as text analyst and critic:

What kind of person, with what interests and values could both write and read this naively and unproblematically? What is this text trying to do to me? In whose interest? Which positions, voices, and interests are at play? Which are silent and absent?

The practice of civic reading, then, harnesses individual and collective resources in order to inquire into social issues with the intention of developing a position or positions for decision making and action. For example, the possibilities and problems of corporate hog farms in Pennsylvania communities required citizens to crack the codes, construct meaning, determine purpose, and recognize interests within legal, scientific, cultural, and economic texts. Although all citizens could bring personal resources to bear on each text encountered, the community members possessed collectively the textual resources to exert power on the decisions within their community, subverting those specialized texts to carry community interests. In all communities, individuals' reading practices were enhanced through the collective action. In some, the civic reading reverted to individual acts, directly after the passage of town ordinances. In other communities, however, the collective civic reading continued, tackling other issues of corporate insurgences into community life. In these communities, the collective continues its dialectical relationship with the personal.

As I mentioned in Chapter 9, the four-resources model pushes on the one best method model of teaching reading as defined by NCLB—state exams and NAEP. At most, that one best method encourages teachers to organize their instruction in order to develop code breaker and text participants, emphasizing phonics (alphabetics, phonemic awareness, and fluency) and comprehension (including vocabulary). Exclusive attention to only those families of practices neglects a variety of cultural and social functions that different types of text perform in and out of school and the ways in which texts represent and legitimize particular values and points of view while quieting and stigmatizing others. This neglect hinders students', and later adults', capabilities to engage in everyday life as citizens, particularly in civic life. Official curriculum, then, forces readers to acquire pragmatic and critical resources away from the classroom and, therefore, favors students who have greater access to demonstrations of sophisticated reading employing all four resources. If we are to fulfill the promise of civic reading, then we must attend to all four resources at all stages and levels of reading education, forgoing the narrowing focus of the century-long project to rationalize reading and reading instruction.

Civic Reading Pedagogy

Following Simon's lead, I use the term *pedagogy* instead of *instruction* to describe teachers' efforts to develop students' civic reading.[23] *Instruction* connotes the intention to transfer information fully formed from teacher to student through the application of technique. The effectiveness of instruction can be measured in some way in order to determine how much information learners have received and retained. The measurement determines the effectiveness of both the instruction and the learning. Instruction, then, entails the selection of content, materials, time, and place as well as procedures, audience, and mode of assessment. Making such choices, the instructor specifies answers to questions such as what knowledge is worth knowing, what it means to know something, how people learn, and what a learner and a learning environment are. These, of course, are political questions that valorize some groups and marginalize others, that sanction some ways of acting and disparage others, and that legitimize some futures and disqualify others. In most educational discourse, the politics of these questions is denied or ignored because instructors assume that their decisions are good for all, or rather, for the good of all.[24] Pedagogy, on the other hand, acknowledges that education is political.

> In other words, talk about pedagogy is simultaneously talk about the details of what students and others might do together and the cultural politics such practices support. To propose a pedagogy is to propose a political vision. In this perspective, we cannot talk about teaching practices without talking about politics.[25]

Some educators across the United States are engaging in civic reading pedagogy and making their work public.[26] While they work with all ages of learners, in various settings, and with different topics, they share the same hope that civic reading practices of the classroom will carry into the public lives of the learners. I know of no official coordination among these educators, but all seem to follow at some level Paulo Freire's attempt to remake the roles of authority, rigor, and context in their teaching.[27] Recognizing the different knowledges and practices among classroom participants (including the teacher), Freirians explore the tension between authority and authoritarianism. They attempt to teach by demonstrating what it means to learn, enabling their learners' knowledge to contribute to the new understandings they develop. In these classrooms, rigor becomes the levels to which participants engage the topic at hand—what types of questions they ask, how attentive they are to tasks and others, and how they change during the processes. Freirians recognize that the contexts of their classrooms have cultural, historical, physical, and temporal dimensions. The teachers and students begin with given parameters, but they are not constrained completely by them. Cultural norms are investigated; history is explored; time becomes a potential ally as well as an enemy; and classrooms expand actually and virtually beyond classroom walls. Although these teachers do not follow a single orthodoxy, they project certain values.

Civic reading pedagogy should be:

Participatory: Learners must be subjects, not objects, in the development of curricula and the processes of learning.

Critical: The nature of the curricula leads to analysis and questioning of the sociopolitical, cultural, and economic realities that shape our lives.

Situated: The point of entry to that analysis is through learners' daily experiences.

Dialogic: The processes of learning are inquiries that engage both learners and teacher in the construction of new knowledge through discussion and conversations.

Desocializing: The curricula and processes of learning seek to identify and explore the effects of society on learners and teacher.

Democratic: Although authority cannot be shared equally between teacher and students, hierarchical relations are reduced by the other pedagogical values and through socially negotiated meanings.

Interdisciplinary: Situated experiences of the curricula require broad thinking across traditional subject categories.

Activist: Consciousness-raising and skill development are put in service to transformative projects of recognition and redistribution.[28]

Vivian Vasquez begins *Negotiating Critical Literacies with Young Children* with "A critical literacy curriculum needs to be lived."[29] The book presents her account of promoting civic reading among three- to five-year-old students during a single year in a public school setting. Students' work and the curriculum as lived were recorded in "audit trails"—maps of events and texts that represented the students' efforts to use reading in order to explore rain forests, the environment, gender, fairness, the media, and everyday issues of concern. The representations were artifacts that students gathered, chose, or created in order to keep track of their activities for their own use as well as to inform their parents and the school community. Vasquez shares photographs of portions of these trails as annotated time lines of both the simple activities and the development of more sophisticated understandings of the power of reading within even the youngest among her students. I know of no more graphic challenge to Piagetian structural notions of children's capabilities than

Vasquez's audit trails. The tracks demonstrate concern, understanding, and action among children who have been traditionally considered to be incapable of demonstrating interest, attention, or logical thought at these levels. Given the opportunity, her students displayed their developing knowledge of all four resources without privileging one above the others.

Although the book was written after the school year's end, Vasquez tells the story of her emerging understanding of the possibilities of civic reading as it was conceived and negotiated during a school year. In that way, she presents the challenges to her thinking, pedagogy, and social actions in and out of the classroom. Her accounts work deeply into the inquiries of her students around the code of reading and the meanings of text. They brought an awareness of genre to the discussions as they posed and participated in the creation of texts to represent what they had learned. And through interesting selection (initially by Vasquez), they began to recognize that texts do not present a unified message; rather, multiple texts are necessary to develop any understanding of a topic. With remarkable attention to detail, Vasquez charts children's progress as they harnessed and developed these four families of practice during the year. She ends her book with her classes' advice to next year's kindergartners: "You can be strong from your brain."

Randy and Katherine Bomer offer a conversation about their attempts to move social justice to the center of their curricula in elementary and secondary school classrooms.[30] In *For a Better World: Reading and Writing for Social Action*, they present a case for extending their interests in process approaches to literacy teaching to an overtly progressive pedagogy.

> Some classrooms include a lot of talk about skills, some talk about following instructions, some talk about standards imposed by outside agencies. Then again, some classrooms talk about beautiful language and aesthetic pleasure, some talk about personal memories, and some talk about self-expression and creativity. Though any of these things might come up in our classrooms, we have been working to place important concepts about social justice at the center of our discourse. Though we work on skills and discuss what others have said about standards, we talk more about difference and fairness. Though we talk about personal memories, we try to explore more how those memories illuminate aspects of culture and social relationships. In other examinations of language, we are concerned more than before with how power relationships bring out some features while silencing others. Holding democracy at the center of our conversations transforms the images and themes we see in books, the topics we write about, and the ways we look at the world.[31]

The Bomers invite readers to take steps from code and meaning to pragmatic and critical resources by listing topics and strategies and then providing classroom evidence in order to substantiate their choices. Their concepts for civic reading are extensive and compelling: groups, power, taking things for granted (naturalization), fairness and justice, voice and silence, multiple perspectives (different sides of stories), representations (showing what people are like), gender, race, class, money, labor, language, intimate relationships and families, relationships to nature, violence and peace, and acting alone or together (individualism and collectivism). Each issue is supported by examples of how teachers and students might find points of entry to engage the topic. Their points are illustrated through classroom examples in which pedagogical strategies encourage students to take up these issues and to act on them within their classrooms and communities. The Bomers' flowchart representations of differing conceptions of the reading process provide teachers with a graphic means for understanding how students can come to understand that what appear to be personal problems are often actually social issues that warrant group action.

In a much less ambitious treatment of civic reading, Maureen McLaughlin and Glenn DeVoogd describe ways in which critical, pragmatic, and meaning resources develop simultaneously and enhance one another.[32] The crux of McLaughlin and DeVoogd's pedagogy is designed around issues of recognition with problem-posing questions, which are posed in order to draw students' attention to the representations of groups in texts written for children. These questions serve as templates for teachers and students in order to interrogate text: Who or what is in the text? Who or what is missing from the text? What is marginalized? What does the author want you to think? What story might an alternative text tell? and How can information from the text be used to promote justice? Unfortunately, at times, the authors seem to overspecify how these questions could be put to use by supplying example (but complete) lesson plans for particular books. This step demonstrates a certain lack of respect for teachers' intellect and creativity and gives the impression that civic reading could be packaged and sold to teachers. However, the examples could serve as invitations to some teachers who might consider the civic concepts that the authors introduce in the first two chapters to be too complicated for their understanding. Although to some, such confusion might suggest more theoretical work, McLaughlin and DeVoogd present examples to illustrate similarities with and differences from typical instructional practices. In the terms of traditional American reading instruction, *Critical Literacy: Enhancing Students' Comprehension of Text* should be considered a primer for civic reading pedagogy.

Critical Literacy/Critical Teaching: Tools for Preparing Responsive Teachers offers a unique approach to civic reading pedagogy, blending coding and meaning resources with pragmatic and critical practices within a university literacy lab.[33] Cheryl Dozier, Peter Johnston, and Rebecca Rogers write and edit a polyphonic treatment of a decade-long research project in which university faculty, schoolteachers, and children identified as struggling at school collaborated to develop and maintain a civic reading pedagogy that helped teachers become more sensitive to issues of justice as they developed ways to help students gain greater control over coding and meaning resources. Although it is decidedly a story of success, the authors do not shy away from the tensions between the traditions of remedial reading instruction and their desires to act against what appeared to be the systematic bias against certain social groups within those traditions. They are candid about the politics of the decisions they negotiated with their university, schools, teachers, parents, and students in order to continue the project.

Dozier, Johnston, and Rogers make their argument in two ways. First, they describe their theoretical and practical work to defamiliarize the traditional curriculum of the university literacy lab, offering both political and pedagogical criticisms. They are candid about their struggles to reconcile what appear at first to be contrary notions—Marie Clay's theories about the need to accelerate struggling readers' rates of learning with hybrid theories of critical literacy.[34] They discuss their invitations to teachers to join in defining that curriculum, finally choosing teacher inquiry as the mechanism to help teachers connect their teaching with students' everyday lives. Second, they demonstrate the democratic elements of their pedagogy, by stepping back to allow the teacher-researchers from the university lab to speak for themselves. These contributors write cogently about their projects and are positioned in the book in order to illustrate the sixteen tools invented to "set up the conditions where teachers notice, theorize, productively (self-) critique, and build a sustaining community."[35]

Perhaps the best source for information on civic reading, pedagogy, or progressive education in general is Rethinking Schools.[36] Founded in 1986, this collective of Milwaukee teachers has developed into a vocal force in school reform by publishing a quarterly journal, preparing collections of articles as readers on specific topics, and sponsoring seminars for teachers who hope to make their civic pedagogy more public. The group began with local concerns about textbooks, funding, and unions, creating a newspaper that informed Milwaukee teachers about their position and struggles. These early efforts were tied to union work and alliances with other community organizations seeking recognition and redistribution of the cities' educational and civic resources. While the scope of their efforts and participation has grown during the past twenty years, this organization of practicing teachers remains close-knit and clearly focused. On its website, Rethinking Schools characterizes its vision for schools.

Schools are about more than producing efficient workers or future winners of the Nobel Prize for science. They are the place in this society where the children from a variety of backgrounds come together and, at least in theory, learn to talk, play and work together.

Schools are integral not only to preparing all children to be full participants in society, but also to be full participants in this country's ever-tenuous experiment in democracy. That this vision has yet to be fully realized does not mean it should be abandoned.[37]

Each issue of the organizations journal has much to help teachers understand and use civic reading as a weapon of critique and a tool of possibilities.[38] For example, the twentieth-anniversary issue included historian Howard Zinn on the development of pedagogies of resistance; Professor Ken Goodman on NCLB and Reading First policies, which he labels the pedagogy of the absurd; Oakland intervention coordinator and teacher coach Elizabeth Jaeger on the detrimental consequences of following scripted lessons during reading instruction; and Portland OR high school English teacher Linda Christensen on how print reading strategies can be taught by treating photographs as text. Christensen's photographs represented the Chilpancingo region in Tijuana, Mexico. Her students worked to decode the images, find meaning in them, place them in social life, and determine their (and the photographer's) politics. She ends her piece:

> My students didn't travel to Mexico with me. They didn't stand on the banks of Río Alamar, smell the acrid odor of a town drowning in toxins, see the rash on Lourdes's arms. But sitting in a classroom near the banks of the Columbia River, they learned how to step into a picture and connect with a community on the other side of the border and question why it's OK for a U.S. corporation to leave toxic waste behind, and discover how women organizing in local communities can tackle giants—and win.[39]

This process of engaging in civic reading with a sense of hope is apparent in every Rethinking Schools publication. Take, for example, the organization's publication *Rethinking Globalization: Teaching for Justice in an Unjust World*, which has a photograph of Earth with a bar code superimposed for its cover.[40] Editors Bill Bigelow and Bob Peterson, a high school and an elementary school teacher, address the purpose of the book directly—to help people of all ages to engage in civic reading about a globalized economy. They bring together articles, poems, photographs, cartoons, songs, and interviews that challenge the government and business position projected daily across mainstream media. They suggest that teachers and students place these texts beside the ones that typically surround them in order to enhance their development and use of the four resources while trying to make sense of globalization. Offering a clear demonstration of civic reading by two teachers, *Rethinking Globalization* provides hundreds of examples and resources that other teachers might employ with their students. Most encouraging are the suggestions of how teachers and students can join other social groups to act on the new knowledge they construct. With an emphasis on collective effort, Biglow and Peterson present ways in which their and other classes of students have used civic reading to participate in living democracy.

What Now?

In the face of domestic and global threats to democracy, many Americans are attempting to live democratically and resist government and business promotions of a thinner version. They recognize that thin democracy offers the rhetoric of freedom and equality without the reality of either in any sense beyond consumerism. For most Americans even consumer choice is limited by economic realities—attention Wal-Mart shoppers! Overt acts to enforce the thin version (e.g., eavesdropping on phone calls, limits on abilities to sue corporations, secrecy in government information, intimidation of the media, and incentives to outsource jobs) have encouraged these Americans to step into the contradictions in order to name them and struggle to reorient democratic practices. The individuals and groups seek to define freedom as the right and capacity to contribute to the discussions and determinations of life's alternatives rather than to simply choose among the alternatives that experts set for them.[41] Moreover, these citizens work toward an equality that will permit all Americans to be recognized and heard, to engage in decision-making processes, and to reap the benefits of the products of America. Although stimulated by the immediacy of the current threats to democracy, they recognize that there was no golden past in America when living democracy worked for all. In this way, their actions seek to illuminate the underlying problems of a market-driven society, to show how those problems affect other peoples' lives, to demonstrate how current policies and practices are not the only way, or the natural way that things must be, and to act on their convictions and new knowledge to bring about change.

The researchers and educators I have mentioned in this chapter and many more as well elevate their responsibilities as citizens to the same level as their responsibilities as teachers and recognize that living democracy requires civic reading.[42] They work to develop a pedagogy that can reorient schooling toward that end. Although the havoc of NCLB captures much of their attention and alerts more teachers and parents to immediate threats to public schooling, these individuals and groups appear poised to push past NCLB's less delicate version of the basal panopticon of the previous century in order to examine and resist market-driven reading instruction. The federal government's demands for adequate yearly progress, reading coaches, and enhanced instructional scripts increase administrators' power of surveillance upon both teachers and students, ensuring the fidelity of the commercially prepared design but significantly limiting teachers' and students' understandings of and capacities for reading toward democracy. As they and more researchers, teachers, and parents identify the origins of NCLB within the century-long project to enforce the one best method to render the outcomes of reading instruction more predictable, and therefore profitable, for business, all will move closer to developing strategies that could make civic reading the rationale for reading programs in American public schools.

This book is my attempt to help make those connections and to identify some of the contradictions between the rhetorical promises for reading and reading education and the design and practices currently available in nearly all classrooms in the United States. Since the first edition of *Broken Promises*, more educators and researchers have joined the project to defeat the rationalization of reading education and to invigorate a civic reading toward living democracy. Their work provides context, texture, and extensions to mine and points to the multitude of ways to enter this struggle. The stakes are high, and the work is daunting, but ultimately, it seems that the meanings and realities of democracy are at stake. They and I invite you to join.

Notes

Introduction

1. Comment made during his speech at forum sponsored by the Council of Excellence in Government Washington, D.C., 2002.

2. As quoted in J. Kozol *Still Separate, Still Unequal: America's Educational Apartheid. Harper's Magazine* 311, 2005, 79.

3. H. Mann. *Report No. 12 of the Massachusetts School Board* 1848. usinfo.state.gov/usa/infousa/facts/democracy

4. R. Allington. *Big Brother and the National Reading Curriculum.* (Portsmouth, NH: Heinemann, 2002) 282.

Chapter One

1. Traditional histories of reading instruction include E. Cubberly's *Public Education in the United States* (Boston: Houghton Mifflin, 1934), M. Mathews' *Teaching to Read* (Chicago: University of Chicago, 1966), and N. B. Smith's *American Reading Instruction* (Newark, DE: International Reading Association, 1986).

2. As quoted in W. Smith, ed., *Theories of Education in Early America 1635–1819* (Bobbs Merrill, 1973), 15.

3. See L. Cremin's *American Education: The Colonial Experience, 1607–1783* (New York: Harper and Row, 1970), 176–77. In *Literacy in Colonial New England* (New York: Norton, 1974), K. Lockridge disputes Cremin's response to the American wilderness hypothesis by arguing that most New England colonists were already prone toward literacy and schooling before they came to the colonies because they practiced some form of Protestantism, which required them to know the word of God as written in the Bible.

4. Cubberly, *Public Education*, 18.

5. Ibid., 18–19.

6. See S. Cohen's *A History of Colonial Education, 1606–1776* (New York: Wiley, 1974). Cohen suggests that educational legislation did not apply equally to all Americans, particularly not for females, Native Americans, Africans, and African Americans. In seventeenth-century New England, these groups were often taught to read and write, although few went beyond petty schools to grammar schools. A 1710 version of the 1642 Massachusetts apprenticeship law stipulated that "females should be taught to read as they may be capable" (71). Most legislation that permitted girls to participate in schooling was forty to fifty years behind that for boys. In many colonies it was against the law to teach slaves or Native Americans to read or write.

7. See G. Murphy's "Massachusetts Bay Colony: The Role of Government in Education (Ph.D. diss., Radcliffe College, n.d.). In *The Social Ideas of American Educators* (Scribner, 1935), M. Curti argues that the separation of petty schools from grammar schools in 1647 was the first indication that schooling in America was not going to be democratic because

it served to perpetuate the class structure of European society. Upon completing petty school, most children were placed in apprenticeships, while only the boys from wealthy homes went on to the grammar schools. Curti maintains that even the reading and writing instruction favored the wealthy since they attended private schools with relatively highly educated masters, while poorer children received less adequate instruction at petty schools held in a kitchen.

8. R. Venezky, "A History of the American Reading Textbook," *Elementary School Journal*, 86 (1987): 247–65.

9. See L. Levy, ed., *Cato's Letters: Unabridged Reproductions, 1755* (New York: DaCapo, 1971). In *The American School, 1642–2000* (New York: McGraw-Hill, 2000), J. Spring presents an interesting discussion of the early challenges to the close association of church and schooling in the United States and England. He suggests that the impetus for *Cato's Letters* was R. Molesworth's *An Account of Demark as It Was in the Year 1692* (Gentofte, Denmark: Rosenkilde and Bagger, reprinted in 1976), in which Molesworth argues that literacy and education designed to promote submission to authority were the direct causes of the authoritarian government of Denmark. Molesworth questioned both church and government sponsorship of schooling on ideological grounds.

10. As quoted in L. Lemisch, ed., *Benjamin Franklin: The Autobiography and Other Writings* (New York: Signet, 1961).

11. T. Jefferson, "A Bill for the More General Diffusion of Knowledge" in *The Writings of Thomas Jefferson,* ed., P. Ford, 221 (New York: Putnam, 1893).

12. B. Finkelstein, "Governing the Young: Teachers' Behaviors in American Primary Schools, 1820–1880, A Documentary History." (PhD diss., Teachers College, Columbia University, n.d.).

13. C. Barton, *The Story of My Childhood* (New York: Baker and Taylor, 1907), 30.

14. Finkelstein, "Governing the Young," 26.

15. Ibid., 102.

16. O. S. Minard, *Recollections of the Log Schoolhouse Period* (New York: Free, 1905), 21.

17. R. Felton, *Country Life in Georgia in the Days of My Youth* (Atlanta, GA: Index Printing, 1919), 59–60.

18. Finkelstein, "Governing the Young," 25.

19. *McGuffey's Pictoral Eclectic Primer* (Chicago: Wilson, Hinkle, 1867), 12.

20. R. Mosier's *Making the American Mind: Social and Moral Ideas in the McGuffey Readers* (New York: Russell and Russell, 1965) provides an early study of the hidden curriculum in schools. He contends that the contents of the readers profoundly affected the American public, popularizing previously unacceptable social and moral ideas about capitalism, which furthered the cause of industrialists and the wealthy.

21. W. H. McGuffey, *McGuffey's Eclectic Fourth Reader* (Chicago: Wilson, Hinkle, 1837), 221.

22. W. H. McGuffey, *McGuffey's Eclectic Third Reader* (Chicago: Wilson, Hinkle, 1856), 13.

23. Finkelstein, "Governing the Young," 142–43.

24. N. Dearborn, "The Oswego Movement in American Education" (PhD diss., Teachers College, Columbia University, n.d.), 44.

25. E. Sheldon as quoted in M. Barnes, ed., *The Autobiography of Edward Austin Sheldon* (New York: Ives-Butler, 1911), 121.

26. Finkelstein, "Governing the Young," 148.

27. Dearborn, "The Oswego Movement," 80.

28. See L. Cuban. *How Teachers Taught, 1880–1990* (New York: Teachers College Press, 1993).

29. L. Cuban. *How Teachers Taught.* Cuban argues that most educational innovations have floundered because they disrupt the historically constructed routine of textbook-oriented delivery of instruction. Because all teachers are trained into this routine and all innovations must past through the classroom, Cuban is pessimistic about the possibilities of change within schools.

30. See L. Cremin's *The Transformation of the School: Progressivism in American Education, 1876–1957.* (New York: Vintage, 1961).

31. F. Parker, *Talks on Teaching* (New York: Kellogg, 1883), 84.

32. C. Adams, "The New Departure in the Common Schools of Quincy," reprinted in *Elementary School Journal* 35 (1935): 500.

33. L. Patridge, *The Quincy Method Illustrated* (New York: Kellogg, 1889).

34. Patridge, *The Quincy Method Illustrated*, 367.

35. Ibid., 219.

36. C. Adams was the president of the Quincy School Board. As quoted in J. Campbell, *Colonel Francis W. Parker: The Children's Crusader* (New York: Teachers College Press, 1965), 92.

37. Adams, "The New Departure," 503–4.

38. See J. M. Rice's *The Public School System of the United States* (New York: Century, 1893).

39. Rice, *The Public School System*, 2.

40. Cremin, *The Transformation*, 49.

41. Rice, *The Public School System*, 26.

42. Ibid., 57–58.

43. Ibid., 176–77.

44. Ibid., 147.

45. Ibid., 153.

46. Ibid., 17–18.

47. Ibid., 21.

48. Ibid., 224.

49. Although Rice was generous in his praise for Indianapolis, Minneapolis, and St. Paul schools, he saved his superlatives for Francis Parker and his colleagues: "Of all the schools that I have seen, I know of none that shows so clearly what is implied by an educational ideal as the Cook County Normal School" (*The Public School System*, 209–10).

50. Cremin, *The Transformation*, 94.

Chapter Two

1. See J. Lears' *Fables of Abundance: A Cultural History of American Advertising.* (New York: Basic, 1994).

2. See K. Phillips' *Wealth and Democracy* (New York: Broadway, 2002). Of course many people did not enjoy any form of prosperity, particularly immigrants and minorities. My point here is to give some texture to the rising expectations of many Americans during this period when Horatio Alger stories were so popular and when the accumulation of wealth seemed to be the main attraction of the American dream.

3. See S. E. Morrison and H. S. Commager's *The Growth of the American Republic* (New York: Oxford University Press, 1969).

4. Phillips, *Wealth and Democracy*.

5. See A. Schlesinger's *The American Reformer* (New York: Atheneum, 1960) and G. Kolko's *The Triumph of Conservatism: A Reinterpretation of American History, 1890–1916* (New York: Free, 1963).

6. See R. Hofstader's *Age of Reform* (New York: Knopf, 1956).

7. A. Carnegie, speech at the dedication of the Cooper Union in New York City, 1900.

8. W. H. McGuffey, *New Revised Eclectic Second Reader* (New York: Winthrup B. Smith, 1843), 64.

9. See R. Callahan's *Education and the Cult of Efficiency* (Chicago: University of Chicago Press, 1962). Callahan suggests that the public comparison between business and schooling was extremely effective in bringing about changes in public education because school administrators depended on good public will in order to keep their jobs (vulnerability thesis). Since power in most communities resided with business interests, superintendents' quick attempts to implement scientific management makes sense.

10. W. C. Bagley, *Classroom Management* (New York: MacMillan, 1911), 2.

11. B. Franklin, as quoted in B. Hindle's *The Pursuit of Science in Revolutionary America* (Chappel Hill: University of North Carolina Press, 1956), 1.

12. K. Pearson, *The Grammar of Science* (New York: MacMillan, 1896), 22. Several decades later, in *Sources of Science in Education* (New York: Liveright, 1928), John Dewey argued against the adaptation of procedures from physical science to study social issues. First, Dewey agreed with William James, who doubted if a science of pedagogy patterned after physical science was possible because there was a qualitative difference between physical and social phenomena. Second, Dewey thought that teachers—not educational experts—should use the scientific method to better their instructional practice on a continuous basis while they worked. In fact, Dewey considered education science a dialectical process in which "any portion of ascertained knowledge that enters into the heart, head and hands of educators . . . renders the performance of educational functions enlightened. . . . But there is no way to discover what is more truly enlightened except by the continuation of the educational act itself. The discovery is never made, it is always in the making" (76–77).

13. E. L. Thorndike, *The Principles of Teaching Based on Psychology* (New York: A. G. Seeler, 1906), 265.

14. E. L. Thorndike, "Intelligence and Its Uses," *Harper's Magazine* 140 (1919–20): 235.

15. See H. Rugg's *That Men May Understand* (New York: Harper, 1941). The law of identical elements and interest in the science of pedagogy led Thorndike and his students to design and market tests for arithmetic (1908), handwriting (1910), spelling (1913), drawing (1913), reading (1914), and language ability (1916).

16. Thorndike, *The Principles of Teaching*.

17. E. L. Thorndike, *Animal Intelligence* (New York: MacMillan, 1898), 105.

18. See D. Nelson's *A Mental Revolution* (Columbus: Ohio State University Press, 1992); R. Kanigel's *The One Best Way* (New York: Viking, 1997); A. Gabor's *The Capitalist Philosophers* (New York: Times Business, 2000); and M. Banta's *Taylored Lives* (Chicago: University of Chicago Press, 1993). These authors suggest that Taylor's scientific management did not often follow his prescribed method. More often, he was forced to

simplify the procedures in order to meet production and profit quotas. Under those conditions, Taylor used his judgment to determine how quickly and in what ways workers should do their jobs. Under Taylor's supervision, labor-management relations were often strained. Because of labor union actions in response to scientific management, the federal government held hearings in 1912 to determine whether or not scientific management constituted unfair employment practices.

19. F. W. Taylor, "The Present State of the Art of Industrial Management," *The American Magazine* 71 (December 6, 1912), 4.

20. F. W. Taylor, as quoted in H. Kliebard's *The Struggle for the American Curriculum, 1893–1958* (New York: Routledge, 1986), 53.

21. See L. Cremin's *The Transformation of the School: Progressivism in American Education, 1876–1957* (New York: Vintage, 1961).

22. Certainly, the New Education, as championed by Dewey and William Kirkpatrick generally, and by Laura Zirbes and Jeanette Veatch in reading, flourished in some schools, although "in small, mostly private schools" (L. Cuban, *How Teachers Taught*, 1880–1990 [New York: Teachers College Press], 31). Its major effect came from the ability of some traditionalists to accommodate some elements of the New Education into their methods and language without really threatening traditional educational goals. Accordingly, classrooms became less formal and rigid, but teachers and textbooks remained at the center of schooling. This ability to incorporate elements of innovative methods into traditional methods is how elementary education has appeared to change with the times while remaining essentially the same.

23. F. Spaudling, as quoted in R. Callahan's *Education*, 1962, 74.

24. H. Wilson, ed., *Minimum Essentials in Elementary School Subjects—Standards and Current Practices*, 14th Yearbook of National Society for the Study of Education (Bloomington, IL: Public School, 1915). H. Holmes, "Time Distribution by Subjects and Grades in Representative Cities"; R. Jones, "Standard Vocabulary, p. 176"; S. A. Courtis, "Standards in Rates of Reading," p. 183; W. S. Gray, "Selected Bibliography upon Practical Tests of Reading Ability"; J. F. Hosic, "The Essential Literature."

25. H. Wilson, ed., *Second Report of the Committee on Minimum Essentials in Elementary School Subjects* W. S. Gray, "The Relation of Silent Reading to Economy in Education," 31; O. Munson and J. Hoskinson, "Library and Supplementary Reading Books Recommended for Use in Elementary Schools," 34.

26. H. Wilson, ed., *Third Report of the Committee on Economy of Time in Education*, 17th Yearbook of the National Society for the Study of Education, Part 1 (Bloomington, IL: Public School, 1918). E. Housh, "An Analysis of the Vocabularies of Ten Second-Year Readers," 45.

27. E. Horn, ed., *Fourth Report of the Committee on Economy of Time in Education*, 18th Yearbook of the National Society for the Instruction Study of Education, Part 2 (Bloomington, IL: Public School, 1919), 7–8. According to Horn, these summaries of scientific information on specific elementary school subjects had not been published previously. After the fourth report, the *Elementary School Journal* began to publish an annual summary beginning in 1920. For reading, William S. Gray increased his summary of 35 studies to a book-length document in 1925 describing 436 studies.

28. See L. Cremin's *The Transformation of the School* (New York: Vintage, 1961).

29. F. Freeman, "Principles of Method in Teaching Writing as Derived from Scientific Investigation," in *Fourth Report of the Committee on the Economy of Time in Education*

ed. E. Horn (Bloominton, IL: Public School, 1919). E. Horn, "Principles of Method in Teaching Spelling as Derived from Scientific Investigation."

30. W. S. Gray, "Principles of Method in Teaching Reading as Derived from Scientific Investigation," in *Fourth Report*, ed. E. Horn, 30, 37.

31. Ibid., 41, 41. A comparison of Gray's "Principles" with two other documents gives some indication of the conservative nature of his recommendations. First consider Emma Davis' "Fourth Grade Reading Directions for Teachers in Cleveland Ohio" (in *On the Teaching of English in Elementary and High Schools*, 5th Yearbook of the National Society for the Study of Education, Brown, ed. G. Brown [Bloominton, IL: Public School,1906]). Davis outlined two types of recommended reading instruction, which she called intensive and extensive reading. Without benefit of the scientific method, Davis' prescriptions for teachers closely resembled Gray's, although she overemphasized oral reading. She suggested that teachers feature content over elocution, word study with phonics for primary grades and syllabication and structural analysis for intermediate grades, initial silent reading for independent practice, testing for comprehension, and simple texts for rate training. All of these practices were later recommended by Gray in his scientific summary.

A second source of comparison is John and Evelyn Dewey's *Schools of Tomorrow* (New York: Dutton, 1915), which described reading instruction designed for the New Education. At the elementary school associated with the University of Missouri, "the pupils learn to read and write and figure only as they feel the need of it to enlarge their work about trees, plants, and animals or in the study of their own food, shelter, and clothing" (44–45). "The hour devoted to stories is no more a reading and writing lesson than all the rest of the day's work. During this period, the teacher and the children tell stories to each other; not stories they have studied from their primers, but stories that they already know, that they have listened to, or read because they enjoyed them. . . . Soon they want to learn a new group of stories, and then quite naturally, they go to the school library, pick out a storybook and read. It has been found that the first grade pupils read from twelve to thirty books during the year, the second grade pupils read from twenty-five to fifty. In this way, they learn to read" (49).

32. Charles Judd, dean of the University of Chicago's School of Education and editor of the *Elementary School Journal*, devoted space in several issues of the 1919 volume in order to discuss the lag time between educational science and textbook design and content. Included among these essays was a publisher's response to criticism in which he argued that publishers were responsible only to the marketplace and did not attempt to lead teachers in any direction. If scientific textbooks were sought, then there first must be a market for them. However, as early as 1902, John Dewey accused publishers of manipulating school curricula through their publishing and advertising practices.

33. W. Bagley, Introduction to *New Materials of Instruction*, 19th Yearbook of the National Society for the Study of Education, ed. G. Whipple, 11 (Bloominton, IL: Public School, 1920).

34. See R. Venezky, "A History of the American Reading Textbook," *Elementary School Journal* 87; 1987, 247–65; N. B. Smith, *American Reading Instruction*, (New York: Silver Burdett, 1934); F. Bass, *Lessons for Beginners in Reading* (Boston: D. C. Heath, 1901); Butler Series, *The Second Reader* (Philadelphia: Butler, 1883), 15; S. Sprague, *Lights to Literature* (New York: Rand McNally, 1898), 3; E. Cyr, *The Cyr Readers* (Boston: Ginn, 1901); and J. Baldwin and I. Bender, *Reading with Expression, 7th Reader* (Chicago: American Book, 1911), 5–6.

35. N. B. Smith, *American Reading Instruction*, 2nd ed. (Newark, DE: International Reading Association, 1965), 169. Venezky argues that Smith's history fails to identify the beginning of teachers' guidebooks in the 19th century. He writes, "separate teacher's mauals did not become commonplace until the 1920s, but the pattern for such texts was established in the late 1880s and early 1890s with the publication of Ballard's *Synthetic Method* and

Ward's *Rational Method in Reading*" ("A History," 253). However, as I will argue in later chapters, these 19th-century guidebooks were not based on scientific evidence and, therefore, offered only a simple form of control—someone else's opinion—which teachers could easily ignore. The guidebooks of the 1920s were marketed with scientific authority and were tied to teacher evaluation.

36. M. Hardy, *First Grade Manual for The Child's Own Way Series* (Chicago: Wheeler, 1926), 5–6. The study mentioned was A. Gates, "Problems in Beginning Reading," *Teachers College Record* (1925): 78–91.

37. C. Bryce and R. Hardy, *Teachers' Manual for the Newsons Readers Playtime Primer*, (New York: Newson, 1927), 6.

38. As early as 1925, Lehah Crabbs developed an equation for determining teachers' efficiency of instruction through their students' scores on standardized tests (*Measuring Efficiency in Supervision and Teaching*, Teachers College Contribution to Education, Columbia University New York No. 175). Since tests were designed to examine students' knowledge of what was taught (following the law of identical elements), and test designers' definition of what was taught was the information that was included in students' textbooks, this method of supervision through test scores applied pressure on teachers to follow the guidebooks closely during their reading instruction.

Chapter Three

1. The six studies were published in a variety of reading journals: "On Mastery Learning: Some Unwarranted Constraints Placed on Teachers During their Reading Instruction," *Substance* 8 (1982): 5–7, 11; "The Use of Commercial Reading Materials in American Elementary Schools," *Reading Research Quarterly* 19 (1983): 68–85; "Merit Pay, Formal Rationality, and the Teacher's Role During Reading Instruction," *Reading Research Quarterly* 21 (1986): 20–35; "Conflict or Consensus: Views of Reading Curricula and Instruction Within One Instructional Setting," *Reading Research and Instruction* 26 (1986): 31–49; "Commercial Reading Materials, Technological Ideology, and the Deskilling of Teachers," *Elementary School Journal* 87 (1987): 307–29; and "Class Size, Reading Instruction, and Commercial Materials," *Reading Research and Instruction* 28 (1989): 18–24.

2. *Ideology* is a controversial term because it was used in the Soviet Union in order to justify Stalinist policy and vulgar Marxism. In this text, I use the term to mean a discursive and significatory mechanism that may occlude, legitimize, naturalize, or universalize a set of ideas in a variety of different forms in order to mystify others about the origins and connections of a specific phenomenon.

3. Rationalization is carefully explained in M. Weber's *The Theory of Social and Economic Organization* (New York: Free, 1964) and R. Heilbronner's *The Nature and Logic of Capitalism* (New York: Norton, 1985).

4. There are many good books on the rationalization of law, medicine, and other public and private institutions. See Z. Baumann's *The Individualized Society* (New York: Polity, 2001); N. Klien's *No Logo* (New York: Picador, 1999); and C. Lemert's *Social Things* (New York: Rowman and Littlefield, 1997).

5. See R. Brisbin, *A Strike Like No Other Strike: Law and Resistance During the Pittston Coal Strike, 1989–1990* (Baltimore, MD: Johns Hopkins University, 2002) and A. Mudrosh, ed., *Remediation of Abandoned Surface Coal Mine Sites* (New York: Springer, 2002).

6. H. Marcuse, "Some Social Implications of Modern Technology," published originally in 1941. Reprinted in *The Essential Frankfort School Reader*, eds. A. Arato and E. Gebhardt, 151 (New York: Monthly Review, 1987).

7. R. Anderson et al., *Becoming a Nation of Readers* (Washington DC: National Institute of Education, 1985), 120.

8. G. Lukacs is credited with anticipating humanistic Marxism before Marx's early works were published. His *History and Class Consciousness* (Cambridge, MA: MIT Press, 1970) is considered the founding document in western Marxism. See M. Berman's *Adventures in Marxism* (New York: Verso, 2000) for a overview of humanistic Marxism and Lukacs' contribution.

9. E. B. Huey, *The Psychology and Pedagogy of Reading* (Cambridge, MA: MIT Press, 1908), 9 (reprinted in 1968).

10. E. C. Lagemann, *An Elusive Science: The Troubling History of Education Research* (Chicago: University of Chicago, 2000).

11. H. Donovan, "Use of Research in the Teaching of Reading" *Elementary English Review* (1928): 106–7.

12. See M. Austin and C. Morrison, *The First R* (New York: Wiley, 1963) and A. Barton and D. Wilder, "Research and Practice in the Teaching of Reading," in *Innovations in Education*, ed. M. Miles (New York: Teachers College Press, 1964).

13. The National Society for the Study of Education yearbooks are a rich source of information about reading, research, instruction, testing, and policy. W. S. Gray, ed., *Report of the National Committee on Reading*, 24th Yearbook (Bloomington, IL: Public School, 1925) p. 121; W. S. Gray, ed., *The Teaching of Reading: A Second Report from the National Committee on Reading* 36th Yearbook (Chicago: University of Chicago, 1937); A. Gates, ed., *Reading in the Elementary School*, 48th Yearbook (Chicago: University of Chicago, 1949); P. Witty, ed., *Development in and Through Reading*, 60th Yearbook (Chicago: University of Chicago, 1961); H. Robinson, ed., *Innovation and Change in Reading Instruction*, 67th Yearbook (Chicago: University of Chicago, 1968); A. Purves and O. Niles, ed., *Becoming Readers in a Complex Society*, 83rd Yearbook (Chicago: University of Chicago, 1984); N. Nelson and R. Calfee, ed., *The Reading-Writing Connection*, 97th Yearbook (Chicago: University of Chicago, 1998).

14. Gray, *The Teaching of Reading*, 90–91, 102.

15. Gray, *The Teaching of Reading*, Chapter 6.

16. These statements were made by G. Hildreth, 56, P. McKee, 131, and G. Whipple, 217, in Gates, *Reading in the Elementary School*.

17. These states of qualified support for basals span twenty-three years from V. Herrick in Witty, *Development in and Through Reading*, 173; to M. Wittick in H. Robinson, *Innovation and Change*, 124; to J. Chall and S. Conrad in A. Purves and O. Niles, *Becoming Readers*, 213.

18. J. Harris, H. Donovan, and T. Alexander *Supervision and Teaching of Reading* (Boston: Johnson, 1927), 446.

19. D. Durrell, *Improving Reading Instruction* (New York: World, 1940), 22; E. L. Dolch, *Teaching Primary Reading* (New York: Garland, 1950), 319.

20. P. Shannon, "The Treatment of Commercial Reading Materials in College Reading Methods Textbooks," *Reading World* 23 (1983): 147–57.

21. R. Aukerman, *The Basal Approach to Reading* (New York: Wiley, 1981).

22. P. Shannon, "A Retrospective Look at Teachers' Use of Commercial Reading Materials," *Language Arts* 59 (1982): 844–53.

23. See N. Frame, "The Availability of Reading Materials for Teachers and Pupils at the Primary Level," *English Education* 41 (1964): 262–68; C. Hill and K. Methot, "Making

an Important Transition," *Elementary English* 51 (1974): 842–45; and J. Veatch, "Structure in the Reading Program," *Elementary English* 44 (1967): 252–57 for arguments concerning why the fact that there was no statistical difference between alternatives and basals meant that teachers should use the alternatives. W. S. Gray, "New Issues in Teaching Reading," *Elementary English Review* iv (1993) 162–64; E. Betts," A Study of Vocabulary of First Grade Basal Readers," *Elementary English Review* 16 (1939) 65–69. E. L. Dolch," How Much Word Knowledge Do Children Bring to Grade One?" *Elementary Education Review* 13 (1936), 177–83. A Gates, "Needed in Research in Reading," *Elementary English Review* 13 (1936) 306–10. G. Yoakam, "Unsolved Problems." *Elementary English* 31 (1954), 427–30.

24. See G. Bond, "First Grade Studies," *Elementary English* 43 (1966): 464–70; E. Fry, "Comparing the Diacritical System, ITA, and a Basal Reading Series," *Elementary English* 43 (1966): 607–11; and W. Sheldon and D. Lashinger's 1968, 1969, and 1971 summaries of reading research in *Elementary English*.

25. G. Bond and R. Dykstra, "The Cooperative Research Program in First-Grade Reading Instruction," *Reading Research Quarterly* 2 (1967): 5–142.

26. J. Readence and D. Barone, ed., Special Issue on First-Grade Studies—30 Years After, *Reading Research Quarterly* 32 (1997): 340–445.

27. See Anderson's *Becoming a Nation of Readers*, for example.

28. J. Hoffman and N. Roser edited a special issue (*Elementary School Journal* 87 (1987): 244–410) devoted to basal readers and their use in schools, which demonstrates the supportive skepticism of the reading experts at the time. The quotes are from that issue: Chall, 244; Duffy, Roehler, and Putnam, 360; Farr, Tulley and Powell, 281.

29. J. Squires, "The History of the Profession" in *The Handbook of Research on Teaching the English Language Arts*, ed. D. Lapp and J. Flood, 3–18 (Mahwah, NJ: Erlbaum., 2003).

30. B. Jerrolds, *Reading Reflections: The History of the International Reading Association* (Newark, DE: International Reading Association, 1977), 13, 24.

31. K. Goodman, P. Shannon, Y. Freeman, and S. Murphy, *Report Card on Basal Readers* (Katonah, NY: Richard C. Owen, 1989).

32. R. Anderson, J. Osborn, and R. Tierney, *Learning to Read in American Schools: Basal Readers and Content Texts* (Mahwah, NJ: Erlbaum, 1984), ix.

33. See B. Rosenshine and R. Stevens, "Classroom Instruction in Reading," 745–98 and W. Otto, A. Wolf, and R. Eldridge "Managing Instruction" 199–828, both published in *Handbook of Reading Research*, ed. P. D. Pearson (New York: Longman, 1984).

34. D. Levine, ed., *Improving Student Achievement Through Mastery Learning* (San Francisco: Jossey-Bass, 1985), 1.

35. M. Katims and B. F. Jones, *Chicago Mastery Learning: Theory, Research and Assessment in the Inner City*. (paper presented at the Annual Convention of the International Reading Association, New Orleans, 1981).

36. P. Shannon, "Mastery Learning in Reading and the Control of Teachers and Students," *Language Arts* 61 (1984): 484–93.

37. P. Shannon, "Teachers' and Administrators' Thoughts on Changes in Reading Instruction Within a Merit Pay Program Based on Test Scores," *Reading Research Quarterly* 21 (1986): 20–35. Quote 28.

38. J. Hoffman, "Teacher and School Effects in Learning to Read," in *Handbook of Reading Research*, vol. II, ed. R. Barr et al., 911–50 (New York: Longman, 1991).

39. L. Cuban, "Transforming the Frog into a Prince: Effective School Research, Policy and Practice at the District Level," *Harvard Educational Review* 54 (1984): 129–51.

40. A. Barton and D. Wilde, "Research and Practice in the Teaching of Reading," in *Innovations in Education,* ed. M. Miles (New York: Teachers College, 1964).

41. P. Johnston, "Assessment in Reading," in *Handbook of Reading Research,* ed. P. D. Pearson, 147–83.

42. E. L. Thorndike, "The Measurement of Ability in Reading," *Teachers College Record* 15 (1914): 1.

43. R. Allington, "Oral Reading," in *Handbook of Reading Research,* ed. P. D. Pearson, 829–65.

44. A. Gates, "The Measurement and Evaluation of Achievement in Reading," in *The Teaching of Reading,* ed. W. S. Gray, 374.

45. E. House, "Evaluation as Scientific Management in United States School Reform," *Comparative Education Review* 22 (1978): 388–401; M. McLaughlin, *Evaluation and Reform* (Chicago: Ballinger, 1975).

46. J. Chall and J. Squires, "The Publishing Industry and Textbooks," in *Handbook of Reading,* vol. II, ed. R. Barr, M. Kamil, P. Mosenthal, and P. D. Pearson, 124 (New York: Longman, 1991).

47. N. B. Smith, *American Reading Instruction* (Newark, DE: International Reading Association, 1965).

48. K. Goodman in *Report Card on Basal Readers,* 51–52.

49. Basal author Richard Allington wrote this statement in a signed editorial evaluation of an article I had submitted for publication in 1986.

50. R. Farr, M. Tulley, and D. Powell, "The Evaluation and Selection of Basal Readers," *Elementary School Journal* 87 (1987): 267–81.

51. K. Goodman in *Report Card on Basal Readers,* 48–50.

52. During the 1980s, basal companies merged in order to increase their share of the textbook market. For example, Ginn and Company merged with Silver Burdett publishing and acquired Allyn and Bacon's textbook division. Harcourt, Brace, and Jovanovich purchased Holt, Rinehart, and Winston. Macmillan bought Harper and Row, Lippincott, and Laidlaw. Nonpublishing Gulf and Western Oil Corporation owned the new Ginn conglomerate. Time Life acquired Scott Foresman. By the turn of the twentieth century, three companies own 80 percent of the market, although each company marketed more than one basal.

53. T. Jefferson, "A Bill for the More General Diffusion of Knowledge," in *The Writings of Thomas Jefferson,* ed. P. Ford, 121 (New York: Putnam, 1893).

54. C. Kaestle and M. Smith, "The Federal Role in Elementary and Secondary Education, 1940–1980," *Harvard Educational Review* 52 (1982): 384.

55. See J. Spring's *The American School, 1642–2000* (New York: Longman, 2001) for an overview of the exclusion and inclusion of women, minorities, and the poor in American schools.

56. The Reagan adminstration commissioned the *Nation at Risk* report in 1983 with the original intention of dissolving the U.S. Department of Education but found that neoliberal forces sought a more profound federal presence in public schools in order to reform them in the image of new corporate management theory.

57. H. L. Donovan, "How to Select Textbooks," *Peabody Journal of Education* 18 (1924): 2.

58. G. Whipple, ed., *The Textbook in American Education*, 30th Yearbook of the National Soceity for the Study of Education (Bloomington, IL: Public School, 1931).

59. W. Coffey, "Judicial Opinion on Textbook Selection," in G. Whipple, *The Textbook in American Education*, 386.

60. J. D. Marshall, "With a Little Help from Some Friends: Publishers, Protesters, and Texas Textbook Decisions," in *The Politics of the Textbook*, ed. M. Apple and L. Christian-Smith, 56–77 (New York: Routledge, 1991).

61. J. D. Marshall, "With a Little Help," 68

62. V. Lannie, *Henry Barnard: American Educator* (New York: Teachers College Press, 1974); D. Tyack, R. Lowe, and E. Hansot, *Public Schools in Hard Times: The Great Depression and Recent Years* (Cambridge, MA: Harvard University Press, 1984); W. Bennett, *James Madison Elementary School: A Curriculum for American Schools* (Washington DC.: Government Printing Office, 1988).

63. A. McGill-Franzen, "Policy and Instruction: What is the Relationship?" *Handbook of Reading Research,* vol. III, ed. in M. Kamil, P. Mosenthal, P. D. Pearson, and R. Barr, (Mahwah, NJ: Erlbaum 2000), 889–908.

64. E. House, "Evaluation as Scientific Management," 388–401.

65. W. Becker, "Teaching Reading and Language to the Disadvantaged—What We Have Learned from Field Research," *Harvard Educational Review* 47 (1977): 518–43.

66. J. Readence and D. Barone, Special Issue on First-Grade Studies, 340–445.

67. G. Bond and R. Dykstra as quoted in P. D. Pearson, special issue on First-Grade Studies —30 Years After, *Reading Research Quarterly* 32 (1997): 428.

68. A. Rivilin and M. Timpane, *Should We Give Up or Try Harder? Planned Variation Education* (Washington, DC: Brookings Institution, 1967), 12–13.

69. R. Glazer, Foreword to R. Anderson et al. Becoming a Nation of Readers, viii.

Chapter Four

1. Edward Bellamy was educated as a lawyer, but he never practiced law. Rather, he became a journalist and novelist. *Looking Backwards—2000 to 1887* (Boston: Houghton Mifflin, 1888) was his fourth novel and his first overtly political work. In the book, he intuited a humanistic Marxism before that portion of Marx's work had been translated into English. Its publication captured the rising criticism of contemporary materialism, and more than one million copies were sold during the first five years. Nationalist clubs formed across the country to promote the nationalization of public services. In 1893, Bellamy published *Equality*, a novel to explain his answers to criticisms of *Looking Backwards*.

2. Lester Frank Ward was raised in poverty and began factory work at age twelve. He was self-taught but eventually earned degrees in medicine and law. He is considered the first sociologist and was called the American Aristotle because of his broad knowledge and interests. In *Dynamic Sociology* (New York: Appleton, 1883, 2 volumes), Ward argued for a planned society with a government responsible for universal education, freedom from poverty, and happiness for all.

3. Ward, *Dynamic Sociology*, 596.

4. J. M. Rice, *The Public School Systems of the United States* (New York: Century, 1893), 49.

5. John Dewey believed that education was the catalyst for democracy by developing democratic habits among young and old alike. From 1885 to the end of the World War I,

Dewey tested his philosophical beliefs in schools. The quote is from "The Need for an Industrial Education in an Industrial Democracy," volume 10, *Middle Works of John Dewey* (Carbondale: Southern Illinois University Press, 1983), 139.

6. Col. Francis Wayland Parker was injured during the American Civil War and spent part of his recuperation time studying education in Germany. When he returned, he became superintendent of schools in Quincy, Massachussetts, in 1875. Between 1876 and 1880, thirty thousand visitors passed through Quincy schools to see the Quincy method in practice. The quote is from Parker's *Talk on Pedagogics* (New York: Kellogg, 1884), 1.

7. Parker, *Talk on Pedagogics*, 408.

8. Lelia Patridge spent a year at the Quincy schools and recorded her observations in *The 'Quincy Method' Illustrated* (New York: Kellogg, 1885), 452–53.

9. Charles Quincy Adams explained the Quincy method in "The New Departure in the Common Schools of Quincy," which was reprinted in *Elementary School Journal* 35, (1935): 495–504. The quote is from the last two pages of the article.

10. J. Dewey, *The Ethics of Democracy* (Ann Arbor, MI: Michigan Register, 1888), 26.

11. J. Dewey, *The School and Society* (Chicago: University of Chicago Press, 1899), 19–20.

12. Katherine Mayhew and Ann Edwards were sisters and teachers at Dewey Laboratory School in Chicago. They later wrote about their experiences in *The Dewey School* (New York: Appleton-Century, 1936). The two quotes are from pages 380 and 381.

13. M. Johnson, *Thirty Years with an Idea* (Tuscalossa: University of Alabama Press, 1938), 70; M. Johnson, *Youth in a World of Men* (New York: John Day, 1929), 128.

14. In 1913 and 1914, John Dewey's daughter traveled to nearly a dozen schools promoting the New Education across the country. She published her observations and her father's analysis in *Schools of Tomorrow* (New York: Dutton, 1915), 36.

15. William Kilpatrick was a colleague of John Dewey's at Teachers College, Columbia University, and one of the founding members of the Educational Frontier. The Educational Frontier was a group of radical educators during the 1930s who thought that teachers should act to make society more democratic and egalitarian. Kilpatrick believed that the project method provided the pedagogy for that work. W. Kilpatrick, *Foundations of Method* (New York: Macmillan, 1925), 213.

16. In 1883, Caroline Pratt began teaching at sixteen in a one-room schoolhouse in Fayetteville, New York. She won a scholarship to Teachers College in 1892 for courses in kindergarten methods and industrial arts. She worked seven years as a manual training instructor at the Normal School for Girls in Philadelphia, during which time she met Helen Marot and began to investigate the working and living conditions of the poor. She moved to New York City and worked at three teaching jobs simultaneously at a private school and two settlement houses, where she worked out the general philosophy of the City and Country School. C. Pratt and J. Stanton, *Before Books* (New York: Adelphi, 1826), 79.

17. Freudianism was a driving force in the New Education during the 1920s. Teachers were urged to recognize the students' unconscious as the real source of motivation for their actions. Schooling was to help students sublimate their repressed emotions into socially useful channels. One interpretation of Freud's writings suggested that teachers were to use their understandings of students' interests, instincts, and tendencies to help them develop a basis for their own reflective behavior. Another suggested that schools should shift their focus from intellect to students' emotions in order to help students cope with personal and social problems. Margaret Naumburg was a champion of this second

position. She challenged Dewey, accusing him of missing the "essence of human life" by ignoring the individual's struggles against society's confinement. M. Naumburg, *The Child and the World* (New York: Harcourt, Brace, 1928), 14.

18. H. Mearns, *Creative Youth* (New York: Doubleday, 1925), 26, 79.

19. H. Rugg and A. Shumaker, *The Child-Centered School: An Appraisal of the New Education*, (Yonkers, NY: World Book, 1928).

20. Guy Whipple, *The Activity Movement*, 33rd Yearbook of the National Society for the Study of Education, Part 2 (Bloomington, IL: Public School).

21. Ibid., 77, 87.

22. J. Dewey, How Much Freedom in the New Schools? (*New Republic*, 58, 1930, 203-206). Quotes are from the last two pages.

23. L. Cuban, *How Teachers Taught*, 2d ed. (New York: Teachers College Press, 1993).

24. A. Bester, *Backwoods Utopias* (Philadelphia: University of Pennsylvania, 1950); R. Flesch, *Why Johnny Can't Read* (New York: Harper and Row, 1957); A. Lynd, *Quackery in the Public Schools* (Boston: Little, Brown, 1953); A. Rickover, *Education and Freedom* (New York: Dutton, 1959), 24.

25. Some of the educational utopian books of the 1960s were G. Dennison, *The Lives of Children* (New York: Vintage, 1969); N. Hentoff, *Our Children Are Dying* (New York: Viking, 1966); J. Heardon, *The Way It'd Sposed to Be* (New York: Bantam, 1968); J. Holt, *How Children Learn* (New York: Pittman, 1964); H. Kohl, *36 Children* (New York: Signet, 1967); J. Kozol, *Death at an Early Age* (New York: Bantam, 1967); and P. Lopate, *Being with Children* (New York: Bantam, 1971).

26. R. Barth and C. Rathbone, "Information Education—the Open School," *Center Forum* 16 (1969), 74.

27. J. Kozol, *Free Schools* (Boston: Houghton Mifflin, 1972).

28. G. Dennison, *The Lives of Children*, 93.

29. J. Holt, *Freedom and Beyond* (New York: Dutton, 1972), 229.

30. Founded by Herb Kohl in 1967, the Teachers and Writers Collaborative believed that writers could make a unique contribution to the teaching of writing in public schools. "Teachers and Writers Collaborative. Manifesto of the Huntting Conference," reprinted in *Teaching the Unteachable*, H. Kohl, (New York New York Review of Books, 1966), 11.

31. F. Smith, *Psycholinguistics and Reading* (New York: Holt, Rinehart, Winston, 1973), vi.

32. With guest editors James Hoffman and Nancy Roser, the *Elementary School Journal*, which started in the Dewey Laboratory School, devoted a special issue to whole language. P. David Pearson was included as a moderately supportive critic of whole language. P. David Pearson, "Reading the Whole Language Movement," *Elementary School Journal* 90 (1989), 233.

33. K. Goodman, *What's Whole in Whole Language?* (Portsmouth, NH: Heinemann, 1986), 76.

34. See C. Edelsky, B. Altwerger, and B. Flores, *Whole Language: What's the Difference?* (Portsmouth, NH: Heinemann, 1991).

35. N. Atwell, "Around the Dinner Table," in *Breaking Ground: Teachers Relating Reading and Writing in the Elementary School*, ed. J. Hansen, T. Newkirk, and D. Graves, (Portsmouth, NH: Heinemann, 1985), 231.

36. M. Halliday, *Learning How to Mean* (New York: Elsevier, 1975).

37. Edelsky, Altwerger and Flores. *Whole Language*, 37.

38. L. Rief, "Apprenticeship at Four or Fourteen," in *Workshop 2: By and for Teachers, Beyond the Basal*, ed. N. Atwell, (Portsmouth, NH: Heinemann, 1990), 132.

39. See K. Goodman, P. Shannon, Y. Freeman, and S. Murphy, *The Report Card on Basal Readers* (Katonah, NY: Richard C. Owen, 1988).

40. See J. Willinsky, *The New Literacy: Redefining Reading and Writing in the Schools* (New York: Routledge, 1990).

41. B. Fisher, "Children as Authorities on Their Own Reading," in *Workshop 2*, ed. Atwell, 39.

42. See L. Rosenblatt, "The Reading Transaction: For What?" in *Literacy in Process*, ed. B. Power and R. Hubbard (Portsmouth, NH: Heinemann, 1991).

43. See K. M. Pierce and C. Gilles, ed., *Cycles of Meaning: Exploring the Potential of Talk in Learning Communities* (Portsmouth, NH: Heinemann, 1993).

44. See E. Brinkley, "What's Religion Got to Do with Attacks on Whole Language?" in *In Defense of Good Teaching*, ed. B. Power and R. Hubbard (York, ME: Stenhouse, 1998).

45. See B. Cambourne, *The Whole Story: Natural Learning and the Acquisition of Literacy in the Classroom* (New York: Scholastic, 1988).

46. See J. Lindfors, *Children's Language and Learning* (New York: Pearson, 1987).

47. See H. Giroux, "Critical Literacy and Student Experience: Donald Graves' Approach to Literacy," in *Becoming Political: Readings and Writings in the Politics of Literacy Education*, ed. Patrick Shannon (Portsmouth, NH: Heinemann, 1992).

48. See Chapter 5 in C. Weaver, *Understanding Whole Language* (Portsmouth, NH: Heinemann, 1990), and C. Edelsky, "Whose Agenda Is It Anyway?" *Educational Researcher* 19, 8 (1990): 7–11.

49. Deborah McGriff was assistant superintendent of Milwaukee Schools. D. McGriff, as quoted in B. Peterson, "Basal Adoption Controversy Continues into Second Year," *Rethinking Schools* 3, 1 (1988): 9.

50. See B. Berghoff, K. Egawa, J. Harste and B. Hoonan, *Beyond Reading and Writing: Inquiry, Curriculum and Multiple Ways of Knowing* (Urbana, IL: National Council of Teachers of English, 2000).

51. See S. Hall, ed., "*Representations: Cultural Prepresentations and Signifying Practices*, (Thousand Oaks, CA: Sage, 1997).

52. B. Hoonan, "Nathaniel," in *Beyond Reading and Writing*, ed. B. Berghoff, et al., 50.

53. K. Goodman, "I Didn't Found Whole Language," in *Distinguished Educators On Reading: Contributions That Have Shaped Effective Literacy Instruction*, ed. N. Padak et al., (Newark, DE: International Reading Association, 2000), 14.

54. J. Dewey, *Human Nature and Conduct* (New York: Henry Holt, 1922), 167–68.

55. J. Newman, ed., *Whole Language: Theory in Use* (Portsmouth, NH: Heinemann, 1985), 2.

56. These new authorities—mostly women and teachers—complemented and extended the work of Kenneth and Yetta Goodman, Donald Graves, Judith Newman, Frank Smith, and Dorothy Watson.

57. B. Honig, "The California Reading Initiative," The New Advocate 1, 4 (1988): 235.

58. Honig, "The California Reading Initiative," 239.

59. T. Shannon, "Supervising Change: Moving Away from Basals," in *Basal Readers: A Second Look*, ed. P. Shannon and K. Goodman, 196 (Katonah, NY: Richard C. Owen, 1994).

60. See C. Weaver and L. Henke, ed., *Supporting Whole Language: Stories of Teacher and Institutional Change* (Portsmouth, NH: Heinemann, 1992).

61. See M. Rosecky, "Implementing PCRP: Fact or Fiction," (paper presented at the Pennsylvania Council of Teachers of English, Lehigh University, 1981).

62. S. Lytle and M. Botel, *The Pennsylvania Framework for Reading, Writing, and Talking Across the Curriculum* (Harrisburg: Pennsylvania Department of Education, 1989), 1, 22, 139.

63. P. D. Pearson, "Reading the Whole Language Movement," *Elementary School Journal* 90 (1989): 234.

Chapter Five

1. "The Federal Report: Ketchup Set to Pour Again in School Lunch Rules," editorial *Washington Post*, October 30, 1981, A29.

2. "Bumble Lives," editorial *New York Times*, October 7, 1981, A 26.

3. Heinemann Educational Books made its name in America from publishing books to inform teachers interested in whole language and process writing. After 2002, it also began to publish books under the firsthand imprint with prescribed lessons for teachers to use in their classrooms, apparently working against the advice of the early authors. In fact, some of the early authors, such as Nancie Atwell, Lucy Calkins, and Ralph Fletcher, have recently published scripted lessons for teachers to follow. Although Heinemann continues to publish books that promote teachers' authority, these recent volumes suggest the power of the drift in the market toward books that contribute to the real rationalization of reading education.

4. The titles of some of the books that took the role of reading education in social and economic activities of the 1980s and 1990s give some indication of the skepticism concerning the government's and businesses' position on this matter. David Beliner and Bruce Biddle wrote *The Manufactured Crisis: Myths, Fraud and the Attack on America's Schools* (New York: Addison Wesley, 1995), Jeff McQuillan published *The Literacy Crisis?* (Portsmouth, NH: Heinemann, 1998) and Gerry Coles authored *Reading Lessons: The Debate Over Literacy* (New York: Hill and Wang, 1998). Each demonstrated, using the government's own statistics, that reading test scores were not falling, current students read better than their predecessors, and schools, although not without flaws, were performing well with middle- and upper-class students and struggling with minority and poor students.

5. R. Kirk, *The Conservative Mind* (New York: Free, 1963).

6. H. Kliebard, *Changing Course: American Curricular Reform in the Twentieth Century* (New York: Teachers College Press, 2002) and P. Shannon, *Reading Poverty* (Portsmouth, NH: Heinemann, 1998).

7. T. Bell, Education Policy Development in Reagan Administration 68, *Phi Delta Kappan* (1986): 488.

8. C. Murray, *Losing Ground: American Social Policy 1950–1980* (New York: Basic, 1985).

9. R. Herrnstein, *IQ in the Meritocracy* (Boston: Atlantic-Little, 1974) was the precursor for R. Herrnstein and C. Murray, *The Bell Curve: Intelligence and the Class Structure in American Life* (New York: Free, 1994).

10. W. Simon, *A Time for Truth* (New York: Reader's Digest, 1978), 230.

11. J. Spring, *Political Agenda for Education* (Mawtauk, NJ: Erlbaum, 2002), 39.

12. D. Hood, Head Start, Policy Analysis No. 187 (New York: Cato Institute, 1992).

13. D. Ricci, *The Transformation of American Politics: The New Washington and the Rise of Think Tanks* (New Haven, CT: Yale University, 1993).

14. S. Blumenfeld, "The Whole Language Fraud," *The New American* 8 (1982): 6–8.

15. P. Schlafly, "How and Why I Taught My Children to Read," *Eagle Forum Report* 14 (1981): 1–4.

16. P. Shannon, "Talking Back to Critics," *Teachers Networking* 10 (1991): 12–14.

17. W. Armstrong, *Illiteracy: An Incurable Disease or Educational Malpractice* (Washington DC: Government Publishing Office, 1989).

18. As quoted in K. Goodman, *In Defense of Good Teaching* (York, ME: Stenhouse, 1998), 7.

19. R. Hofstader, *Anti-intellectualism in American Life* (New York: Knopf, 1964), 135.

20. As quoted in R. Reed, *Active Faith* (New York: Free, 1996), 111.

21. S. Diamond, *Spiritual Warfare: The Politics of the Christian Right* (Boston: South End, 1989); B. Reed, ed., *Nothing Sacred: Women Respond to Religious Fundamentalism and Terror* (New York: Nation, 2002).

22. S. Jacoby, *Freethinkers: A History of American Secularism* (New York: Metropolitan, 2004).

23. R. Thoburn, *The Children Trap* (Fort Worth, TX: Dominion, 1986).

24. S. Blumenfeld, "More Problems with Whole Language," *Blumenfeld Education Newsletter*, February 1992, 1.

25. M. Chapman, *Why Not Teach Intensive Phonics?* (Pensacola, FL: Becka, 1986), 14.

26. Visit the Christian Coalitions website www.cc.org for a better understanding of the relationship between the religious right and the various levels of government.

27. W. Bennett, *What Works: Research about Teaching and Learning* (Washington DC: Government Printing Office, 1984), 2.

28. Ibid., 8., W. Bennett, *First Lessons: A Report on Elementary Education in America* (Washington DC: Government Printing Office, 1986), 14; and W. Bennett, *James Madison Elementary School: A Curriculum for American Schools* (Washington DC: Government Printing Office, 1988), 36.

29. Bennett, *First Lessons*, 39.

30. W. Bennett, *Our Children and Our Country: Improving America's Schools and Affirming Common Culture* (New York: Touchstone, 1988), 9.

31. W. Bennett, *The De-Valuing of America: The Fight for Our Culture and Our Children* (New York: Simon and Schuster, 1992), *The Index of Leading Cultural Indicators: Facts and Figures of the State of American Society* (New York: Touchstone, 1994, second edition 1999), *Body Count: Moral Poverty and How to Win America's War Against Crime and Drugs* (New York: Simon and Schuster, 1996), and *The Death of Outrage: Bill Clinton and the Assault on American Ideals* (New York: Free, 1998). Bennett's edited *Book of Virtues: A Treasure of Great Moral Stories* (New York: Simon and Schuster, 1993) began a marketing empire with multiple editions of the book for various audiences, a website, and a television program on the Public Broadcasting Service's stations.

32. As quoted in Stephen Mansfield, *The Faith of George W. Bush* (New York: Tarcher, 2003), 23, 47.

33. National Commission on Excellence in Education. *A Nation at Risk: The Imperative for Educational Reform* (Indianapolis: Indiana Teacher Federation, 1983), 7.

34. T. Bell, *The Thirteenth Man* (New York: Free, 1998), 114.

35. R. Reagan, "A 'Nation at Risk' Report," White House press release, April 3, 1983.

36. C. Lugg, "For God and Country: Reagan and Education" (unpublished diss., Penn State University, 1995).

37. National Commission on Excellence in Education, *A Nation at Risk*, 13.

38. Between 1983 and 1985, eleven reports of school reform were published: College Board, *Academic Preparation for College: What Students Need to Know and Be Able to Do* (New York College Board, 1983); Education Commission of the States, *Action for Excellence: Task Force on Education for Economic Growth* (Washington DC: Education Commission of the States, 1983); Business-Higher Education Forum, *America's Competitive Challenge: A Report to the President of the United States from the Business Education Forum*, (Washington DC: Business-Higher Education Forum, 1983); J. Goodlad, *A Place Called School: Prospects for the Future* (New York: McGraw-Hill, 1984); National Science Foundation, *Educating Americans for the Twenty-First Century: A Plan of Action for Improving Mathematics, Science and Technology Education for all American Students So That Their Achievement Is the Best in the World by 1995* (Washington DC: National Science Foundation, 1983); Carnegie Foundation for Advancement of Teaching, *High School: A Report on Secondary Education in America* (New York: Carnegie Foundation for Advancement of Teaching,1983); *High Schools and the Changing Workplace: The Employer's View* (Washington DC: National Academy of Science, National Academy of Engineering, Institute of Medicine, Committee on Science, Engineering, and Public Policy, 1984); T. Sizer, *Horace's Compromise: The Dilemma of the American High School* (New York: Basic, 1984); Committee for Ecomonic Develpment, *Investing in Our Children: Business and the Public Schools*, (Washington DC: Committee for Economic Development, 1985); C. Finn, *Making the Grade: Report of the Twentieth Century Fund Task Force on Federal Elementary and Secondary Education Policy* (New York: Twentieth Century Fund, 1983).

39. C. Peters, *A Neoliberal Manifesto* (Washington DC: Washington Monthly, 1983), 21.

40. R. Marshall and M. Tucker, *Thinking for a Living* (New York: Basic, 1992), 17.

41. R. Reich, *Tales of a New America* (New York: Times, 1987).

42. Marshall and Tucker, *Thinking for a Living*, 46.

43. *Educating America: State Strategies for Achieving the National Goals: Report of the Task Force on Education* (Washington, DC: National Governors Association, 1990), 12.

44. Ibid., 23.

45. M. Smith and B. Scholl, "The Clinton Human Capital Agenda," *Teachers College Record* 96 (1995): 389–404.

46. President William Clinton, speech in Wyandotte, Michigan, August 27, 1996.

47. See J. Edmondson, *America Reads: A Critical Policy Analysis* (Newark: DE: International Reading Association, 2001); J. Edmundson, "Asking Different Questions: Critical Analyses and Reading Research," In *Reading Education Policy*, ed. P. Shannon and J. Edmondson (Newark, DE: International Reading Association, 2005); J. Fitzgerald, "Can Minimally Trained College Student Volunteers Help Young At-Risk Children Read Better?" *Reading Research Quarterly* 36 (2001): 28–47.

48. These definitions are quoted verbatim from the Reading Excellence Act of 1998, which can be viewed at thomas.loc.gov.

49. As quoted in S. Mansfield, *The Faith of George W. Bush* (New York: Tarcher, 2004), 77.

50. W. Haney, "The Myth of the Texas Miracle in Education," *Education Policy Analysis Archives* 8 (2000): 127–159; M. Carnoy, S. Loch, and T. Smith, "Do Higher State Test Scores in Texas Make for Better High School Outcomes?" (paper presented at the American Educational Research Association, April 2001).

51. George W. Bush, speech in Louisville, Kentucky, February 27, 2001.

52. D. Grissmer, A. Flanagan, J. Kawata, and S. Williamson, *Improving Student's Achievement: What State NAEP Test Scores Tell Us* (Washington DC: RAND, 2000).

53. F. Hess, "Refining or Retreating? High Stakes Accountability in the States," in *No Child Left Behind? The Politics and Practice of School Accountability*, ed. P. Peterson and M. West (Washington DC: Brookings Institution, 2003) 55–79.

54. Ibid., 2003, 65.

55. P. Shannon, "Philadelphia Freedom," *Reading Teacher* 56 (2002): 48–54.

56. Edison Schools, *Strengthening the Performance of Philadelphia School District,* October 2001, www.philaedfund.org/pdfs/completereport.pdf.

57. G. R. Lyon, S. Shaywitz, B. Shaywitz, and V. Chabra, "Evidence-Based Reading Policy in the United States: How Scientific Research Informs Instructional Practices," in *Brookings Papers on Education Policy 2005*, ed. Diane Ravitch (Washington DC: Brookings Institution, 2005).

58. G. Bracey, *Setting the Record Straight* (Portsmouth, NH: Heinemann, 2004).

59. See the exchange: J. Edmondson and P. Shannon, "Reading First Initiative in Rural Pennsylvania Schools," M. Opuda, "NCLB—A Threat or a Challenge to Public Education"; M. Arnold, "Taking the Road Less Traveled"; and P. Shannon and J. Edmondson, "A Rejoinder to Opuda and Arnold," *Journal of Research in Rural Education* 18, (2003): 31–45.

60. R. Ingersol, *Teacher Turnover, Teacher Shortages, and the Organization of Schools: Center for the Study of Teaching and Policy* (Seattle: Washington University, 2004).

61. G. Whitehurst, speech to the White House Conference on Preparing Tomorrow's Teachers, March 2002.

62. D. Monk, "Memo Update," (Pennsylvania State University, University Park, PA, September 20, 2004).

63. Abraham Flexner's report was submitted to the Carnegie Foundation in 1914; see www.carnegiefoundation.org/eLibrary/flexner_report.pdf. A. Beck, "The Standardization of American Medical Schools," *Journal of American Medical Association*, 291 (2004): 2139–49.

64. See R. Allington ed., *Big Brother and the National Reading Curriculum: How Ideology Trumped Evidence* (Portsmouth, NH: Heinemann, 2003); D. Berliner, "If the Underlying Premise for No Child Left Behind Is False, How Can That Act Solve Our Problems?" in *Saving Our Schools: Saying No to No Child Left Behind,* ed. K. Goodman, P. Shannon, Y. Goodman, and R. Rapoport (San Francisco: RJR, 2004, 167-84); and G. Bracey, "14th Bracey Report on the Condition of Public Schooling," *Phi Delta Kappan*, 86 (2004): 149–67.

Chapter Six

1. A. Scharf, "Scripted Talk," *Dollars and Sense* 249 (2003): 35–37, 53.

2. R. Leidner, *Fast Food, Fast Talk: Service Work and the Routinization of Everyday Life* (Berkeley: University of California, 1993), 14.

3. Scharf, "Scripted Talk," 36.

4. What is often referred to as supervision in industry is more a form of discipline for workers. The gaze of the supervisor becomes a constant concern for workers who worry

about their work behaviors and how they might be interpreted. Workers begin to monitor their actions without the supervision. Michel Foucault wrote about this internalization of the supervisory gaze as governmentality in which authority achieves compliance among subjects without coercion. M. Foucault, "Governmentality," in *The Foucault Effect: Studies in Governmentality,* ed. G. Burchell, C. Gordon, and P. Miller (Chicago: University of Chicago Press, 1991), 87–104.

5. Scharf, "Scripted Talk," 37.

6. U.S. Department of Labor, *Tomorrow's Jobs—2004 to 2014,* December 20, 2005 (www.bls.gov/oco/oco2003.html).

7. "The quality of teachers in our schools affects every aspect of our society, from jobs to national security. The nation will not continue to lead or to create new jobs if we persist in viewing teaching—the profession that makes all other professions possible—as a second-rate occupation." L. Gerstner, *Teaching at Risk,* Teaching Commission Report. (Washington DC: The Teaching Commission, 2004) 1.

8. G. Hull, *Changing Work, Changing Workers: Critical Perspectives on Language Literacy and Skills* (Albany: State University of New York Press, 1997).

9. D. Tyack and L. Cuban, *Tinkering Toward Utopia: A Century of Public School Reform* (Cambridge, MA: Harvard University Press, 1995).

10. An Unfinished Journey: The Legacy of Brown and Narrowing of the Achievement Gap, *Phi Delta Kappan* 85, (May 2004). See the entire issue.

11. P. Shannon, *Reading Poverty* (Portsmouth, NH: Heinemann. 1998).

12. C. Goldin, "The Human Capital Century and American Leadership: Virtues of the Past," *Journal of Economic History* 65, (2001): 263–92.

13. J. E. Bowsher, *Educating America: Lessons Learned in the Nation's Corporations* (New York: John Wiley and Sons, 1989), 1.

14. C. Goldin, "The Human Capital Century," *Education Next* 2003 (www.educationnext.org /20031/73.html).

15. M. Tucker and R. Marshall, *Thinking for a Living: Education and the Wealth of a Nation* (New York: Basic. 1993).

16. The Conference Board, *Ten Years After "A Nation at Risk,"* Report #1041 (New York: Conference Board, 1993).

17. M. Tucker, *Redesigning America's Schools: The Public Speaks* (New York: Carnegie Forum on Education and the Economy, 1986).

18. Visit the Business Roundtable website (www.brtable.org) for a positive assessment of this connection, or read K. Emery and S. Ohanian, *Why Is Corporate America Bashing Our Public Schools?* (Portsmouth, NH: Heinemann, 2004) for a critical evaluation.

19. D. Doyle, *The Education Summit: What Does It Mean for Education Reform?* Archives of Thomas Fordham Foundation (1996) (www.edexcellence.net/institute).

20. J. J. Lagowski, "The Education Summit: A Different Signal," *Journal of Chemical Education* 73 (1996): 383–87.

21. See the explanation of the writing of national English language arts standards in Chapter 7.

22. For example, the University of Pittsburgh's Learning Research and Development Center designed the original protocol for measuring the alignment between standards and testing for English language arts that Achieve used to judge states' progress.

23. See Achieve's website for a complete overview of institutions' involvement in public schools: www.achieve.org.

24. T. Henry, "Taking Measure of the US Education Summit," *USA Today*, September 27, 1999, A1, 9.

25. National Education Summit, *1999 Summit Action Statement,* adopted October 1, 1999 (www.achieve.org).

26. A. F. Ryan, "2005 National Education Summit on High Schools: The American Diploma Project Network," Achieve press release, February 21, 2005 (www.achieve.org).

27. See B. Altwerger, ed., *Reading for Profit: How the Bottom Line Leaves Kids Behind,* (Portsmouth, NH: Heinemann) and R. Allington, ed., *Big Brother and the National Reading Curriculum: How Ideology Trumped Evidence* (Portsmouth, NH: Heinemann).

28. Since the Reagan administration, federal social welfare programs have been under assault. Consider President Clinton's end of welfare as we know it and President Bush's reform of Medicare drug policies and attempt to privatize Social Security. The social safety net in the United States is getting smaller and smaller.

29. K. Goodman, P. Shannon, Y. Freeman, and S. Murphy, *Report Card on Basal Readers: A Report to the NCTE Commission on Reading* (Katonah, NY: Richard C. Owen, 1988).

30. J. Baumann, "Basal Reading Programs and the Deskilling of Teachers: A Critical Examination of the Argument, " *Reading Research Quarterly* 27 (1992): 390–98; R. Allington, "Letter to the Editors: Reply to Shannon," *Reading Research Quarterly* 28 (1993): 216; J. Flood and D. Lapp, "Types of Writings Included in Basal Reading Programs," in *Literacy Theory and Research,* ed. J. Zutell, S. McCormack, M. Connolly, and P. O'Keefe Chicago: National Reading Conference, 1990), 141–50; J. Hoffman, S. McCarthy, J. Abbott, C. Christian, L. Corman, C. Curry, M. Dressman, B. Elliot, D. Mathews, and D. Sable, "So What's New in the New Basals?" *Journal of Reading Behavior* 26, (1990): 47–73.

31. P. D. Pearson ed., *Handbook of Reading Research* (New York: Longman, 1984).

32. J. Chall and J. Squire, "The Publishing Industry and Textbooks," in *Handbook of Reading Research, vol. II,* ed. R. Barr, M. Kamil, P. Mosenthal, and P. D. Pearson (New York: Longman, 1991), 120–46.

33. B. Honig, "The California Reading Initiative," *The New Advocate* 1 (1988): 235–40.

34. P. Shannon and K. Goodman ed., *Basal Readers: A Second Look* (Katonah, NY: Richard C. Owen, 1994); P. Crawford, "Reading Bound: A Deconstruction of the Basal Teachers' Manual" (unpublished diss., Pennsylvania State University, 1995).

35. Although much has been written about the rise and strengths of whole language, few writers have addressed the politics of its rise and fall. Critics argue that the lack of a specific definition for whole language means that the philosophy is incoherent, but advocates of whole language reply that whole language is to be defined by the individuals who practice its assumptions of reading, language, and learning. It is therefore unfortunate the proponents of whole language did not provide a more proactive attack on the publishing industry's efforts to absorb whole language within its materials.

36. J. McQuillan, *The Literacy Crisis: False Claims, Real Solutions* (Portsmouth, NH: Heinemann, 1998).

37. E. Brinkley, "What's Religion Got to Do with Attacks on Whole Language?" in *In Defense of Good Teaching: What Teachers Need to Know About the Reading Wars,* ed. K. Goodman (York, ME: Stenhouse, 1998) 57–71.

38. J. Edmondson, "Policymaking in Education: Understanding Influences on the Reading Excellence Act," *Education Policy Analysis Archives* 13 (2005): 148–63. (www.epaa.asu.edu).

39. P. Shannon, *iSHOP, You Shop: Raising Questions About Reading Commodities* (Portsmouth, NH: Heinemann).

40. R. Anderson, *Becoming a Nation of Readers* (Washington, DC: National Institute for Education, 1985); J. Dole and J. Osborn, "Elementary Language Arts Textbooks: A Decade of Change," in *Handbook of Research on Teaching of the English Language Arts*, 2d ed., ed. J. Flood, D. Lapp. J. Squires, and J. Jensen (New York: Longman, 2003).

41. See D. C. Simmons and E. J. Kame'enui, *A Consumer's Guide to Evaluating a Core Reading Program Grades K–3: A Critical Elements Analysis* (Eugene, OK: Institute for the Development of Educational Achievement, 2003) (www.reading.uoregon.edu/curricula/core_program.php).

42. E. Garen, "Scientific Flimflam: A Who's Who of Entrepreneurial Research," in *Reading for Profit: How the Bottom Line Leaves Kids Behind*, ed. B. Altwerger (Portsmouth, NH: Heinemann), 21–32.

43. Andrew Brownstein and Travis Hicks produced reports on application of scientifically based research in the selection of core reading programs and testing tools within the federal Reading First Program: "When Research Goes to Market?" and "Reading First Under Fire," *Title I Monitor* (August 2005) (www.title1online.com/libraries/title1online /news).

44. S. Metcalf, "Reading Between the Lines," in *Education, Inc: Turning Learning into a Business*, ed. A. Kohn and P. Shannon (Portsmouth, NH: Heinemann, 2004), 49–57.

45. B. Miner, "Testing Companies Mine for Gold," *Rethinking Schools* 19 (Winter 2004–5), 5–8.

46. T. Toch, *Margins of Error: The Testing Industry in the NCLB Era* (Washington, DC: Education Sector, 2006).

47. G. Toppo, "Reading First: Reading Program Raises Questions for Lawmakers," *USA Today*, September 7, 2005, A 4.

48. K. K. Manzo, "States Pressed to Refashion Reading First Grant Designs," *Education Week*, September 7, 2005 (www.educationweek.org/articles/2005/09/07/02read).

49. As quoted in Toch, *Margins of Error.* Statement made on December 18, 2002, 19.

50. D. Mezzacappa, "Vallas Critical of Tutoring Options," *Philadelphia Inquirer*, October 26, 2003, C1.

51. Nina Rees, "Tutor.com: Virtual Relief for Homework Headaches," *The Education Innovator* 3 (February 22, 2005): 1.

52. A. Das and A. Paulson, "Need a Tutor? Call India," *USA Today*, July 22, 2005, C1.

53. S. Pines, executive director of the Education Industry Association as quoted in G. Toppo. Offshare Learning Online. *USA Today* (August 30, 2005), A5.

Chapter Seven

1. *Educational Sciences Reform Act of 2002*, HR 3801, 107th Congress, see Thomas.loc.gov.

2. A spirited debate over the federal definition of education science was published as a special issue of the *Educational Researcher* (31, 2002, 8). The commentaries vary from Feuer, Towne, and Shavelson's unenthusiastic support to St. Pierre's note that the definition erases all poststructuralist research on education. In between these extremes, Berliner argued that positivism is impossible in schools because too many variables are beyond researchers' control.

3. F. Bacon, *The New Organon* (1620) (www.constitution.org/bacon/nov_org.html).

4. P. Watson, *Ideas: A History of Thought and Invention* (New York: Harper Collins, 2005).

5. F. Bacon, *The New Atlantis* (1626) (www.consititution.org/bacon/new_atlantis.html).

6. D. Carnine, "Campaigns for Moving Research into Practice," *Remedial and Special Education* 20 (1999): 2–6, 35.

7. K. McCollum Clark, "National Council of Teachers of English, Corporate Philanthropy, and National Education Standards" (unpublished diss., Pennsylvania State University, 1995).

8. National Council of Teachers of English, press release, October 13, 1992.

9. P. D. Pearson, "Standards for the English Language Arts: A Policy Perspective," *Journal of Reading Behavior* 25 (1993): 457–75.

10. M. Myers, "Work Worth Doing," *NCTE Council Chronicle* (June 1994): 24.

11. J. Emig, as quoted in "Emig Sees Proposed Federal Panel as Intruding in Standards Process," *NCTE Council Chronicle* (June 1993): 6.

12. Pearson, "Standards," 471–72.

13. Ibid., 462.

14. W. Staub, "Standards for English: The Hands on Work Begins," *NCTE Council Chronicle* (June 1993): 1.

15. "US Standards Project Refines Framework," *IRA Reading Today* (December 1993): 31.

16. McCollum Clark, "National Council," 148.

17. K. Diegmueller "English Group Loses Funding for Standards," *Education Week* May 4, 1994, 1, 9.

18. J. Elson, "History, the Sequel," *Time Magazine*, November 7, 1994, 64.

19. Diegmueller, "English Group Loses Funding," 9.

20. Pearson, "Standards," 473.

21. B. Grossen, *30 Years of Research on Reading: What We Know About How Children Learn to Read,* (Santa Cruz, CA: Center for the Future of Teaching and Learning, 1997).

22. R. Allington and H. Woodside-Jiron, "The Politics of Literacy Teaching: How 'Research' Shaped Educational Policy," *Educational Researcher* 28 (1999): 4–13.

23. See R. Allington and H. Woodside-Jiron, "Thirty Years of Research on Reading: When Is a Research Summary Not a Research Summary," In *In Defense of Good Teaching*, ed. K. Goodman (York, ME: Stenhouse, 1998) 143–58; G. Coles, *Misreading Reading: The Bad Science That Hurts Children* (Portsmouth, NH: Heinemann, 2000); and D. Taylor, *Beginning to Read and the Spin Doctors of Science* (Urbana, IL: National Council of Teachers of English, 1998).

24. Grossen, *30 Years of Research*, 4.

25. J. Carlilse and E. Heibert, "Context and Contribution of the Research at the Center for Improvement in Early Reading Achievement," *Elementary School Journal* 105 (2004): 133.

26. Grossen, *30 Years of Research*, 5.

27 Grossen, *30 Years of Research*, 2.

28. Research studies that Grossen reviewed as inconsequential were K. Dahl and P. Freppon, "A Comparison of Inner-City Children's Interpretations of Reading and Writing Instruction in the Early Grades in Skill Based and Whole Language Classrooms," *Reading Research Quarterly* 30 (1995): 50–74; P. Freppon, "Children's Concepts of the Nature and Purpose of Reading in Different Instructional Settings," *Journal of Reading Behavior* 23 (1991): 139–63; W. Kasten and B. Clarke, *Reading/Writing Readiness for Preschool and Kindergarten Children* (Sanibel, FL: Education Research and Development Center, ERIC

ED 312 041, 1989); E. McIntyre and P. Freppon, "A Comparison of Children's Development of Alphabetic Knowledge in a Skills Based and Whole Language Classroom," *Research in the Teaching of English* 28 (1994): 391–417; H. Ribowsky, "The Effects of Code Emphasis and Whole Langauge Approach Upon Emergent Literacy of Kindergarten Children," (Alexandria, VA: ERIC ED 269 720, 1985); and C. Stice and N. Bertrand, *Whole Language and the Emergent Literacy of at Risk Children: A Two Year Study* (Nashville, TN: ERIC ED 324 636, 1990).

29. Grossen, *30 Years of Research,* 9-14.

30. L. Moats, *Teaching Reading Is Rocket Science* (Washington, DC: American Federation of Teachers. 1999).

31. K. Manzo, "More States Moving to Make Phonics the Law," *Education Week*, April 29, 1998, 24.

32. J. McDaniels, C. Sims, and C. Miskel, "The National Reading Policy Arena," *Education Policy* 15 (2001): 92–114.

33. J. McDaniels and C. Miskel, "Stakeholder Salience: Business and Educational Policy," *Teachers College Record* 104 (2002): 325–56.

34. B. Taylor, R. Anderson, K. Au, and T. Raphael, "Discretion in the Translation of Research to Policy: A Case from Beginning Reading," *Educational Researcher* 29 (2000): 16–26.

35. Policy-driven work is based on functionalist social theory in which the human body is used as metaphor for the working of complex social systems. Like the body, schools require the coordination of several systems to maintain a healthy status quo. If a problem arises in one part of a body, causing ill health, then other systems begin to troubleshoot the system of that part in order to regain a healthy norm. Policy-driven work is designed so that reading researchers and educators will gather and use data in order to address the problems in reading education and then to inform the executive branch of schools so that healthy policy can be directed to all schools to maintain reading education generally. Policy-driven work has four tenets: (1) Policy is the search for the one best method, which is effective and efficient for the largest possible context, (2) policymaking is a rational process used to solve the problems within existing reading education systems, (3) policy decisions are based on means-ends analysis, and (4) policy analyses should rely on empirical investigations and mathematical reasoning. See P. Shannon and J. Edmondson, ed., *Reading Policy* (Newark, DE: International Reading Association, 2005).

36. Taylor et al., "Discretion in the Translation," 23.

37. S. Strauss, "An Open Letter to Reid Lyon," *Educational Researcher* 30 (2001): 26–33.

38. Strauss, "An Open Letter," 30.

39. Critical policy action rejects the policy-driven assumptions that science provides the only legitimate knowledge and is not satisfied to accept the prevailing ideas, actions, or social conditions unthinkingly or from habit. Rather, advocates engage in relentless criticism of all exisiting conditions in order to address the questions Why are things the way they are? How did they become this way? Who benefits from their continuation? and How can we redistribute those benefits more widely? These questions require critical educators and researchers to delve into the histories of the intentions, interests, and values of groups participating in policy decisions, to listen to the individuals and groups affected by policy to understand its consequences psychologically and socially, and to examine the social structures that enable policymaking and institutional behaviors. Unlike a policy-driven approach, critical policy action requires an advocacy stance for change in the status quo. Critical policy action has four tenets: (1) Policy is the authoritative allocation of values

to maintain social, economic, and/or political status quo, (2) policymaking is a political negotiation among groups of unequal power, (3) policy decisions are expressions of power in which advantages are maintained, (4) policy is the product of historically conditioned social relations that are often hidden from view by common sense understandings of the way things are that can be overcome through self-reflective social action.

40. S. E. Zorinsky (R NE), Amendment to 1986 Human Services Reauthorization Act, *Congresstional Record* 132, 90: 1.

41. During William Bennett's service as secretary of education for the Reagan administration, the government produced *What Works: Research About Teaching and Learning* (Washington, DC: U.S. Department of Education) which featured research that supported the administration's position on education policy and practice. See G. Glass, "What Works: Politics and Research," *Educational Researcher* 16 (1987): 5–10 for a thorough critique of Bennett's intentions with this document.

42. P. D. Pearson, Foreword to *Beginning to Read*, ed. M. Adams, ix (Cambridge, MA: MIT Press, 1990). The statement appeared in the original printing of the book and was deleted from subsequent printings.

43. The cover of the summary reads: *Beginning to Read: Thinking and Learning About Print by Marilyn Adams: A Summary* (Urbana: Center for the Study of Reading, Reading Research and Education Center, University of Illinois at Urbana-Champaign, 1990). On the title page the publishers acknowledge that the summary was prepared by Steven Stahl, Jean Osborn, and Fran Lehr.

44. M. Adams, "Response to My Critics," *Reading Teacher* 44 (1991): 390.

45. J. Baumann, ed., "Beginning to Read: A Critique by Literacy Professionals and a Response by Marilyn Adams," *Reading Teacher* 44 (1991): 370–95.

46. P. Shannon, "Politics of Beginning to Read," *Reading Teacher* 44 (1991): 386. M. Adams, "Response," *Reading Teacher* 44 (1991): 394.

47. C. Snow, S. Burns, and P. Griffin, ed., *Preventing Reading Difficulties in Young Children* (Washington, DC: National Academy Press, 1998), 116.

48. P. D. Pearson, "A Historically Based Review of Preventing Reading Difficulties in Young Children," *Reading Research Quarterly* 34 (1999): 245.

49. J. Gee, "Critical Issues: Reading and the New Literacy Studies: Reframing the National Academy of Sciences Report on Reading," *Journal of Literacy Research* 31 (1999): 355–74.

50. Gee. "Critical Issues," 369.

51. C. Snow, "On the Limits of Reframing," *Journal of Literacy Research* 32 (2000): 119.

52. See J. Edmondson, "Policymaking in Education: Understanding Influences on the Reading Excellence Act," *Education Policy Analysis Archives* 13 (2005): 148–63.

53. S. J. Samuels made this statement during the Hall of Fame Members Speak About No Child Left Behind, May 3, 2006, International Reading Association Convention, Chicago.

54. J. Cunningham, "The National Reading Panel Report," *Reading Research Quarterly* 36 (2001): 326–55.

55. J. Edmondson and P. Shannon, "The Will of the People," *Reading Teacher* 55 (2002): 452–55.

56. Cunningham, "The National Reading Panel Report," 236.

57. See E. Garan, "Beyond Smoke and Mirrors: A Critique of the National Reading Panel Report on Phonics," *Phi Delta Kappan* 82 (2001): 36–46. Again the summary of a federal report removed the nuance and qualifications in its advocacy of the government's position on reading education.

58. See R. Allington ed., *Big Brother and the National Reading Curriculum: How Ideology Trumped Evidence* (Portsmouth, NH: Heinemann, 2002), G. Coles, *Reading the Naked Truth: Literacy, Legislation and Lies* (Portsmouth, NH: Heinemann, 2003), and S. Strauss, *Linguistics, Neurology, and the Politics of Phonics: The Silent E Speaks Out* (New York: Erlbaum, 2004).

Chapter Eight

1. F. Fukuyama, *The End of History and the Last Man* (New York: Free, 2006), reprint ed.

2. G. W. F. Hegel, *The Philosophy of History* (Buffalo, NY: Prometheus, 1990). reprint ed. Hegel explained history as the continuous unfolding of the idea of freedom in a progression toward conditions that would enable all to develop to their full capacity. Later he would write that the Prussian state achieved the end of this progression during the 1820s, invoking criticism that Hegel had lost his revolutionary drive in order to achieve the comforts of a secure position within the status quo.

3. In *State Building: Governance and World Order in the 21st Century* (Ithaca, NY: Cornell University, 2004), Fukuyama acknowledges the United States' War on Terror, in which weak states enable small groups to interrupt free markets and democracy as a test of the resolution of history.

4. F. Nietzsche, *Thus Spoke Zarathustra: A Book for Everyone and Nobody*, trans. G. Parkes (New York: Oxford University, 2005), 78.

5. N. B. Smith, *American Reading Instruction* (Newark, DE: International Reading Association, 2002).

6. *American Reading Instruction* was originally published in 1934 and was updated in 1965, 1986, and 2002. The 1986 edition was edited by Smith's former graduate student, H. Alan Robinson. The 2002 edition has a prologue by Richard Robinson, an epilogue by Norman Stahl, and an extension by P. David Pearson.

7. This consensus on the one best method for teaching reading is summarized in G. R. Lyon, S. Shaywitz, B. Shaywitz, and V. Chhabra, "Evidence-Based Reading Policy in the United States: How Scientific Research Informs Instruction," *Brookings Papers on Education Policy* 1 (2005): 209–50.

8. G. W. Bush, speech at Glen Burnie Elementary School, January 9, 2006.

9. These reading experts presented speeches concerning deskilling under No Child Left Behind policy during the International Reading Association Convention in Toronto, May 3, 2007.

10. G. Coles, *Reading the Naked Truth: Literacy, Legislation and Lies,* (Portsmouth, NH: Heinemann, 2004).

11. B. Feller, "States Don't Meet Teacher Goals: Some Face Loss of Federal Funds," *Centre Daily Times*, May 13, 2006, A8.

12. Assistant Secretary of Elementary and Secondary Education Henry Johnson, as quoted in B. Feller, "States Don't Meet," A8.

13. See www.ets.org/readingspecialist.

14. B. Armbruster, F. Lehr, and J. Osborn, *Put Reading First: The Research Building Blocks for Teaching Children to Read,* (Washington, DC: Partnership for Reading, 2001).

15. Classic works on the benefits of parent talk upon children's learning to read include S. B. Heath, *Ways with Words* (New York: Cambridge University, 1983); C. D. Gaines and D. Taylor, *Growing Up Literate* (Portsmouth, NH: Heinemann, 1988); and G. Wells, *Meaning Makers* (Portsmouth, NH: Heinemann, 1985).

16. In addition to the Heath's, Taylor's, and Well's work on social class and language, see V. P. Gates, *Other People's World: Cycles of Low Literacy* (Cambridge, MA: Harvard University Press, 1997) and L. Moll, C. Amanti, and N. Gonzales, ed., *Funds of Knowledge* (Mahwah, NJ: Erlbaum, 2005).

17. H. Graff, *The Labrynths of Literacy: Reflections on Literacy Past and Present* (Pittsburgh: University of Pittsburgh, 1995).

18. In this condition, *highly qualified* would be tied to the teacher-as-researcher movement, in which teachers pose and address questions about their teaching by systematically gathering, analyzing, and interpreting evidence from their communities, schools, and classrooms.

19. See G. Ladson-Billings, *Dreamkeepers: Successful Teachers of African American Children* (San Francisco: Jossey-Bass, 1997); J. Oakes, *Teaching to Change the World* (New York: McGraw-Hill, 2004); and W. Ayers, *To Teach: The Journey of a Teacher* (New York: Teachers College Record, 2001).

20. K. Manzo, "Reading Programs Bear Similarities Across the States," *Education Week*, February 4, 2004 (edweek.or/ew/ewstroy.cfm?slug21Read.h23).

21. V. Strauss, "Phonics Pitch Irks Teachers U.S.: Cont. U.S.: Denies It's Pushing Commerical Products," *Washington Post*, September 10, 2002, A01. Department of Education Office of Inspector General. The Reading First Program's Grant Application Process-Final Inspection Report ED-OIG/I13-F0017 (September 2006). Confirm that conflict of interest and bias directed the early administration of the Reading First Initiative.

22. Elaine Meeks, principal of Cherry Valley School in Polson, Montana, as quoted in B. Reed, "A Tale of Two Schools: Reading Instruction in the Real World," *Northwest Education Magazine* (Summer 2004) (www.nwrel.org./nwedu/09-o4/tale.php).

23. J. Edmondson and P. Shannon, "Reading First Initiative in Rural Pennsylvania," *Journal of Research in Rural Education* 18 (2003): 31–44.

24. A. Gawande, *Complications: A Surgeon's Notes on an Imperfect Science* (New York: Picador, 2003).

25. See J. Dewey, *The Quest for Certainty: A Study of Relation of Knowledge and Action* (New York: Kessinger, 2005 [originally 1929]) and N. Postman, *Technopoly: The Surrender of Culture to Technology* (New York: Vintage, 1993).

26. For example, see R. Sylwester, "When You Don't Understand the Brains You're Trying to Teach," *Brain Connection* (April 2000) (www.brainconnection.com/topics/?mon=col/sylwester00apr); "President Promotes Reading First Initiative in Florida," press release, October 17, 2002 (www.whitehouse.gov/news/release/2002/10/2002/017.5.html); L. Moats, *Teaching Reading Is Rocket Science* (Washington, DC: American Federation of Teachers, 1999).

27. McGraw-Hill reading textbook sale prospectus, media.corporate-if.net/media files/IROL /96/96/96562/book05/Education.pdf.

28. Ibid., 24.

29. C. Dudley-Marling and P. Paugh, "The Rich Get Richer and the Poor Get Direct Instruction," in *Reading for Profit: How the Bottom Line Leaves Kids Behind*, ed. B. Altwerger (Portsmouth, NH: Heinemann, 2005), 156–71.

30. Ibid., 166.

31. The statistical success of this approach to reading instruction is presented in Chapter 9.

32. Wright Group/McGraw-Hill, Wright Group Literacy (New York: McGraw-Hill, 2004).

33. Harcourt Reading/Language Arts Programs, Harcourt Trophies (Orlando, FL: Harcourt, 2005).

34. P. David Pearson, "A Historically Based Review of Preventing Reading Difficulties in Young Children," *Reading Research Quarterly* 34 (1999): 245; B. Taylor, R. Anderson, K. Au, and T. Raphael, "Discretion in the Translation of Research to Policy: A Case from Beginning Reading," *Educational Researcher* 29, (2000): 16–26.

35. SRA Open Court Reading (Columbus, OH: McGraw-Hill, 2003).

36. SRA Reading Mastery (Columbus, OH: McGraw-Hill, 2005).

37. R. Land and M. Moustafa, "Scripted Reading Instruction: Help or Hinderance?" in *Reading for Profit: How the Bottom Line Leaves Kids Behind,* ed. B. Altwerger 65 (Portsmouth, NH: Heinemann, 2005).

Chapter Nine

1. The Associated Press articles appeared in our local newspaper between April 18 and April 21, 2006: M. Rubinkam, "Schools Not Reporting Scores of Scores," F. Bass, N. Z. Dixon, and B. Feller, "No Child Leaves Test Loopholes"; B. Feller, "Parents More Optimistic than Teachers"; B. Feller, "Suppliers Cash in on Law." Although the authors suggest better oversight is needed, they do not probe the possible reasons for teachers' and schools' search for reasonable expectations for reporting of student test scores.

2. In a series of books, George Lakoff argues that politicians construct positions within rhetorical metaphors that couch their values within more acceptable contexts. He describes the three-decade rise of conservative politics as the best example of this practice. G. Lakoff, *Moral Politics: How Liberals and Conservatives Think* (Chicago: University of Chicago, 2002), 2d ed.; *Metaphors We Live By* (Chicago: University of Chicago, 2003), 2d ed.; and *Don't Think About an Elephant: Know Your Values and Frame the Debate* (New York: Cheslea Green, 2004).

3. See K. Phillips, *Wealth and Democracy* (New York: Broadway, 2002), and J. Lardner, ed., *Inequality Matters: The Growing Economic Divide in America and Its Poisonous Consequences* (New York: New, 2006).

4. D. Berliner, "Our Impoverished View of Educational Reform," *Teachers College Record* 107 (2005): 56–87.

5. L. Guinier, *Meritocracy, Inc.: How Wealth Became Merit, Class Became Race, and a College Education Became a Gift from the Poor to the Rich* (New York: Basic, 2007).

6. As quoted in R. Parrish, "The Meritocracy Myth: An Interview with Lani Guinier," *Dollars and Sense* 263 (Jan/Feb. 2006): 5.

7. J. Kozol, *The Shame of the Nation: The Restoration of Apartheid Schooling in America* (New York: Crown, 2005).

8. G. Orfield, *Schools More Separate* (Cambridge, MA: Harvard University Civil Rights Project, July 17, 2001).

9. U.S. Census Bureau. Current Population Reports: Series P60-222, Detailed Poverty Table 3 (ferret.bis.census.gov/mano/032004/pv.toc).

10. See M. R. Rank, *One Nation Underprivileged: Why American Poverty Affects Us All* (New York: Oxford University, 2005).

11. Center for Budget and Policy Priorities, "Number of Uninsured Americans Continued to Rise in 2004," August 30, 2005 (www.cbpp.org/8-30-05health.htm).

12. Children's Defense Fund, "State of America's Children," (2005) (www.childrensdefense.org /publications/greenbook/).

13. For similar conclusions, see G. Bracey, "No Child Left Behind: Just Say No," (2005) (geraldbracey.org) and D. Meiers and G. Wood, ed., *Many Children Left Behind: How the No Child Left Behind Is Damaging Our Schools and Our Children* (Boston: Beacon, 2004).

14. R. Hernnstein and C. Murray, *The Bell Curve: Intelligence and Class Structure in American Life* (New York: Free, 1994), 520.

15. This is a statistical as well as an actual consequence. Schools with more diversity have a greater chance of one group failing to reach proficiency and triggering the school improvement sanctions. The finding is also a national trend. See T. Kane and D. Staiger, "Unintended Consequences of Racial Subgroup Rule," in *No Child Left Behind: The Politics and Practices of School Accountability,* ed. Peterson and West (Washington, DC: Brookings Institution, 2003), and J. Kim and G. Sunderman, *Large Mandates and Limited Resources: State Responses to the NCLB and Implications for Accountability,* final report (Cambridge, MA: Harvard Civil Rights Project, February 9, 2004).

16. Thousands of school districts across the country have been placed in the "needs improvement category." See G. Sunderman and J. Kim, *Inspiring Vision, Disappointing Results: For Studies on Implementing the NCLB Act,* final report (Cambridge, MA: Harvard Civil Rights Project, Februrary 9, 2004); J. Lee and G. Orfield, *Tracking Achievement Gaps and Assessing the Impact of NCLB on the Gaps,* final report (Cambridge, MA: Harvard Civil Rights Project, June 14, 2006); and G. Sunderman, *The Unraveling of No Child Left Behind,* final report (Cambridge, MA: Harvard Civil Rights Project, February 13, 2006), which found that the federal government has started to make individual accommodations for states and school districts to avoid even larger numbers of schools being classified as "needs improvement."

17. For an overview of political values in educational policy, see P. Shannon and J. Edmondson, eds., *Reading Education Policy* (Newark, DE: International Reading Association).

18. For an overview of conservative positions on these groups, see R. Kirk, *The Conservative Mind: From Burke to Elliot* (Chicago: Regency, 1953); C. Murray, *Losing Ground: American Social Policy from 1950 to 1980* (New York: Basic, 1985); and G. Schneider, ed., *Conservatism in America Since 1930* (New York: New York University, 2003).

19. See Chapter 22, "A Place for Everyone," in *The Bell Curve,* in which Herrnstein and Murray present their economic and social case for excluding individuals with tested low cognitive ability from advanced schooling and high-paying jobs in order to improve the lives of the individuals and society. J. Blanchard, a former Arizona State Senator, reported that no public or private institution offered a bid to manage the Many Farms school in the Chinle School District deep in the Navajo Nation because no one believed the students could succeed under NCLB. The Beliefs of Politicians. College Reading Association, Pittsburgh, PA (October 26, 2006)

20. J. Green and M. Winters, *Study of the Florida Program to End Social Promotion,* final report (Education Research Office, New York: Manhattan Institute, November 2004).

21. A. Russo, "Social Promotion in Chicago," *Education Next* 6 (Winter 2005): 41–45.

22. M. West and P. Peterson, "The Politics and Practices of Accountability," in *No Child Left Behind: The Politics and Practices of School Accountability,* ed. P. Peterson and M. West (Washington, DC: Brookings Institution, 2003).

23. P. Zock, *Doomed to Fail: The Built in Defects of American Education* (Chicago: Ivan R. Doe, 2004).

24. C. Goldin, "The Human Capital Century," *Education Next* 4 (Winter 2003): 73–79.

25. Z. Bauman, *Wasted Lives: Modernity and Its Outcasts* (Cambridge, UK: Polity, 2004).

26. Personal communication, March 14, 2006.

27. There are growing data of consequences for youth who drop out or are pushed out of high schools. See B. Dohrn, "Look Out Kid; It's Something You Did," in *Zero Tolerance: Resisting the Drive to Punishment in Our Schools*, ed. W. Ayers, B. Dohrn, and M. Ayers (New York: Basic, 2001); P. Noguera, "Schools, Prisons, and Social Implications of Punishment: Rethinking Disciplinary Practices," *Theory into Practice* 42 (2003): 341–50; C. Robbins, "Expelling Hope: Zero Tolerance and the Attack on Youth, Schooling, and Democracy," (unpublished diss., Pennsylvania State University, 2005).

28. Criticisms vary in severity from the Center on Education Policy, "From Capital to Classroom: Year 4 of NCLB," 2006 (www.cep-dc.org.nclb/year4/press) to FairTest, "Leaving Children Behind," (www.fairtest.org/facts/NCLB). Most criticisms concentrate on the hours of test preparation curricula.

29. F. Hess, "Refining or Retreating? High Stakes Accountability in the States," in *No Child Left Behind* ed. Peterson and West, 55–79; G. Sunderman, *The Unraveling*.

30. R. Allington, *Big Brother and the National Reading Curriculum* (Portsmouth, NH: Heinemann. 2002).

31. P. Freebody and A. Luke, "Literacy Programs: Debates and Demands of Cultural Contexts," *Prospects: Australian Journal of TESOL* 5 (1990): 7–16. Updated in *Literacy Futures* (Queensland, Australia, 2002).

32. A. Luke and P. Freebody, "Further Notes on Four Resources Model" (August 1999) (www.readingonline.org/research/lukefreebody.html).

33. P. Noguera, "Preventing Violence in Schools Through the Production of Docile Bodies," *In Motion Magazine* (June 17, 1999) (www.inmotionmagazine.com/pedro31.html).

34. A. H. Dyson, *Brothers and Sisters Learn to Write: Popular Literacies in Childhood and School* (New York: Teachers College Press, 2003); V. P. Gates, *Other People's Words* (Cambridge, MA: Harvard University, 1997); C. C. Lilly, *Reading Families: The Literate Lives of Urban Children* (New York: Teachers College Press, 2003); V. Vasquez, *Negotiating Critical Literacies with Young Children* (Mawtauk, NJ: Erlbaum, 2004); L. Moll, C. Amanti, and N. Gonzales, ed., *Funds of Knowledge: Theorizing Practices in Households and Classrooms* (Mawtauk, NJ: Erlbaum, 2005); T. McCarty, ed., *Language, Literacy, and Power in Schooling* (Mawtauk, NJ: Erlbaum, 2005).

35. See S. Lee, *Up Against Whiteness: Race, School, and Immigrant Youth* (New York: Teachers College Press, 2005); N. Lopez, *Hopeful Girls/Troubled Boys: Race and Gender Disparity in Urban Schools* (New York: Routledge, 2002); and P. Shannon *text, lies & video tape: stories about life, literacy, and learning* (Portsmouth, NH: Heinemann, 1995).

Chapter Ten

1. See E. Frank, *The Raw Deal: How Myths and Misinformation About the Deficit, Inflation, and Wealth Impoverish America* (Boston: Beacon, 2004); and W. Greider, *The Soul of Capitalism: Opening Paths to a Moral Economy* (New York: Simon and Schuster, 2003).

2. See W. Brasch, *America's Unpatriotic Acts: The Federal Government's Violation of the Constitution and Civil Rights* (New York: Peter Lang, 2005); G. Palast, *The Best Democracy Money Can Buy* (New York: Plume, 2004); K. Phillips, *American Theocracy: The Peril and Politics of Radical Religion, Oil and Borrowed Money in the 21st Century* (New York: Viking,

2006); and R. Putnam, *Bowling Alone: The Collapse and Revival of American Community* (New York: Simon and Schuster, 2001).

3. R. Hira and A. Hira, *Outsourcing America: What's Behind Our National Crisis and How We Can Reclaim American Jobs* (New York: AMACON, 2005).

4. Chairman of the Federal Reserve Board Ben Bernanke as quoted in P. Krugman, "Graduates Versus Oligarchs," *New York Times*, February 27, 2006, A23.

5. I. Becker and R. Gordon, *Where Did the Productivity Growth Go? Inflation Dynamics and the Distribution of Income* (Washington, DC: Brookings Panel on Economic Activity, September 8, 2005).

6. A. Blinder, "Offshoring: The Next Industrial Revolution," *Foreign Affairs* 85 (2006): 276–94.

7. See J. Anyon, *Radical Possibilities: Public Policy, Urban Education, and a New School Movement* (New York: Routledge, 2005) and D. Meier and G. Woods, *Many Children Left Behind: How the No Child Left Behind Act Is Damaging Our Children and Schools* (Boston: Beacon, 2004).

8. Perhaps there has always been a tension between activist citizenship that questions authority and the notion that patriots support the position of government authority without question. During my lifetime the cold war, Vietnam War, and several invasions in the Middle East and Central and South America have brought this tension to the surface. Since 2001, the War on Terror has accentuated the tension, even leading to the commercialization of symbols of support. See D. W. Orr, *The Last Refuge: Patriotism, Politics and the Environment in an Age of Terror* (New York: Island, 2005).

9. J. Allen, ed., *Class Actions: Teaching for Social Justice in Elementary and Middle School* (New York: Teachers College, 1999); C. Edelsky, ed., *Making Justice Our Project: Teachers Working Toward Critical Whole Language Practice* (Urbana, IL: National Council of Teachers of English, 1999). See also www.rethinkingschools.org; www.soundout.org; www.whatkidscando.org; www.forumforyouthinvestment.org; and www.freechild.org.

10. F. M. Lappe, *Democracy's Edge: Choosing to Save Our Country by Bringing Democracy to Life* (San Francisco: Jossey-Bass, 2006).

11. P. Shannon, "The Practice of Democracy and Dewey's Challenge," *Language Arts* 82 (2004): 16–25.

12. C. Mouffee, *The Return of the Political* (New York: Verso, 1993), 65.

13. The Voting Rights Act of 1965 was renewed in 2006 amid evidence-based claims that millions of African American voters were disqualified illegally during the 2000 and 2004 presidential elections. See R. Simon, *Divided We Stand: How Al Gore Beat George Bush and Lost the Presidency* (New York: Crown, 2001) and R. Kennedy, "Was the 2004 Election Stolen?" *Rolling Stone Magazine* (June 1, 2006): 58–64.

14. C. Mouffee, "Politics, Democratic Action, and Solidarity," *Inquiry* 38 (1995): 107.

15. P. Bachrach and A. Botwinich, *Power and Empowerment: A Radical Theory of Democratic Participation* (Philadelphia: Temple University, 1992).

16. Mouffee, "Politics, Democratic Action," 107.

17. P. Shannon, E. Duvall, J. Edmondson, L. Ortega, N. Westbrook, and E. Wyble, "Reframing No Child Left Behind," *Language Arts* (in press).

18. R. Putnam, *Democracies in Flux: The Evolution of Social Capital in Contemporary Society* (New York: Oxford, 2004); C. West, *Democracy Matters: Winning the Fight Against Imperialism* (New York: Penguin, 2004); G. Lakoff, *Whose Freedom? The Battle Over*

America's Most Important Idea (New York: Farrar, Strauss and Giroux, 2006); S. B. Porath, *Citizenship Under Fire: Democratic Education in Times of Conflict* (Princeton, NJ: Princeton University, 2006).

19. H. Giroux, *Schooling and the Struggle for Public Life* (Boulder, CO: Paradigm, 2005); J. Anyon, *Radical Possibilities: Public Policy, Urban Education, and a New School Movement* (New York: Routledge, 2005); J. Edmondson, *Prairie Town: Redefining Rural Life in the Age of Globalization* (Boulder, CO: Rowman and Littlefield, 2003); R. Powell, *Literacy as a Moral Imperative* (Boulder, CO: Rowman and Littlefield, 1999); C. Edelsky, *With Literacy and Justice for All: Rethinking the Social in Language and Education* (Mahwah, NJ: Erlbaum, 2006); J. Charlton, *Nothing About Us Without Us* (Berkeley: University of California, 2000); V. Romero, *Alienated: Immigrant Rights, the Constitution and Equality in America* (New York: New York University, 2005); D. Taylor, *Toxic Literacies: Exposing the Injustice of Bureaucratic Texts* (Portsmouth, NH: Heinemann, 1996); C. Prendergast, *Literacy and Racial Justice: The Politics of Learning After Brown v. Board of Education* (Carbondale: Southern Illinois University Press, 2003.

20. A. Luke and P. Freebody, "A Map of Possible Practices: Further Notes on the Four Resources Model," *Practically Primary* 4 (1999): 5.

21. See G. Hull, ed., *Changing Work, Changing Workers: Critical Perspectives on Language, Literacy, and Skills* (Albany: State University of New York, 1997); J. Larson and J. Marsh, *Making Literacy Real: Theories and Practices for Learning and Teaching* (Thousand Oaks, CA: Sage, 2005); and B. Perez, *Sociocultural Context of Language and Literacy* (Mahwah, NJ: Erlbaum, 2004).

22. A. Luke and P. Freebody, "The Social Practices of Reading," in *Constructing Critical Literacies: Teaching and Learning Textual Practice,* ed. S. Muspratt, A. Luke, and P. Freebody, (Cresskill, NJ: Hampton, 1997), 214.

23. R. Simon, *Teaching Against the Grain: Text for a Pedagogy of Possibility* (Westport, CT: Bergin and Garvey, 1992).

24. L. Weis, C. McCarthy, G. Dimitriadis, *Ideology, Curriculum, and the New Sociology of Education: Revisiting the Work of Michael Apple* (New York: Routledge, 2006).

25. R. Simon, "Empowerment as a Pedagogy of Possibility," in *Becoming Political Too: Reading and Writings in the Politics of Literacy Education,* ed. P. Shannon, (Portsmouth, NH: Heinemann, 2001), 143.

26. I am able to discuss only a few of the educators. In addition to the authors cited in this chapter, consider the following authors: Deborah Appleman, Cathy Compton Lilly, Barbara Comber, Barbara Flores, Lee Heffernan, Hillary Janks, Terry McCarthy, Donaldo Macedo, Jabari Mahiri, and Connie White.

27. P. Freire, *Pedagogy of Freedom: Ethics, Democracy, and Civic Courage* (Boulder, CO: Rowman and Littlefield, 2000).

28. I. Shor, *Working Hands and Critical Minds: A Paulo Freire Model for Job Training* (Chicago: Alternative School Network, 1988).

29. V. Vasquez, *Negotiating Critical Literacies with Young Children* (Mahwah, NJ: Erlbaum, 2004), 1.

30. R. Bomer and K. Bomer, *For a Better World: Reading and Writing for Social Action* (Portsmouth, NH: Heinemann, 2001).

31. Bomer and Bomer, "For a Better World," 6.

32. M. McLaughlin and G. DeVoogd, *Critical Literacy: Enhancing Students' Comprehension of Text* (New York: Scholastic, 2004).

33. C. Dozier, P. Johnston, and R. Rogers, *Critical Literacy/Critical Teaching: Tools for Preparing Responsive Teachers* (New York: Teachers College, 2005).

34. The authors address this apparent contradiction with a unique take on agency that might open the option of the four-resources model to advocates of skills programs. Dozier, Johnston, and Rogers argue that readers' agency is enhanced by their ability to negotiate text at the code level, making them more in control of their efforts with text. When coupled simultaneously with consideration of meaning, pragmatics, and critical resources, skills instruction for the authors becomes responsive teaching of civic reading. "Agentive learning best occurs in the process of actually accomplishing a valued task or participating in a valued activity. This is not to say that an aspect might not be taken out of the activity and rehearsed separately on some occasions, provided that the rehearsal is seen as part of, and contributing to, the ongoing action." *Critical Literacy/Critical Teaching*, 17

35. Dozier, Johnston, and Rogers, *Critical Literacy/Critical Teaching*, 33.

36. The site www.rethinkingschools.org includes a complete inventory of the group's publications and a search engine to help locate specific articles.

37. See www.rethinkingschools.org/about/history.shtml.

38. *Rethinking Schools* 20 (Spring 2006). C. Capellaro, "A Pedagogy of Resistance: An Interview with Howard Zinn," 19–21; K. Goodman, "Pedagogy of the Absurd," 30–33; E. Jaeger, "Silencing Teachers in an Era of Scripted Reading," 39–42; L. Christensen, "Reading Chilpancingo," 60–64.

39. Christensen, "Reading Chilpancingo," 63.

40. B. Bigelow and B. Peterson, ed., *Rethinking Globalization: Teaching for Justice in an Unjust World* (Milwaukee: Rethinking Schools).

41. See "On Freedom" in C. W. Mills, *Sociological Imagination* (Chicago: University of Chicago, 1959) and P. Shannon, *iSHOP/You Shop: Raising Questions About Reading Commodities* (Portsmouth, NH: Heinemann, 2001).

42. See the work of Donna Alverman, Gerry Coles, Curt Dudley-Marling, James Gee, Kris Gutierrez, Joanne Larson, Cynthia Lewis, Elizabeth Moje, David O'Brien, and Arlette Willis.

Index

Buswell, G., 54, 55
Business involvement, 17, 18–21, 55–
    56, 69–71, 142–143, 165, 190–191,
    195, 206–210, 212, 217, 230–231
Business roundtable, 131–134, 138
Butler and Company, 31

C
CIERA, 155, 157–158
CTB/McGraw-Hill, 139
California Department of Education,
    vii, 63, 91–93, 136, 154, 189
Calloway, B., 46
Calkins, L., 91
Carnegie, A., 19, 20, 21
Carnegie Foundation, 123
Carnegie Forum on Education and
    Economy, 130
Carnine, D., 147–148
Castle Bill, 145
Cato Institute, 101
Cato's Letters, 5
Cattell, J., 53
Chall, J., 44, 47, 55, 67
Charlton, J., 221
Cheney, L.,102
Chicago mastery learning , 50–51
Child centered teaching, 11–14
Children's Defense Fund, 196
Children's school, 78–79
Christensen, L., 229
Christian coalitions, 103
Christian fundamentalists, 100, 102–
    105, 123, 213
Church, S., 91
Citizens for Excellence in Education,
    105
City and country school, 78
Civic life, 215–221
Civic reading, 221–223
Civic reading practices, 224–230
Classroom management, 21
Clinton, B., xii, 110, 112–113, 116, 215
Clay, M., 228
Coalition for Evidence Based Policy, viii

Coding practices, 222
Coffey, W., 63
Coles, G., xii
Colonial period, 2–6
Comenius, 12, 16
Committee on Materials in Education,
    31
Committee on Measurement in
    Educational Products, 31
Compassionate conservatism, xii
Congressional record, 152
Connecticut colony, 2
Conservativism, 97, 98–108, 123,
    203–210
Copeland, K., 91
Cook County Normal School, 14, 26
Core reading program, vii, xii, 137–
    138, 175–191, 207–208
Council of Chief State School Officers,
    152
Cremin, L., 17, 26
Critical practices, 223
Cuban, L., 10–11, 34, 52, 81
Cunningham, J., 164

D
D. C. Heath, 31, 48
DIBELS, 141
DISTAR, 66
DRTA, 58
Dartmouth conference, 149
Darwinism, 22, 69–70
Dearborn, W., 53
DeVoogd, G., 227
Democracy, xiii, xiv, 62, 71–76, 166–
    167, 194, 214–231
Dennison, G., 82–83
Deskilling, 168
Dewey, E., 77
Dewey, J., 26, 30, 71, 73–76, 78, 80, 82,
    84, 90, 95
Dick and Jane, 1–2, 58, 98
Disaggregated test scores, 192–210
Dolch, E., 44–45, 46
Donovan, H., 42